YOU
CAN
BE
HOLY

YOU CAN BE HOLY

Charles Finney

Whitaker House

YOU CAN BE HOLY

ISBN: 0-88368-060-2
Printed in the United States of America
Copyright © 1985 by Whitaker House
Images © 1995 PhotoDisc, Inc.

Whitaker House
30 Hunt Valley Circle
New Kensington, PA 15068

6 7 8 9 10 11 12 13 14 / 06 05 04 03 02 01 00 99 98 97

CONTENTS

Chapter 1

DISCOVERING THE WAY OF SALVATION

"Sirs, what must I do to be saved? And they said, Believe on the Lord Jesus Christ"—Acts 16:30,31.

"Of him are ye in Christ Jesus, Who of God is made unto us wisdom, and righteousness, and sanctification, and redemption"—1 Corinthians 1:30.

The gospel plan of salvation is by faith, not works. Originally, the human race was to be saved by perfect and eternal obedience to the law of God. Adam was the natural head of the human race, and his sin has involved us in its consequences. But his sin is not literally accounted *our* sin. He stood as our natural head, and his sin has resulted in the sin and ruin of his descendants.

"By one man's disobedience many were made sinners" (Romans 5:19). When Adam fell, the law offered no hope of salvation.

Then *the plan* that had been provided by God's foresight for saving mankind by mere grace was revealed. Salvation was now placed on a new foundation by a covenant of *redemption*. You will find this covenant in the 89th Psalm and other places in the Old Testament. This is a covenant between the Father and the Son regarding the salvation of mankind and is the foundation of another covenant—the covenant of grace.

God's Covenant Relationship

In the covenant of redemption, man is merely the subject of the covenant. The parties are God the Father and God the Son. In this covenant, the Son is made the head or representative of His people. Adam was the *natural* head of the human family, and Christ is the *covenant* head of His Church.

The covenant of grace was founded on this covenant of redemption. Made with men and revealed to Adam after the fall, it was more fully revealed to Abraham. With Jesus Christ as Mediator of this covenant of grace (in opposition to the original covenant of works), salvation was now by faith. The obedience and death of Jesus Christ was regarded as the reason any individual could be saved, not an individual's personal obedience.

But Christ's obedience was not performed *for us*. As a man, He had to obey for Himself. If He did not obey, He became personally a transgressor. Yet there is a sense in which it may be said that His obedience is reckoned to our account. His obedience has highly honored the law, and His death has fully satisfied

8

the demands of public justice. *Grace* (not justice) has reckoned His righteousness to us. If He had obeyed the law strictly *for us,* justice would have accounted His obedience to us. We could have obtained salvation *by right* instead of asking for it through grace.

Only in this sense is salvation accounted ours: that He, being God and man, voluntarily assumed our nature and layed down His life to make atonement. This casts such a glory on God's law that grace is willing to consider His obedience ours, as if we were righteous.

Christ is also the covenant head of those who believe. He is not the natural head, as Adam was, but our *covenant* relationship to Him is such that whatever is given to Him is given to us. Whatever He is and whatever He has done, either as God or man, is given to us by covenant. The Church, as a body, has never understood the fullness and richness of this covenant. All there is in Christ is ours in the covenant of grace.

We receive this grace by faith. Nothing we can do makes us deserving of this righteousness. But as soon as we exercise faith, all that is contained in the covenant of grace becomes ours. This is why the inspired writers make so much of faith. Faith is our part of the covenant. It is the eye that discerns, the hand that takes hold, and the medium by which we become possessed of the blessings of the covenant. By faith the soul actually becomes *possessed* of all that is embraced in that act of faith. If there is not enough faith received to break the bonds of sin and set the soul at liberty, it is because the act has not embraced enough of what Christ is and what He has done.

Covenant Benefits

I have referred to the verse from Corinthians for the purpose of discussing the fundamental things contained in this covenant of grace. "Of him are ye in Christ Jesus, who of God is made unto us wisdom, and righteousness, and sanctification, and redemption." But what is meant? How and in what sense is Christ our wisdom, righteousness, sanctification, and redemption?

Jesus is often called the *Wisdom of God.* In the Book of Proverbs, He is called *Wisdom.* But how is He made to *us* wisdom?

First, we have all the benefits of His wisdom; and if we exercise faith, we are certain to be directed by it. He is the infinite source of wisdom, and we are partakers of His wisdom and have it guaranteed to us. If we trust in Him, we may have it as certainly as if we had it originally ourselves. This is what we need from the gospel and what the gospel must furnish to suit our needs.

Any man who thinks his own theorizing and speculating are going to bring him to any right knowledge of God knows nothing at all. His carnal, earthly heart can no more study the realities of the subject than the heart of a beast. "What man knoweth the things of a man, save the spirit of man which is in him? even so the things of God knoweth no man, but the Spirit of God" (1 Corinthians 2:11). What can we know, without experience, about the character or Spirit of God?

Do you say, "We can reason about God"? What if we do reason? What can reason do here? Suppose I should undertake to teach a pure intellectual what it is to love. I could reason and philosophize with him about love. Yet it is impossible to make a pure intellectual understand what love is unless he has actually experienced it! It's like talking about colors to a man born blind. He hears the word, but what idea can he attach to it? To get the idea of the difference of colors into his mind is impossible. The term is a mere word.

One whose mind has not experienced Christianity may reason about it. He may prove the perfections of God as he would prove the theory of gravity. But the spirit and life of the gospel can no more be carried to the mind by mere words, without experience, than love to an intellectual or colors to a man born blind. You may explain the law and crush him with conviction, but to give the spiritual meaning of things without the Spirit of God is absurd.

Jesus is made to us *righteousness*. Righteousness means holiness or obedience to law, and sanctification means the same. What distinction, therefore, did Paul have in mind?

Christ is our *outward* righteousness. His obedience is, under the covenant of grace, accounted to us. He didn't obey *for us,* and God doesn't consider us righteous because our Substitute has obeyed; but, as a matter of *grace*, we are treated as if *we* had obeyed.

Some people think that the righteousness of Christ is attributed to us in such a way that we are considered as having always been holy. It was once argued that righteousness was imputed to us and that we had a right to *demand* salvation because of justice. My view of the matter is entirely different: Christ's righteousness becomes ours by *gift.* God has united us to Christ and on His account treats us with favor.

For example, imagine that a father has done some service to his country, and the government rewards him. And not only is the individual himself rewarded but his entire family, because they are his children. Human governments do this, and the reason for it is very plain.

Christ's disciples are similarly considered one with Him. The Father is highly delighted with the service He has done the Kingdom, and He accounts Christ's righteousness to them as if it were their own. In other words, God treats them just as He would treat Christ Himself.

Please bear in mind that I am now speaking of *outward* righteousness—the reason why God accepts and saves believers in Christ. This reason includes both the obedience of Christ to the law and His obedience unto death.

The Author Of Holiness

Sanctification is inward purity or holiness. Jesus is our inward purity. The control that He exercises over us—His Spirit working in us—sheds His love abroad in our hearts, and through faith we are made holy.

When I say that Christ is our sanctification, or our holiness, I mean that He is the *author* of our holiness. He not only makes it available to us, by His atonement and intercession, but by His direct contact with the soul He produces holiness. He is not the remote but the immediate cause of our being sanctified. He works in us by the influences of His Spirit in a way perfectly consistent with our freedom.

Sanctification is received *by faith*. By faith Jesus is received and enthroned as King in our hearts. When the mind yields to Christ, it is led by His Spirit and guided and controlled by His hand. The act of the mind that throws the soul into the hand of Christ for sanctification is faith. Nothing is necessary except for the mind to sever any confidence in itself and to give itself up to be led and controlled by Him.

Imagine a child who offers his hand to his father to have him lead wherever he pleases. If the child is distrustful or unwilling to be led, or if he has confidence in his own wisdom and strength, he will break away and try to run alone. But if all that self-confidence fails, he will come and give himself up to his father again to be led entirely at his will. Similarly, by faith an individual gives his mind up to be led and controlled by Jesus Christ. He ceases from his own efforts and leaves himself in the hands of Christ for sanctification.

Jesus is our *redemption*. This refers to the Jewish practice of redeeming estates or relatives that had been sold for debt. When an estate had been sold out of the family or an individual had been deprived of liberty for debt, they could be redeemed by paying a price. There are frequent allusions in the Bible to this practice of redemption.

While we are in our sins, under the law, we are sold as slaves in the hand of public justice. We are bound over to death and have no possible way to redeem ourselves from the curse of the law. But Christ Himself is the price of our redemption. He has redeemed us from the curse of the law, being made a curse for us. He redeems us from the power of sin.

God's Unmerited Favor

Under this covenant of grace, *works of law* have no more to do with our salvation than if we had never existed. One must differentiate between salvation by works and salvation by grace. Salvation by grace is founded on a reason entirely separate from and out of ourselves. Under the law, salvation depended on ourselves. Now we *receive* salvation as a free gift. Jesus Christ is the sole author, founder and reason for our salvation.

14

Our own holiness does not enter at all into the reason for our acceptance and salvation. We are not indebted to Christ for a while, until we are sanctified, and then stand in our own righteousness. However perfect and holy we may become, Jesus Christ will forever be the sole reason why we are not in hell. However holy we may become, it will be forever true that we *have sinned*. In the eye of justice, nothing in us short of our eternal damnation can satisfy the law. But Jesus Christ remains the sole ground of our salvation.

Faith in Christ puts us in possession of Jesus. He was the very blessing promised in the Abrahamic covenant. Throughout the Scriptures, He is held forth as the sum and substance of all God's favors to man. He is the bread of life, the water of life, our strength, and our *all*.

Faith puts the mind in possession of these blessings. It annihilates those things that stand in the way of our relationship with Christ. He says, "Behold, I stand at the door, and knock: if any man hear my voice, and open the door, I will come in to him, and will sup with him, and he with me" (Revelation 3:20).

Why don't we receive Christ as our wisdom? Because we depend on our own wisdom and think we know the things of God. As long as we depend on this, we keep the door shut. Throw open the door and give up your wisdom. When we are empty of any available knowledge concerning the way of salvation, then Jesus will teach us. Until we do this, there is a door between us and Christ. We have something of our own instead of coming and throwing ourselves perfectly into the hands of Jesus.

How does faith put us in possession of the righteousness of Christ? Until our mind takes hold of the righteousness of Christ, we are engaged in working out a righteousness of our own. Until we cease entirely from our own works and throw ourselves on Jesus for righteousness, we cannot come to Him. He won't patch up our own righteousness to make it suitable. If we depend on our prayers, our tears, our charities, or anything we have done, He will not receive us. But the moment an individual takes hold of Jesus, he receives all Christ's righteousness through grace.

This is also true in regard to holiness and redemption. Until an individual receives Christ, he does not cease from his own works. The moment the mind yields itself up to Jesus, the responsibility is His. The believer by faith pledges Christ for his obedience and holiness. When the mind properly recognizes Christ and receives Him in unwavering faith, nothing is left contrary to the law of God.

Whenever you come to Christ, receive Him for all that He is—wisdom, righteousness, sanctification, and redemption. Nothing but unbelief can hinder you from enjoying it all *now*. No preparation will help. You must receive salvation as the *free gift* of grace.

True faith always works by love, purifies the heart, and overcomes the world. Whenever you find

16

any difficulty in your way, you have a lack of faith. No matter what happens to you outwardly—if you find yourself backsliding or if your mind is confused—unbelief is the cause and faith is the remedy. If you lay hold of Jesus and keep hold, all the devils in hell can never drive you away from God or put out your light.

Chapter 2

TRUE AND FALSE REPENTANCE

"For godly sorrow worketh repentance to salvation not to be repented of: but the sorrow of the world worketh death. For behold this self-same thing, that ye sorrowed after a godly sort, what carefulness it wrought in you, yea, what clearing of yourselves, yea, what indignation, yea, what fear, yea, what vehement desire, yea, what zeal, yea, what revenge! In all things ye have approved yourself to be clear in this matter" — 2 Corinthians 7:10-11.

True repentance involves a change of *opinion* respecting the nature of sin followed by a corresponding change of *feeling* toward sin. Feeling is the result of thought. When this change of opinion produces a corresponding change of feeling, if the opinion is right and the feeling corresponds, this is true repentance. Godly sorrow, which God requires, must spring from His views of sin.

To one who truly repents, sin looks very different than it does to him who has not repented. Instead of looking desirable or fascinating, it looks odious and detestable. He is astonished that he ever could have desired such a thing. Impenitent sinners may look at sin and see that it will ruin them because God will punish them for it. But it still appears in itself desirable. They love it. If it could end in happiness, they would never think of abandoning their sin.

But one who truly repents looks at his own conduct as perfectly hateful. He looks back and exclaims, "How detestable and worthy of hell my sin was."

Sinners don't see why God threatens sin with such terrible punishment. They love it so much that they cannot see why God thinks it is worthy of everlasting judgment. When sinners are strongly convicted, they see sin in the same light as a Christian does. Then all they need is a corresponding change in feeling to be saved.

Many sinners reflect on their relationship to God and know that they deserve eternal death, but their *heart* doesn't agree with God's opinions. This is the case with the demons and wicked spirits in hell. A change of opinion is indispensable to true repentance and always precedes it. There may be a change of opinion without repentance, but no genuine repentance occurs without a change of opinion.

The unsaved sinner thinks it utterly incredible that sin deserves everlasting death. He may be fully changed, however, to see that sin injures himself and everybody else and that there is no remedy but universal abstinence. Even the devil knows this is true.

The word rendered "repentance" implies a change of opinion in regard to the just outcome of sin. The careless sinner has almost no right ideas about the just punishment of sin. Even if he admits in theory that sin deserves eternal death, he does not believe it. If he believed it, it would be impossible for him to remain a careless sinner. He is deceived if he supposes that he honestly holds the opinion that sin deserves the wrath of God *forever*.

The truly awakened and convicted sinner sees clearly that sin deserves everlasting punishment from God. To him it is simply a matter of fact.

A Change Of Heart

In true repentance there must be a corresponding change of feeling. This change of feeling respects sin in its nature, its functions, its tendencies, and its outcome. The individual who truly repents not only sees sin as detestable, vile, and worthy of abhorrence, but he hates it in his heart. A person may see sin to be hurtful and abominable and still love it, desire it, and cling to it. But when he truly repents, he wholeheartedly abhors and renounces it.

This is the source of those tears of sorrow which sometimes break out when Christians see sin in its true nature. When a believer views sin in relation to God, he feels like weeping. Fountains of sorrow gush forth, and he wants to get down on his face and pour out a flood of tears over his sin.

When a believer views sin in its tendencies, it awakens a burning desire to stop it and save people from their sins. His heart is set on fire, and he prays with all his might to pull sinners out of hell and save them from the awful consequences of sin. It is as if he saw all the people taking poison that would destroy them. He lifts up his voice and screams, "Beware!"

He has an intellectual conviction that sin deserves everlasting punishment and is amazed that God can forgive him. Instead of thinking it severe or unkind that sinners are sent to hell, he is full of adoring wonder that he is not sent to hell himself. And when he thinks of such a sinner being saved, he feels a sense of gratitude unlike any he has ever known.

If your repentance is genuine, you have a *conscious* change of views and feelings in regard to sin. Can you say this? Do you know that there has been a change in you and that old things are done away and all things have become new?

Where repentance is genuine, the prevailing tendency to repeat sin is gone. If you have truly repented, you do not now love sin. You do not now abstain from it through fear or to avoid punishment but because you hate it. Look at the sins you used to practice. How do they appear to you? Do they look pleasant, and would you really love to practice them again if you dared? If you do have the disposition to sin left, you are only convicted. Your *opinions* of sin may be changed, but if the love of that sin remains, you are still an impenitent sinner.

The Scripture says, "Godly sorrow worketh repentance." Godly sorrow produces a reformation of *conduct*. Otherwise it is like saying that repentance produces repentance. But repentance must be a change of mind that produces a change of conduct and ends in salvation. Have you forsaken your sins? Or are you still practicing them? If so, you are still a sinner. You may have changed your mind, but if you have not changed your conduct, it is not godly repentance.

Repentance Unto Salvation

Genuine repentance leads to confession and restitution. The thief has not repented while he keeps the money he stole. He may have conviction but no repentance. If he had truly repented, he would go and give back the money. If you have cheated anyone and do not restore what you have taken; or if you have injured anyone and do not undo the wrong, you have not truly repented.

True repentance is a permanent change of character and conduct. The text says it is repentance "not to be repented of." True repentance is so deep and fundamental that the man never changes back again. People often quote it as if it read "repentance that does not *need* to be repented of." But it says, *not to be* repented of and is so thorough that there is no going back. The love of sin is totally abandoned. Any individual who has truly repented has changed his views and feelings and will not change back to the love of sin. The truly penitent sinner exercises feelings of which he will never repent— "unto salvation." The very reason it ends in salvation is because it will not be repented of.

False repentance is the sorrow of the world: sorrow for sin arising from worldly considerations and motives connected with the present life. At most false repentance has respect for the individual's own happiness in a future world and has no regard for the true nature of sin.

False repentance is not founded on a change of opinion like true repentance. A person may see the evil consequences of sin from a worldly point of view, and it may fill him with anxiety. He may see that it will greatly affect his character or endanger his life. If his secrets were found out, he would be disgraced—this may fill him with fear and distress. People often have this kind of sorrow when some worldly consideration is at the bottom of it.

Selfishness is at the root of false repentance. It may be a strong feeling of regret in the mind of the individual. He sees the evil consequences of his actions, and it makes him miserable or exposes him to the wrath of God. Sin may injure his family, his friends, or himself in time or in eternity. All this is pure selfishness.

He may feel remorse of conscience—biting, consuming *remorse*—and no true repentance. It may extend to deep and dreadful fear of the wrath of God and the pains of hell but be purely selfish. All the while there may be no abhorrence of sin and no feelings of the heart convicted of the infinite evil of sin.

False repentance leaves the feelings unchanged and the disposition to sin in the heart unbroken and unsubdued. The feelings about the nature of sin are not changed, and the individual still feels a desire to sin. He abstains from it not from abhorrence of it but from the dread of its consequences.

The individual who has exercised true repentance is willing to admit that he has repented and that he was a sinner. He who falsely repents resorts to excuses and lying to cover his sins and is ashamed of his repentance. He will cover up his sins by a thousand apologies and excuses, trying to smooth them over and diminish their enormity. If he speaks of his past conduct, he always does it in the softest and most favorable terms.

Repentance Unto Death

False repentance leads to death. It makes people commit one sin to cover up another. Instead of that open-hearted breaking forth of humility and frankness, you see a half-hearted confession that confesses nothing.

Are you ashamed to talk about your sins? If so, then your sorrow is only a worldly sorrow. Often sinners avoid conversation about their sins yet call themselves anxious inquirers, expecting to become Christians. The same kind of sorrow is found in hell. No doubt all those wretched inhabitants of the pit wish to get away from the eye of God. No such sorrow is found among the saints in heaven.

Open, genuine sorrow is consistent with true happiness. The saints are happy, yet have a deep, undisguised remorse for sin. But this worldly sorrow is ashamed of itself and is mean and miserable—its end is death.

The change produced by worldly sorrow extends only to those things of which the individual has been strongly convicted. The heart is not changed. You will see him avoid only those obvious sins about which he has been counseled.

Observe a young convert. If he is deceived, you will find only a partial change in his conduct. He is reformed in certain things, but he continues to practice many wrong things. If you become intimately acquainted with him, you will find him strict and quick-sighted in regard to certain things but far from manifesting a Christian spirit in regard to all sin.

Ordinarily, the change produced by false repentance is temporary even in those things which are reformed. The individual is continually relapsing into old sins. The *disposition* to sin is not gone—only checked and restrained by fear. As soon as he has a hope, is attending church, and gets bolstered up so that his fears are relieved, you will see him gradually returning to his old sins.

This was the difficulty with the house of Israel that made them constantly return to idolatry and other sins. They had only worldly sorrow. You see it everywhere in the Church. Individuals are reformed for a time and are taken into a congregation, but then they relapse into their old sins. They call it "getting cold" or backsliding, but the truth is, *they always loved sin.*

This is the foundation of all those flashes and starts in religion that you see so much of. People are awakened and convicted, but soon they settle down in false security and away they go. Perhaps they may keep their guard and won't be turned out of church; but if the foundations of sin are not broken up, they will return to their old ways.

A true convert's most obsessive sins before conversion are the furthest from them now. He is least likely to fall into his old besetting sin because he abhors it most. But if he is deceived and worldly minded, he always tends toward the same sins. The fountain of sin is not broken up. He has not purged iniquity from his heart but has regarded sin in his heart the whole time.

Bondage And Legalism

The change produced by false repentance is not only partial and temporary, it is also forced and constrained. The reformation of one who has true repentance is from the heart. In him the Bible promise is fulfilled. He actually finds that wisdom's "ways are ways of pleasantness, and all her paths are peace" (Proverbs 3:17). He experiences that the Savior's yoke is easy and His burden is light. He has felt that God's commmandments are not grievous but joyous. "More to be desired are they than gold, yea, than much fine gold: sweeter also than honey and the honeycomb" (Psalm 19:10).

But this spurious kind of repentance is very different: it is a legal repentance, resulting from fear and not love. Selfish repentance is anything but a free, voluntary change from sin to obedience. If you have this kind of repentance, you will find that you are conscious that you abstain from sin not because you hate it but from other considerations. You are more motivated by forbiddings of conscience or the fear that you will lose your soul, your hope, or your character than from abhorrence of sin or love of God.

Such people always apologize for sin, evade duty, and think there is no great harm in doing as they do. They love their sins. If there is not some scriptural command of God that they dare not resist, they will continue in sin.

This is not so with true repentance. If a thing seems contrary to the great law of love, the person who has true repentance will hate it and avoid it whether he has a direct command from God for it or not. He sees it is contrary to the law of benevolence, and he would no more do it than he would blaspheme God, steal, or commit any other abomination. The man that has true repentance does not need a "thus saith the Lord" to keep him from oppressing his fellowmen.

False repentance leads to self-righteousness. An

individual may know that Jesus Christ is the only Savior of sinners and may profess to believe in and rely on Him alone for salvation. But he is actually placing ten times more reliance on his *reformation* than on Jesus Christ for his salvation. And if he would watch his own heart, he would know it. He may say he expects salvation by Christ, but he is really building a righteousness of his own.

He supposes his worldly sorrow to be true repentance, and he trusts in it. He takes it for granted that Jesus will save him because he has had sorrow on account of his sins, although he is not conscious that he has never felt any resting in Christ. He felt sorrow, then got relief and felt better. Now he expects to be saved by Christ, when his very consciousness will teach him that he has never relied on Him.

The individual who has this kind of sorrow becomes harder in heart in proportion to the number of times that he exercises such sorrow. If he has strong emotions of conviction but his heart is not broken, the fountains of feeling dry up and his heart is more difficult to reach.

A real Christian who has truly repented is different. Every time you bring the truth to him he becomes more easily affected, excited, and broken under God's blessed Word. His heart gets into the habit of going along with the convictions of his understanding, and he becomes as teachable as a little child.

A Hardening Of Heart

Churches—or individual members—who have only worldly repentance pass through a revival, get waked up, and then grow cold again. Let this be repeated, and you will find them more and more difficult to be roused. Soon they become as hard as millstone, and nothing can ever rally them to a revival again.

On the other hand, some churches and individuals experience true repentance. Let them go through successive revivals, and you will find them growing more and more tender. When they hear the trumpet blow for a revival, they will glow instantly and be ready for the work.

The distinction between true and false repentance is as broad as between light and darkness. The principle is illustrated in sinners, who after passing through repeated revivals, will scoff and criticize. Although the heavens hang with clouds of mercy over their heads, they reject it. If they don't have true repentance, every fresh excitement hardens the heart and makes them more difficult to be reached by the truth.

Some people are thrown into distress whenever the truth is flashed upon their mind. They may not have as much conviction as the real Christian, but the real Christian is filled with peace at the very time his tears are flowing from conviction of sin. And each repeated season of conviction makes him more

and more watchful, tender, and careful, until h
conscience becomes so sensitive that the very a
pearance of evil will offend it. But the other kin
of sorrow, which does not lead to true renunci:
tion of sin, leaves the heart harder than before an
soon sears the conscience like a hot iron.

False repentance is sure to be repented of. Yo
will soon find these people becoming ashamed (
the deep feelings that they had. They do not war
to speak of them, and if they do talk of them it
always lightly and coldly. Perhaps they bustled abou
in time of revival and appeared as busy as anybod
Very likely they were among the extremes in ever
thing that was done. But now the revival is ove
and you find them opposed to new measures, chan;
ing back, and ashamed of their zeal. In fact, *they r*
pent of their repentance!

After they have joined a church, they will b
ashamed of their public repentance. When the heigl
of the revival has gone by, they will begin to ta
about being "too enthusiastic" and the necessity (
being more sober and consistent.

You sometimes find people who profess to b
converted in a revival turning against the very me:
sure, means, and doctrines by which they profe:
to have been converted. Not so with the true Chri:
tian. He is never ashamed of his repentance. The la:
thing he would ever think of being ashamed of :
the excitement he felt in a revival.

Many people have mistaken conviction for cor
version and the sorrow of the world for that godl

sorrow that "worketh repentance to salvation, not to be repented of." I am convinced, after years of observation, that this is the true reason for the present deplorable state of the Church all over the world.

Where Do We Stand?

Many sinners think it is a great trial to give up their ungodly companions and their sins. If they had true repentance, they would not think it any cross to give up their sins. When I first saw young people becoming Christians and joining the Church, I thought it was a good thing because their souls would be saved and they would get to heaven. But at the time repentance seemed to be a very sorrowful thing. I never dreamed then that these young people could ever be truly happy.

It is very common for people who know that Christianity is good to think they cannot be happy in the Church. They do not understand that true repentance leads to an abhorrence of those things that were formerly loved. Sinners do not see that when their young friends become true Christians sinful amusements are crucified.

People who experience false repentance do not know what it is to *enjoy* Christianity. They are not cheerful and happy. They are grieved because they have to withdraw from so many things they love or because they have to give so much money. They are in the fire all the time. Instead of rejoicing in every opportunity of self-denial and rejoicing in truth, the plain truth distresses them. Why? Because their hearts do not love to work for God. If they loved to do their duty, every ray of light that broke in upon their minds from heaven would be welcomed and would make them happier.

Perhaps you think I suppose all true Christians are perfect. There is a radical difference between a backslidden Christian and a hypocrite who has returned to the world. The hypocrite loves the world and *enjoys sin* when he returns to it. He may have fear, remorse, and apprehension about the loss of character; but, after all, he enjoys sin.

The backslidden Christian is different. He loses his first love, then he falls prey to temptation and enters into sin. But he does not love it. It is always bitter to him, and he feels unhappy and homesick. He has, at the time, no Spirit of God to keep him from sin, but he does not love it. He is unhappy, and he feels like a wretch. He is as different from the hypocrite as can be. He can never again *enjoy sin* or delight in the pleasures of the world. Never again can he drink iniquity like water. As long as he continues to wander, he is miserable.

Convicted sinners are afraid to pledge themselves to give up their sins. They tell you they can't promise to do it because they are afraid they won't keep the promise. *They love sin*. The drunkard knows that he loves strong drink. Although he may be constrained to abstain from it, he still craves it. Likewise, the convicted sinner loves sin, and his hold on sin has never been broken—he dares not promise to give it up.

Sinners who have worldly sorrow can now see where the difficulty lies and why they are not converted. Their intellectual views of sin may be such that if their hearts corresponded they would be Christians. Perhaps they think this is true repentance. If they were truly willing to give up all sin, they would not hesitate to pledge themselves to it and have all the world know that they had done it.

If you are willing to give up sin, you are willing to promise to do it and willing to have it known that you have done it. But if you resist conviction and still love your sins, all your convictions will not help you. They will only sink you deeper in hell for resisting them.

Let us pray that this is the evidence that our repentance is genuine: "For behold this selfsame thing, that ye sorrowed after a godly sort, what carefulness it wrought in you, yea, what clearing of yourselves, yea, what indignation, yea, what fear, yea, what vehement desire, yea, what zeal, yea, what revenge! In *all things* ye have approved yourselves to be clear in this matter" (2 Corinthians 7:11).

Chapter 3

TRUE AND FALSE CONVERSION

"Behold, all ye that kindle a fire, that compass yourselves about with sparks: walk in the light of your fire, and in the sparks that ye have kindled. This shall ye have of mine; ye shall lie down in sorrow"—Isaiah 50:11.

Evidently, Isaiah was addressing those who professed to be religious and who flattered themselves that they were in a state of salvation. But their hope was a fire of their own kindling, and the sparks were created by themselves. This discussion will be of no use except to those who are honest in applying it to themselves. If you will do this, I may be able to lead you to discover your true state and, if you are now deceived, direct you to the true path of salvation.

The natural state of men before conversion is pure, unmingled selfishness. They have no gospel benevolence. Selfishness is supremely regarding one's own happiness and seeking one's own good because it is his own. Selfish men place their own happiness above other interests of greater value, such as the glory of God and the good of the universe. That men, before conversion, are in this state is evident from many considerations.

Every man knows that all other men are selfish. All the dealings of mankind are conducted on this principle. If any man overlooks this and tries to deal with people as if they were not selfish, he will be thought deranged.

Benevolence is choosing the happiness of others. In a converted state, man's character becomes benevolent or loving. An individual who is converted is benevolent and not supremely selfish. This is God's state of mind.

We are told that God *is* love. Benevolence comprises His whole character. All His moral attributes are only manifestations of His benevolence. A converted person is in this respect like God. I don't mean that no one is converted unless he is as purely and perfectly benevolent as God is. But his prevailing choice is benevolence. He sincerely seeks the good of others for its own sake. By *disinterested benevolence* I do not mean that a person who is disinterested feels no interest in his object of pursuit. He seeks the happiness of others for their own sake and not for promoting his own happiness.

God is purely benevolent. He does not make His creatures happy for the sake of promoting His own happiness but because He loves their happiness and chooses it for their own sake. Of course He does feel happy in promoting the happiness of His creatures, but He does not do it *for the sake* of His own gratification. The disinterested man feels happy in doing good. If he did not love and enjoy doing good, it would not be virtue in him.

Benevolence is holiness. The law of God requires that "Thou shalt love the Lord thy God with all thy heart, and with all thy soul, and with all thy mind . . . .thou shalt love thy neighbor as thyself" (Matthew 22:37,39). The converted man yields to the law of God; and, as much as he is like God, he is benevolent. It is the leading feature of his character.

True conversion is a change from a state of supreme selfishness to benevolence. It is a change in the end of pursuit and not a mere change in the means of attaining the end. That the converted and the unconverted differ only in the means they use, while both are aiming at the same end, is false. Gabriel and Satan are not *both* aiming to be happy. The archangel does not obey God for the sake of promoting his own happiness.

Motive And Action

A man may change his means and yet have the same end: his own happiness. He may not believe in Jesus or in eternity and yet may see that doing good will be to his advantage in this world. Suppose, then, that his eyes are opened and he sees the reality of eternity. He may take up religion as a means of happiness in eternity. *No virtue* lies in this. It is the *motive* that gives character to the act, not the means employed.

The true and the false convert differ in this. The true convert chooses, as the end of his pursuit, the glory of God and the good of His Kingdom. He views this as a greater good than his own happiness. He is not indifferent to his own happiness but prefers God's glory because it is a greater good. He looks on the happiness of every individual according to its real importance, as far as he is capable of valuing it, and chooses the greatest good as his supreme object.

There are ways in which true saints and deceived people agree and ways in which they differ. They may agree in leading a moral life. The difference is in their motives. The true saint leads a moral life because he loves holiness. The deceived person uses morality as the means to effect his own happiness.

They may be equally prayerful as far as the *form* of praying is concerned. Again, the difference is in their motives. The true saint loves to pray, while the other prays because he hopes to derive some benefit to himself from praying. The true saint expects a benefit from praying, but that is not his leading motive. The other prays from no other motive.

Both may be equally zealous in religion. One may be zealous because his zeal is according to knowledge, and he sincerely desires and loves to promote Christianity for its own sake. The other may show equal zeal to assure his own salvation or because he is afraid of going to hell if he doesn't work for the Lord. He wants to quiet his conscience and doesn't love Christianity for its own sake.

They may be equally responsible to their duties—the true convert because he loves to work for the Lord and the other because he dares not neglect it.

Both may pay equal regard to what is right—the true convert because he *loves* what is right and the other because he knows he cannot be saved unless he does right. He is honest in his business transactions because it is the only way to secure his own interest. He has the reputation of being honest; but if he has no higher motive, he will have no reward from God.

They may agree in their desires, in many respects. They may agree in their desire to serve God. The true convert serves God because he loves the service of God; and the deceived person serves God for the reward, as the hired servant serves his master.

The true saint desires the conversion of souls because it will glorify God. The deceived person desires the favor of God for personal gain. He will be motivated in this just as he is in giving money. A person can give money to a Bible society or a missionary society from selfish motives alone. He can also desire and work for the conversion of souls from purely selfish motives.

Holiness And Selfishness

Both true and false converts may desire to repent. The true convert abhors sin because it dishonors God. The other desires to repent because he knows that unless he does he will be damned.

The true saint desires to obey God to increase in holiness. The false convert desires the rewards of obedience.

They may agree not only in their desires but in their resolutions. Both may resolve to give up sin, obey God, and witness for the Kingdom. They may both resolve it with great strength of purpose but with different motives.

Their designs may be similar. They may both design to glorify God, to convert men, and to extend the Kingdom of Christ. The true saint works from love to God and holiness, and the false convert works for the sake of securing his own happiness. One chooses it as an end, while the other chooses it as a means to promote a selfish end.

Both may design to be truly holy—the true saint because he loves holiness and the deceived person because he knows that he can't be happy any other way.

They may both love the Bible. The true saint loves it because it is God's truth, and he delights in it. The other reads it and applies it to his egocentric hopes.

The true saint loves God because he sees God's character to be supremely lovely and excellent in itself. The other thinks God is his particular friend and is going to make him happy forever. He connects the idea of God with his own interest.

They both may love Christians. The true convert sees in them the image of Christ. The deceived person loves them because they belong to his own denomination or because they are on his side.

They may also agree in hating the same things. They both may hate infidelity and oppose it strenuously—the true saint because it is opposed to God and holiness and the deceived person because it injures his own interests.

The true convert hates sin because it is odious to God, and the deceived person hates it because it is harmful to himself. Many individuals have hated their own sins and yet not forsaken them. Often the drunkard looks back at what he once was and abhors alcohol because it has ruined him. And still he continues to drink, although when he looks at the effects, he feels indignation.

Love Of Saints And Sinners

The true saint graciously opposes sinners and abhors any character or conduct calculated to overthrow the Kingdom of God. The false convert opposes sinners because they contradict his religion.

Both may rejoice in the conversion of souls—the true convert because he has his heart set on it and loves it for its own sake. The deceived person loves it because he thinks he has an advancing concern.

Both the true and false convert may mourn at the lack of zeal in the Church. The true convert is distressed because God is dishonored, and the deceived person grieves because his own soul is not happy.

The true convert enjoys spiritual conversation, but the deceived person hopes to derive some advantage from the saints' company. The first enjoys it because out of the abundance of the heart the mouth speaks. The latter loves to talk about the great interest he feels in religion and the hope he has of going to heaven.

The true saint delights in worship, prayer, hearing the Word of God, and being in communion with God and His saints. The other thinks a religious meeting supports his special hopes. He may have a hundred reasons for loving meetings, yet not because he loves worship in itself.

While both may find pleasure in prayer, the true saint draws near to God and finds delight in communion with Him. No embarrassments keep him from going right to God. The deceived person finds satisfaction in it because it is his duty to pray in secret, and he feels a self-righteous satisfaction in doing it. He may feel a certain pleasure in it, from a kind of excitement of the mind that he mistakes for communion with God.

They both may love God's law. The true saint loves it because it is excellent, holy, just, and good. The other thinks it will make him happy if he loves it.

Although each may consent to the penalty of the law, only the true saint consents to it because he feels it just for God to send him to hell. The deceived person thinks *he* is in no danger from it. He feels a respect for it because he knows that it is right, and his conscience approves it. But he has never consented to it in his own case.

They may be equally liberal in giving to charitable organizations. Two men may give equal sums to a worthy cause but from different motives. One would be just as willing to give even if he knew that no other living person would give. The other gives for the credit of it, to quiet his conscience, or because he hopes to purchase the favor of God.

They may be equally self-denying in many things. Self-denial is not confined to true saints. Look at the sacrifices of the Muslims going on pilgrimages to Mecca. Look at the papists going up and down over the sharp stones on their bare knees until they bleed. But we know that this isn't Christianity. The true saint denies himself for the sake of doing more good to others. He is more set on this than on his own indulgence or his own interest. The deceived person may go to equal lengths from purely selfish motives.

Both may be willing to suffer martyrdom. Read the lives of the martyrs, and you will have no doubt that some were willing to suffer from a wrong idea of the rewards of martyrdom. They would seek their own destruction because they thought it was the sure road to eternal life.

In all these cases, the motives of one class contradicts the other. The difference lies in the choice of different *ends*. One chooses his own interest as his chief end, and the other chooses God's interest. For a person to pretend that both these classes aim at the same end is to say that an impenitent sinner is just as unselfish as a real Christian.

If these two classes are so similar, then how are we to know our own true character? We know that the heart is deceitful above all things and desperately wicked. How do we know if we are seeking God's love and His holiness or whether we are seeking God's favor for our own benefit?

If we are truly seeking benevolence and holiness, it will appear in our daily transactions. If selfishness rules our conduct there, as sure as God reigns, we are truly selfish. If we are selfish with men, then we are selfish with God. "For he that loveth not his brother whom he hath seen, how can he love God whom he hath not seen?" (1 John 4:20).

Christianity is not merely love to God but to man also. If our daily transactions show us to be selfish, we are unconverted. Otherwise, benevolence is not essential to the faith, and a man can be a Christian without loving his neighbor as himself.

If you are *disinterested*, Christian duties will not be a task to you. You will not labor as if your work were a nuisance. The false convert wouldn't work if he didn't have to. It is a task, and if he takes any pleasure in it, it is for its anticipated results—the support and comfort of his family or the increase of his property.

This is the attitude some people have in regard to Christianity. They act like a sick man taking medicine. They desire its effects, and they know they must have it or die. They would never do it for its own sake. Suppose men love labor like a child loves play. They would do it all day long without any other incentive than pleasure. When Christianity is loved for its own sake, no weariness exists.

If it is a time of general coldness in the church, real converts will still enjoy their own relationship with God. But the deceived person will then invariably be found embracing the world. Then, when true saints rise up and shout about their joy so that Christianity begins to revive, the deceived will soon bustle about and appear even more zealous than true saints. He is impelled by convictions and not affections. When there is no public interest, he feels no conviction. But when the church awakes, he is compelled to stir about to keep his conscience quiet. This is only selfishness in another form.

If you are selfish, your joy will depend mainly on the strength of your hopes of heaven and not on your affections. Your enjoyments are not in the employments of Christianity but of a vastly different kind from those of the true saint. They are mostly from *anticipating*. When you feel very certain about going to heaven, then you enjoy your faith. It depends on your hope and not on your love.

People tell of having no enjoyment in religion when they lose their hopes. The reason is plain. If they loved Christianity for its own sake, their enjoyment would not depend on their hope. A person who loves his job is happy anywhere. And if you loved the employments of Christianity, you would be happy if God put you in hell, provided He let you work for Him there.

Of course, true saints enjoy their hope, but they *think* very little about it. The deceived person, on the contrary, is aware that he does not enjoy his duties. He only enjoys them as a man does who thinks that by hard work he will have great wealth.

The true saint enjoys the peace of God because heaven has already begun in his soul. He not only has the prospect of it, but eternal life has actually begun in him. He has that faith that is the very substance of things hoped for. (See Hebrews 11:1.) He knows that heaven has begun in him and that he is not obliged to wait until he dies to taste the joys of eternal life. His enjoyment is in proportion to his holiness and not in proportion to his hope.

The Obedience Of Love

Another way to tell whether you are selfish in religion is this: the deceived person has only a *purpose* of obedience while the true saint has a *preference* of obedience. This is an important distinction, and I fear few people make it. Multitudes have a purpose of obedience but have no true preference of obedience. Preference is actual choice or obedience of heart. Individuals speak of purposing to obey but fail to do it. And they will tell you how difficult it is to execute their purpose.

On the other hand, the true saint prefers and

chooses obedience. The one has a purpose to obey, like that which Paul had. Before Paul was converted, he had a strong purpose of obedience, but he did not obey because his heart was not in it. (See Romans 7.) The false convert purposes to be holy because he knows that it is the only way to be happy. The true saint chooses holiness for its own sake, and he is holy.

The true convert and the deceived person also differ in their faith. The former has confidence in the character of God that leads him to complete submission to God. Confidence in the Lord's promises depends on knowing God's character.

Human or divine, governments are obeyed on only two principles: fear and confidence. It doesn't matter whether it is the government of a family, a ship, a nation, or a universe. All obedience springs from one of these two principles.

In one case, individuals obey from hope of rewards and fear of the penalty. In the other, they obey from that confidence in the character of the government that works by love. One child obeys his parents from confidence. His faith works by love. The other yields an outward obedience from hope and fear. The true convert has faith to obey God because He loves God. This is the obedience of faith.

The other has only partial faith and partial submission. The devil has partial faith. He believes and trembles. (See James 2:19.) A person may believe that Christ came to save sinners and submit to him to be saved. But does he submit himself to God's government? No! His submission is only on condition that he be saved. It is never with that unreserved confidence in God's whole character that leads him to say, "Let thy will be done."

He only submits to salvation. His religion is the religion of law. The other is gospel faith. One is selfish, and the other is benevolent. Here lies the true difference between the two classes: One is outward and hypocritical, and the other is that of the heart, holy and acceptable to God.

If you are selfish, you will rejoice in the conversion of sinners only when you have a part in it. You will have very little satisfaction when someone else is involved. The selfish person rejoices when he is active and successful in converting sinners because he thinks he will have a great reward. But instead of delighting in it when done by others, he will be envious.

The true saint sincerely delights and rejoices when sinners are converted by others as much as if by himself. Some take interest in revival only when they are connected with it. It seems they would rather have sinners remain unconverted than be saved through an evangelist or a minister of another denomination. The true spirit of a child of God is to say, "Send, Lord, whomever you will—only let souls be saved and your name glorified!"

Living To Glorify God

Regard your own happiness according to its rela

tive value. Put it next to the glory of God and the good of the universe, and then give it the value it deserves. This is precisely what God does. And this is what He means when He commands you to love your neighbor as yourself.

You will in fact promote your own happiness to the degree that you leave it out of view. Your happiness consists mainly in the gratification of virtuous desires. There may be pleasure in gratifying desires that are selfish, but it is not real happiness. But to be virtuous, your desires must be disinterested.

Suppose a man meets a beggar in the street—cold, hungry, and ready to perish. The man's feelings are touched, and he steps into a store to buy the beggar a loaf of bread. At once the countenance of the beggar lights up with unutterable gratitude. The gratification of the man in the act is in exact proportion to his motives. If he did it solely out of love, his gratification is complete in the act itself. But if he did it partly to have it known that he is a charitable and human person, then his happiness is not complete until the deed is known to others.

Imagine a sinner in his sins. He is very wicked and very wretched. Your compassion is moved, and you lead him to Jesus. If your motive was to obtain honor among men and to secure the favor of God, you are not completely happy until the deed is told. But if you wished purely to save a soul from death, then as you see it done your gratification is complete.

If you aim at doing good for its own sake, then you will be happy to the degree that you do good. But if you do good simply to secure your own happiness, you will fail. You will be like the child pursuing his own shadow: he can never overtake it because it always stays just ahead of him.

Suppose in the case I have mentioned, you have no desire to relieve the beggar but simply crave the applause of a certain individual. You will feel no pleasure at all in the relief of the beggar until that individual hears of it and commends it—then you are gratified. But you are not gratified in the thing itself. Or suppose you aim at the conversion of sinners. If it is not love to sinners that leads you to do it, how can the conversion of sinners make you happy? The truth is that God has made man so he must seek the happiness of others or he cannot be happy.

This is the true reason why men, seeking their own happiness and not the happiness of others, fail. It is always just before them. If they would stop seeking their own happiness and work to do good, they would be happy.

Happiness Through Holiness

Christ despised the shame, endured the cross, and regarded the joy set before Him. But what was the joy set before Him? Not His own salvation or happiness but the great good He would do in the salvation of the world. He was perfectly happy in

Himself. The happiness of others was His aim. This was the joy set before Him, and He obtained it.

Where it is said, "We love him because he first loved us" (1 John 4:19), the language plainly suggests two interpretations: either that love to us has provided the way for our return and the influence that brought us to love Him, or that we love Him for His favor shown to ourselves. The latter is not the meaning because Jesus Christ fully refuted the principle in His Sermon on the Mount. "If ye love them which love you, what reward have ye? Do not even the publicans the same?" (Matthew 5:46). If we love God, not for His character but for His favors to us, Jesus Christ calls us reprobate.

The Bible speaks of happiness as the result of virtue, but virtue is not the pursuit of one's own happiness. If a person desires the good of others, he will be happy to the degree that he gratifies that desire.

God loves others. He desires everyone's happiness. And to be like Him, we must aim at and delight in His happiness and glory and the honor and glory of the universe.

God requires *true repentance*—that is, to forsake sin because it is hateful in itself. It is not true repentance to forsake sin on condition of pardon or to say, "I will be sorry for my sins, if you will forgive me." True repentance requires true faith and true submission, not conditional faith or partial submission. This is what the Bible insists.

Many people have different views of the nature of the gospel. Some view it as a matter of *accom-*

modation to mankind in which God has become less strict than He was under the law. This enables them to be fashionable or worldly, and the gospel will come in and make up their deficiencies and save them. The other class views the gospel as a provision of divine benevolence designed to destroy sin and promote holiness. Its whole value consists in its power to make them holy.

From this discussion we can see why some people are much more anxious to convert sinners than to see the Church sanctified and God glorified by the good works of His people. Many feel a natural sympathy for sinners and wish to have them saved from hell. If that is gained, they have no further concern. But true saints are affected by sin because it dishonors God. And they are even more distressed to see Christians sin because it dishonors God more.

Some people don't seem to care how the people of the Church live if they can only see the work of conversion. They are not anxious to have God honored. It shows that they are not motivated by the love of holiness but by mere compassion for sinners.

Chapter 4

TRUE SUBMISSION: A MATTER OF CHOICE

"Submit yourselves therefore to God"—James 4:7.

If you have built your Christian life on a false foundation, your fundamental error was embracing what you thought was the gospel plan of salvation from selfish motives. Your selfish heart was unbroken. This is the source of your delusion, if you are deceived. If your selfishness was subdued, you are not deceived in your hope. If it was not, all your religion is vain, and your hope is vain.

If any of you have a false hope, you are in danger of reviving your old ways. Often false converts, after a season of anxiety and self-examination, settle down again on the old foundation. Their habits of mind have become fixed, and it is difficult to break into a new course. It is indispensable, therefore, if you ever intend to get right, that you see clearly that you have up to now been wrong.

True submission to God is not indifference. No two things can be more opposite than indifference and true submission.

Some suppose that true submission includes the idea of being willing to be sinful for the glory of God. But this is a mistake. To be willing to be sinful is itself a sinful state of mind. And to be willing to do *anything* for the glory of God is to choose not to be sinful. The idea of being sinful for the glory of God is absurd.

Bowing Before God's Will

If we were now in hell, true submission would require that we would be willing to be punished. Then it would be certain that it was God's will. If we were in a world where no provision was made for the redemption of sinners and where our punishment was therefore inevitable, it would be our duty to be willing to be punished. But as it is, genuine submission does not imply a willingness to be punished. It is not the will of God that all be punished, but His will is that all who truly repent and submit will be saved.

True submission consists in perfect acquiescence in all the dealings of God, whether relating to ourselves, to others, or to the universe. Some people think they submit to the providential government of God. But they find fault with God's arrangements in many things. They wonder why God permitted Adam to sin or why He permitted sin to enter the universe at all? Or why He did this or that? Or why He made this, that, thus, or so? In all these cases, supposing we could find no reason at all that would

53

be satisfactory, true submission implies a perfect acquiescence in whatever He has permitted or done.

True submission implies yielding to the precepts of God's moral law. The general precept of God's moral law is "Thou shalt love the Lord thy God with all thy heart, and with all thy soul, and with all thy strength, and with all thy mind; and thy neighbor as thyself" (Luke 10:27). Here we must carefully make the distinction between a formal obedience to God's law and actual submission to it.

Common sense approves of this law. Every devil in hell approves of it. God has made our minds so that it is impossible to be a moral agent and not approve His law. But this is not the yielding I propose.

True acquiescence to God's moral law includes actual obedience. It is vain for a child to *pretend* to yield to his father's commands unless he actually obeys them and vain for a citizen to pretend to agree with the laws of the land unless he obeys them. Men have taken their supreme affection from God and His Kingdom and given it to self-interest. Instead of pressing to do good, as God requires, they have adopted the maxim that "charity begins at home." This is the very point in debate between God and the sinner. The sinner aims at promoting his own interest as his supreme object.

The first idea implied in submission is the yielding of this point. We must stop putting our own interest first and let the interests of God and His Kingdom rise in our affections. We must put them as high above our own interests as their real value is greater. The man who does not do this is a rebel against God.

Suppose a civil ruler wanted to promote the general happiness of his nation and wisely made laws to this end. He would require every subject to do the same. Then suppose an individual set up his own private interest in opposition to the general interest. He is a rebel against the government and against all the interest that the government promotes. Then the first idea of submission, on the part of the rebel, is *giving up that point* and falling in with the ruler and the obedient subjects in promoting the public good.

The law of God absolutely requires that you make your own happiness subordinate to the glory of God and the good of the universe. Until you do this, you are the enemy of God and the universe.

The gospel requires the same as the law. Many maintain that it is right for a man to aim directly at his own salvation and make his own happiness his goal. But God's law requires everyone to prize *God's interest* supremely. Otherwise, Jesus Christ is the minister of sin and came into the world to take up arms *against* God's government.

From the Bible, we see that the gospel requires love to God and man, the same as the law. "Seek ye first the kingdom of God, and his righteousness" (Matthew 6:33). What does that mean? Men have quoted this very text to prove that it is right to seek our own salvation first and to make that the leading object of pursuit. But that is not the meaning.

It requires everyone to make the promotion of the Kingdom of God his *great object.* It means to aim at being *holy.*

Happiness is connected with holiness but is *not* the same thing, and to honor and glorify the Lord is a very different thing from seeking our own interests first.

"Whether therefore ye eat, or drink, or whatsoever ye do, do all to the glory of God" (1 Corinthians 10:31). Indeed! May we eat and drink to please ourselves? No! We may not even gratify our natural appetite for food, except in submission to the glory of God. This is what the gospel requires, for the apostle wrote this to the Church.

Our Savior says, "Whosoever will save his life shall lose it: and whosoever will lose his life for my sake will find it" (Matthew 16:25). If a man aims at his own interest, he will lose his own interest. If saving his own soul is his supreme object, he will lose it. He must make the good of others his supreme object, or he will be lost.

"There is no man that hath left house, or brethren, or sisters, or father, or mother, or wife, or children, or lands, for my sake, and the gospel's, But he shall receive an hundredfold now in this time, houses, and brethren, and sisters, and mothers, and children, and lands, with persecutions; and in the world to come eternal life" (Mark 10:29-30).

Here some people may stumble and say, "There is a reward held out as a motive." But what are we to do? *Forsake self* for the sake of a reward to *self?*

56

No, we must forsake self for the sake of Christ and His gospel, and the *consequences* will be as stated. This is the important distinction.

True Submission Is Love

In Corinthians 13, Paul gives a full description of disinterested love, or charity, without which a person is nothing. Note how much a person may do and still be nothing: "Though I speak with the tongues of men and of angels, and have not charity, I am become as sounding brass, or a tinkling cymbal. And though I have the gift of prophecy, and understand all mysteries, and all knowledge; and though I have all faith, so that I could remove mountains, and have not charity, I am nothing. And though I bestow all my goods to feed the poor, and though I give my body to be burned, and have not charity, it profiteth me nothing" (1 Corinthians 13:1-3).

True gospel benevolence is of this character: "Charity suffereth long, and is kind; charity envieth not; charity vaunteth not itself, is not puffed up, Doth not behave itself unseemly, seeketh not her own, is not easily provoked, thinketh no evil; Rejoiceth not in iniquity, but rejoiceth in the truth; Beareth all things, believeth all things, hopeth all things, endureth all things" (1 Corinthians 13:4-7).

Love has no selfish end but seeks the happiness of others as its great end. Without this kind of benevolence, we know there is *not a particle* of true Christianity.

Many people wonder why the threatenings of the Word of God are given, if it is selfishness to be influenced by fear. Man dreads pain. The Scripture threatenings answer many purposes. One is to arrest the selfish mind and lead it to examine reasons to love and obey God. When the Holy Spirit gets the attention, then He rouses the sinner's conscience and challenges him to consider and decide on the reasonableness and duty of submitting to God.

Is it wrong to be influenced by pleasure and pain? No, it is neither right nor wrong. These susceptibilities have no moral character. Suppose you stand on a cliff: if you throw yourself down, you will break your neck. You are warned against it. Now, if you do not regard the warning but throw yourself down and destroy your life, that will be sin. But heeding the warning is no virtue. It is simply a prudential act. There is no virtue in avoiding danger, although it may often be sinful not to avoid it. To resist the wrath of God is sinful. But to be afraid of hell is not holy, no more than the fear of breaking your neck is holy.

We may seek our own happiness with respect to its real value, and we are to do so. He that doesn't do this commits sin.

But no one can be happy while he makes his own happiness his supreme object. Happiness consists in the gratification of virtuous desires. But to be gratified, the thing must be obtained that is desired. To be happy, therefore, the desires that are gratified must be *right*, and they must be *disinterested* desires.

Two things are indispensable to true happiness. First, there must be virtuous or righteous desire. If the desire is not virtuous, conscience will oppose it, and gratification will be attended with pain. Secondly, the object must be desired for its own sake, or the gratification will not be complete, even if it is attained.

If the object is desired as a means to an end, the gratification will depend on obtaining the end by this means. But if the thing was desired *as an end,* obtaining it would produce true gratification. The mind must not desire its own happiness, for in this way it can *never be attained.* Desires must strive for some other object that is desired for its own sake, and its attainment would result in happiness.

If everyone pursues his own happiness as the ultimate goal, the interests of different individuals will clash and destroy the happiness of all. This is what we see in the world. It is the reason for all the fraud, violence, oppression, and wickedness in earth and hell. As each pursues his own goals, interests clash. The only way to secure our own happiness is to pursue the glory of God and the good of the universe. The question is not whether we should desire and pursue our own happiness at all but whether we should make our own happiness our supreme end.

Rebels In A Holy Empire

We are not simply under a government of naked

law. This world is a province of God's empire. We have rebelled, and by a new and special provision God offers us mercy. The conditions are that we obey the precepts of the law and submit to the justice of the penalty. God's gospel supplements His government of law.

The gospel requires the same obedience as the law. It requires sinners to yield to the *justice* of the penalty. If the sinner were under mere law, it would require that he submit to the *infliction* of the penalty. But man is not and never has been, since the fall, under the government of mere law. He has always known, more or less clearly, that mercy is offered.

It has, therefore, never been required that men be willing to be punished. In this respect, gospel submission differs from legal submission. Under naked law, submission would consist in willingness to be punished. Submission consists in yielding to the justice of the penalty and regarding himself as *deserving* the eternal wrath of God.

The duty of every sovereign is to see that all his subjects submit to his government. If every individual obeys perfectly, his laws will promote the public good to the highest possible degree. Then, if anyone refuses to obey, the ruler must force that rebel to serve the public interest in the best way. If he will not serve voluntarily, he should be made to do it involuntarily.

God is a sovereign ruler, and the submission that He requires is exactly what He must require. He would be neglecting His duty as a ruler if He did not require it. If you have refused to obey this requirement, you are bound to throw yourself into His hands for Him to punish you in the way that will best promote the interests of the universe. You have forfeited all claim to the happiness of the universe or the favor of God. God requires that you acknowledge the justice of His law and leave your future entirely and unconditionally at His disposal. You must submit all you have and all you are to Him.

True submission requires complete acceptance of the terms of the gospel. They are repentance, holiness, faith, perfect trust, and confidence toward God. This leads you, without hesitation, to throw body and soul into His hand to do with you as He thinks good.

To receive Christ as mediator, advocate, atoning sacrifice, ruler, teacher—and in all the offices in which He is presented in God's Word—is true submission. This is true acquiescence to God's appointed way of salvation.

The Church is full of false hopes. Many people embrace what they consider the gospel without yielding to the law. They look at the law with dread and regard the gospel as a scheme to get away from the law. These tendencies have always been seen in men. Many hold to the gospel and reject the law, while others accept the law and neglect the gospel. The truth is that the rule of life is the same in both, and *both require disinterested benevolence.*

If a person thinks that under the gospel he may

give up the glory of God as his supreme object and, instead of loving God with all his heart, and soul, and strength, may make his own salvation his supreme object, his hopes are false. He has embraced another gospel—which is *no gospel at all*.

Submission Unto Salvation

Faith is not believing that *you* will be saved but believing God's Word concerning His Son. He has revealed the fact that Jesus Christ came into the world to save sinners. What you call faith is more properly hope. The confident expectation that you will be saved is an inference from the act of faith and an inference which you have a right to draw when you are conscious of obeying the law and believing the gospel. When you exercise the feelings required in the law and gospel, you have a right to trust in Christ for your *own* salvation.

God wills that every soul be saved. That fact exercises disinterested benevolence. Suppose a man came to me and asked, "What must I do to be saved?" and I told him, "If you expect to be saved, you must despair of being saved"—what would he think? What inspired writer ever gave such direction? The answer is, "Love the Lord thy God with all thy heart," "Repent," "Believe the gospel," and so on. Is there anything here that implies despair?

Sinners do despair before they obtain true peace. But what is the reason? Despair is not essential to true peace. Many anxious sinners despair because they get a false impression that they have sinned away their day of grace or that they have committed the unpardonable sin. Sometimes they despair because they know that mercy will be provided as soon as they comply with the terms, but they find all their efforts at true submission vain. They find they are proud and obstinate and cannot consent to the terms of salvation. Perhaps most individuals who do submit come to a point where they give up all as lost. But is that necessary?

Nothing but their own wickedness drives them to despair. They are unwilling to accept God's mercy. Their despair, then, instead of being essential to true submission is inconsistent. No man ever embraced the gospel while in that state. To say despair is essential to true submission is saying that *sin* is essential to true submission!

Every Christian knows that God desires sinners to be saved. The true ground for salvation is that a man must not seek his own salvation but seek the glory of God.

What did the apostles tell sinners when they asked what they must do to be saved? What did Peter tell them at Pentecost? What did Paul tell the jailer—to *repent,* forsake their selfishness, and believe the gospel. This is what men must do to be saved.

Another difficulty exists in attempting to convert men in this way. It tries to convert them by the law and sets aside the gospel, trying to make them holy without the appropriate influences. Paul tried this way and found it didn't work. In Romans 7, he gives us the result. It drove him to confess that the law was holy and good, and he ought to obey it. It left him crying, "The good that I would I do not: but the evil which I would not, that I do" (Romans 7:19). The law was not able to convert him, and he cried out, "O wretched man that I am! who shall deliver me from the body of this death?" (Romans 7:24).

Here the love of God in sending His Son Jesus Christ is presented to his mind, and that *did* the work. In the next chapter, Paul explains it. "What the law could not do, in that it was weak through the flesh, God sending his own Son in the likeness of sinful flesh, and for sin, condemned sin in the flesh: That the righteousness of the law might be fulfilled in us, who walk not after the flesh, but after the Spirit" (Romans 8:3-4). The whole Bible testifies that only the influence of the gospel can bring sinners to obey the law. The law will never do it.

The Father's Broken Heart

The offer of mercy can be perverted, as every good thing can be, and then it can give rise to selfish religion. And God knew it when He revealed the gospel. But nothing is calculated to subdue the rebellious heart of man other than God's mercy.

There was a father who had a stubborn and rebellious son, and he tried to subdue him by chastisement. He loved his son and longed to have him virtuous and obedient. But the child seemed to harden his heart against his repeated efforts. Finally, the poor father was discouraged and burst into a flood of tears. "My son! What can I do? Can I save you? I have done all that I can to save you! What more can I do?"

The son had never yielded to the rod. But when he saw the tears rolling down his father's cheeks and heard his sobs, he, too, burst into tears. He cried out, "Whip me, Father! But don't cry!" The father had found the way to subdue that stubborn heart. Instead of holding the iron hand of law over him, he poured out his soul before him. And what was the effect? To crush him into hypocritical submission? No, the rod did that. The gushing tears of his father's love broke him down at once to true submission to his father's will.

The sinner braves the wrath of Almighty God and hardens himself to receive the heaviest bolt of thunder. Then he sees the love of his Heavenly Father's heart. When he sees God manifested in the flesh, stooping to take human nature, hanging on the cross, and pouring out his soul in tears, bloody sweat, and death, his heart melts. He cries out, "Do anything else, and I can bear it; but the love of the blessed Jesus overwhelms me."

To be thus influenced is the very nature of the mind. Instead of being afraid to exhibit the love of God to sinners, this is the only way to make them truly submissive. The law makes hypocrites, but only the gospel can draw souls to truly love God.

Chapter 5

THE PURSUIT OF SELFISHNESS

"Love. . .seeketh not her own"—1 Corinthians 13:5.

Charity, or Christian love, "seeketh not her own." The question is not whether it is lawful to have any regard to our own happiness. On the contrary, part of our duty is to regard our own happiness according to its value in the scale with other interests. God has commanded us to love our neighbor *as ourselves.* This plainly makes it a duty to love ourselves and regard our own happiness by the same rule that we regard the happiness of others.

We must regard the promises of God and threatenings of evil as affecting ourselves. But a threat against us is not as important as a threat against a large number of individuals. Imagine a threat of evil against yourself as an individual. This is not as important as if it included your family. Then imagine it extended to the congregation, the state, the nation, or the world. The happiness of an individual, although great, should not be regarded as supreme.

I am a minister. Suppose God says to me, "If you do not do your duty, you will be sent to hell." This is a great evil, and I ought to avoid it. Instead, imagine Him to say, "If your people do not do their duty, they will all be sent to hell. But if you faithfully do your duty, you will save the whole congregation." Is it right for me to be as much influenced by the fear of evil to myself as by the fear of having a whole congregation sent to hell?

Godly Influence Or Fear?

The Bible tells us, "Labor not for the meat that perisheth, but for that meat which endureth unto everlasting life" (John 6:27). This teaches that we are not to value earthly interests at all compared to eternal life.

Our Savior says, "Lay not up for yourselves treasures on the earth, where moth and rust doth corrupt, and where thieves break through and steal: But lay up for yourselves treasures in heaven, where neither moth nor rust doth corrupt, and where thieves do not break through nor steal" (Matthew 6:20-21).

When Christ sent out His disciples, two by two, to preach and to work miracles, they came back full of joy and exultation because they found even the devils yielding to their power. "Lord, even the devils are subject unto us." Jesus answered, "Rejoice not, that the spirits are subject unto you; but rather rejoice because your names are written in heaven" (Luke 10:17,20). Here He teaches that it is a greater good to have our names written in heaven than to enjoy great temporal power, even authority over devils themselves.

The Bible teaches preference of eternal good over temporal good. This is different than regarding our own individual interest as the *supreme object*.

Hope and fear should influence our conduct. But when we are influenced by hope and fear, the things that are hoped or feared should be put into the scale according to their real value in comparison with other interests.

Noah was moved with fear and built the ark. But was it the fear of being drowned himself or fear for his own personal safety that chiefly moved him? The Bible does not say it. He feared for the safety of his family, and he dreaded the destruction of the whole human race.

Good men are influenced by hope and fear. However, this hope and fear respecting their own personal interest is not the controlling motive. This is not affirmed in the Bible. They must be influenced by promises and threats. Otherwise, they could not obey the second part of the law: "Thou shalt love thy neighbor *as thyself*."

Is supreme regard to our own happiness Christianity? Are we to fear our own damnation *more than* the damnation of all other men and the dishonor to God? Are we to aim at securing our own happiness *more than* the happiness of all other men and the glory of God?

All true Christianity consists in being like God—

acting on His principles and grounds and having His feelings towards different objects.

Benevolence And Complacency

The Bible tells us that "God is love" (1 John 4:16). Love is the sum total of His character. All His other moral attributes, such as justice, mercy, etc., are only modifications of this love. His love is manifested in two forms. One is *benevolence*—desiring the happiness of others. The other is *complacency*—approving the character of others who are holy.

God's *benevolence* regards all beings who are capable of happiness. This is universal. He exercises the love of *complacency* toward all holy beings. In other words, God loves His neighbor as Himself. He considers the interests of all beings, according to their relative value, as much as His own. He seeks His own happiness, or glory, as the supreme good— not because it is His own, but because *it is* the supreme good. The sum total of His happiness, as an infinite being, is greater than the sum total of the happiness of all other beings or of any possible number of finite creatures.

Imagine a man that is kind to animals. This man and his horse fall into the river. Now, does true Christian love require the man to drown himself in order to save his horse? No. It would be true benevolence to save himself. His happiness is of much greater value than that of the horse. But the difference between God and all created beings is infinitely greater than between a man and a horse or between the highest angel and the lowest insect.

God, therefore, regards the happiness of all creatures precisely according to their real value. Unless we do the same, we are not like God. If we are like God, we must regard God's happiness and glory in the same light that He does—as the supreme good, beyond everything else in the universe. If we desire our own happiness more than God's happiness, we are unlike God.

To aim supremely at our own happiness is contrary to the Spirit of Christ. We are told that "if any man have not the Spirit of Christ, he is none of his" (Romans 8:9). Jesus, as a man, did not seek His own glory. What was He seeking? Was it His own personal salvation or happiness? No. It was the *glory of His Father* and the good of the universe through the salvation of men. He came to benefit the Kingdom of God—not to benefit Himself. This was "the joy that was set before him," for which He "endured the cross, despising the shame" (Hebrews 12:2).

The sum of the gospel is this: "Thou shalt love the Lord thy God with all thy heart, and with all thy soul, and with all thy strength, and with all thy mind; and thy neighbor as thyself" (Luke 10:27). Benevolence toward God and man is the great requirement. To love the happiness and glory of God above all other things is lovely and desirable and *is* the supreme good.

Some have objected that it is not our duty to seek the happiness of God because His happiness is already secured. Suppose the king of England is perfectly independent of me and is happy without me. Does that make it less my duty to wish him well, to desire his happiness, and to rejoice in it? Because God is happy, independent of His creatures, should we not love His happiness and rejoice in it?

Dying To Self

To seek our own happiness as our supreme end is contrary to the gospel. In 1 Corinthians 13, the apostle begins, "Though I speak with the tongues of men and of angels, and have not charity, I am become as sounding brass, or a tinkling cymbal. And though I have the gift of prophecy, and understand all mysteries, and all knowledge; and though I have all faith, so that I could remove mountains, and have not charity, I am nothing. And though I bestow all my goods to feed the poor, and though I give my body to be burned, and have not charity, it profiteth me nothing" (verses 1-3).

Paul couldn't have expressed the idea that charity (love), or benevolence, is essential to Christianity in stronger language. He lowers his guard on every side and makes it impossible to mistake his views: If a person has no true love, he is nothing.

Paul then shows what the characteristics of this true charity are: "Charity suffereth long, and is kind; charity envieth not; charity vaunteth not itself, is not puffed up, Doth not behave itself unseemly, seeketh not her own, is not easily provoked, thinketh no evil; Rejoiceth not in iniquity, but rejoiceth in the truth; Beareth all things, believeth all things, hopeth all things, endureth all things'' (1 Corinthians 13:4-7).

Here you see that one leading peculiarity of this love is that charity ''seeketh not her own.'' Many passages plainly teach the same thing. ''Whosoever will save his life shall lose it'' (Matthew 16:25). An established principle of God's government is that if a person aims supremely at his own interest, he will lose his own interest.

The same principle is taught later in this epistle: ''Let no man seek his own, but every man another's wealth'' (1 Corinthians 10:24). If you look at the passage, you will see that the word *wealth* is in italic letters, showing that it was added by the translator and is not in the Greek. They could have as easily used the word ''happiness'' or ''welfare'' as wealth.

Paul also says, ''Even as I please all men in all things, not seeking mine own profit, but the profit of many, that they may be saved'' (1 Corinthians 10:33). Therefore, to make our own interest our supreme object is as contrary to the gospel as it is to the law.

A supreme regard to our own happiness is not virtue. Men have always known that to serve God and benefit mankind is what is right, and to seek supremely their own personal interest is not right. Consequently, we see how much pain men take to conceal their selfishness and appear benevolent. Unless his conscience is blunted by sin or perverted by false instruction, any man can see that to place his own happiness above more important interests is sinful.

Right reason teaches us to regard all things according to their *real value*. God does this, and we should do the same. God has given us the ability to reason for the purpose of weighing and comparing the relative value of things. It is a mockery of reason to deny that it teaches us to regard things according to their real value. To aim at and prefer our own interest is contrary to reason.

Chasing After Happiness

Look at the common sense of mankind in regard to what is called patriotism. No man was ever regarded as a true patriot if his object was to observe his own interest. Suppose his object in fighting was to get himself crowned king; would anybody give him credit for patriotism? All men agree that patriotism is when a man fights for his country's sake. The common sense of mankind understands that a reprobate spirit seeks its own things and prefers its own interests to the greater interests of others.

Happiness is the gratification of desire. We must desire something and gain the object we desire. If a man desires his own happiness, the object of his desire will always keep just ahead of him like his shadow. The faster he pursues it, the faster it flies. Happiness is inseparably attached to the attainment of the object desired.

Suppose I desire a thousand dollars. When I get it that desire is gratified and I am happy. But if I desire the thousand dollars for the purpose of getting a watch, a shirt, etc., the desire is not gratified until I get those things.

But suppose the thing I desired was my own happiness. Getting the thousand dollars does not make me happy because that is not the thing my desire was fixed on. And getting the watch, the shirt, and other things will not make me happy either, for they do not gratify my desire.

God has so constituted things and given such laws to the mind that man can *never* gain happiness by pursuing it. This very makeup plainly indicates the duty of *disinterested benevolence*. Indeed, He has made it impossible for them to be happy, except to the degree that they are disinterested.

Imagine two men walking along the street together. They come across a man who has just been run over and lies bleeding by the curb. They pick him up and carry him to the hospital. Their gratification is in proportion to the intensity of their desire for his relief. If one of them felt and cared little about the suffering of the poor man, he would be little gratified. But if his desire to have the man relieved amounted to agony, his gratification would be accordingly.

Suppose a third individual had no desire to relieve the distressed man. Helping him would be no gratification to that person. He could pass right by him and watch him die. He is not gratified at all. Therefore, happiness is in proportion to gratified desire.

In order to make the happiness of gratified desire complete, the *desire itself* must be virtuous. If the desire is selfish, the gratification will be mingled with pain from conflict in the mind.

That all this is true is a matter of consciousness and is proved to us by the very highest kind of testimony we can have. For anyone to deny this is to charge God foolishly as if He had given us a makeup that would not allow us to be happy in obeying Him.

Men may enjoy a certain kind of pleasure that is not true happiness. Pleasure that does not spring from the gratification of a virtuous desire is a delusion. The reason men do not find happiness, when they are all so anxious for it, is that they are *seeking it*. If they would seek the glory of God and the good of the universe as their supreme end, *happiness would pursue them*.

If each individual aimed at his own happiness as his chief end, their interests would unavoidably collide. Universal war and confusion would follow the train of universal selfishness.

Common Sense And Conscience

To maintain that a supreme regard to our own interest is true Christianity is to contradict the ex-

75

perience of the saints. Every true saint knows that his supreme happiness consists in denying himself and regarding the glory of God and the good of others. If he does not know this, he is not a Christian.

Many people who have had a selfish religion have realized their mistake and come to understand true Christianity. I have known hundreds of such cases, and they testify they know now, by experience, that benevolence is true Christianity.

Every impenitent sinner knows he is aiming supremely at his own interest, and he knows that he doesn't have the truth. The very thing that his conscience condemns him for is that he is regarding his own interest instead of the glory of God.

If a supreme regard to our own interest (*because* it is our own) is true Christianity, then it will follow that God is not holy. God regards His own happiness because it is *the greatest good,* not because it is His own. He is love, or benevolence; and if benevolence is not true Christianity, God's nature must be changed.

If a supreme regard to our own happiness is Christianity, then the law should read, "Thou shalt love thyself with all thy heart and with all thy soul and with all thy mind and with all thy strength, and God and thy neighbor infinitely less than thyself."

When we place our happiness first, we must change "Whether ye eat or drink, or whatsoever ye do, do all to the glory of God" to "Do all for your own happiness." Instead of "He that will save his

76

life shall lose it," we find it saying, "He that is anxious to save his own life shall save it; but he that is benevolent and willing to lose his life for the good of others, shall lose it."

The consciences of men would be changed to testify in favor of selfishness and condemn everything concerning love.

Right reason would be made not to weigh things according to their relative value but to decide that our own little interest is of more value than the greatest interests of God and the universe.

The human makeup would be reversed. If supreme selfishness is virtue, the human constitution was made wrong. And if Christianity consists in seeking our own happiness as a supreme good, then the more faith a man has the more miserable he is.

The whole framework of society would have to be changed. The public good would be best promoted when every man is scrambling for his own interest regardless of the interests of others.

The experience of the saints would have to be reversed. Instead of finding that the more love they have, the more happiness they have, they would testify that the more they aim at their own good, the more they enjoy the favor of God.

The impenitent would testify that they are supremely happy in supreme selfishness.

I will not pursue this proof any further. It has been fully proven that to aim supremely at our own happiness is inconsistent with Christianity.

Selfishness Or True Christianity?

Most men do not know what true happiness is, and they seek it in vain. *They do not find it because they are pursuing it.* If they would turn around and pursue holiness, then happiness would pursue them. If they would become disinterested and determine to do good, they could not help being happy. If they choose happiness as an end, it flies away from them. True happiness consists in the gratification of virtuous desires; and if they would set themselves to glorify God and do good, they would find it.

Many say, "Who will take care of my happiness if I do not? If I am to care only for my neighbor's interest and neglect my own, none of us will be happy." That would be true if your concern for your neighbor's happiness was a detraction from your own. But if your happiness consists in doing good and promoting the happiness of others, the more you do for others, the more you promote your own happiness.

It would be selfishness in God if He regarded His own interest supremely because it is His own. Whoever maintains that a supreme regard to our own interest is Christianity maintains that *selfishness* is Christianity.

If selfishness is virtue, then benevolence is sin. They are direct opposites and cannot both be virtue. For a man to set up his own interest over God's interest is selfishness. If this is virtue, then Jesus Christ departed from the principles of virtue.

Those who regard their own interest as supreme and think they are Christians are deceived. I say it solemnly because I believe it is true, and I would say it if it was the last word I was to speak before going to the judgment. As God is true and your soul is going to the judgment, you do not have the Christianity of the Bible if you are selfish.

Are we to have no regard to our happiness? If so, how are we to decide whether it is supreme or not? You may regard it according to its relative value. Is there any real practical difficulty here? I appeal to your consciousness. If you are honest, you know what your *priorities* are. Are your interests on one side and God's glory and the good of the universe on the other? Or are they so closely balanced in your mind that you cannot tell which you prefer? It is impossible! If you are not just as conscious that you prefer the glory of God to your own interest as you are that you exist, you may take it for granted that you are all wrong.

Choosing To Pursue Holiness

If you really regard the glory of God and the good of mankind, your enjoyment will not depend on evidence. Those who are purely selfish may enjoy much in religion, but it is by anticipation. The idea of going to heaven is pleasing to them. But those who are purely benevolent have heaven present in their hearts.

Anyone who had no peace and joy in the Lord

before they had a hope is deceived. How very different is the experience of a true Christian! His peace does not depend on his hope. True submission and benevolence produce peace and joy independent of hope.

Suppose a prisoner is condemned to be hung the next day. Walking his cell and waiting for dawn, he is in great distress. A messenger comes with a pardon. He seizes the paper, turns it up to the dim light coming through his grate, reads the word *pardon,* and leaps for joy. He thinks the paper is genuine. Now suppose it turns out that the paper is counterfeit. Suddenly his joy is all gone.

It is the same in the case of a deceived person. He was afraid of going to hell, and of course he rejoices if he believes he is pardoned. If the devil told him so and he believed it, his joy would be just as great as if it were a reality.

True Christian joy does not depend on evidence. The true Christian commits himself into the hands of God with confidence, and that very act gives him peace. He had a terrible conflict with God, but all at once he yields and says, "God will do right, let God's will be done."

Then he begins to pray and melts before God. That very act affords sweet, heavenly joy. Perhaps he has not thought of a hope. He may go for hours or even days, full of joy in God, without thinking of his own salvation. His joy does not depend on believing that he is pardoned but consists in *a state of mind,* resting in the government of God. In such a state of mind he can not help being happy.

Hope-seekers will always be disappointed. If you run after hope, you will never have a hope good for anything. But if you pursue holiness, then hope, peace, and joy will come naturally. Is your faith the love of holiness, God, and souls? Or is it only a hope? Look at God's whole character and see the reasons why you should love Him. Throw yourself upon Him without reserve and without distrust. Instead of shrinking from Him, come to Him and say, "Father in heaven, you are sovereign and good. I submit to your government and give myself to you—all I have and all I am, body and soul, for time and eternity."

Chapter 6

RELIGION OR SAVING FAITH?

"What shall we say then? That the Gentiles, which followed not after righteousness, have attained to righteousness, even the righteousness which is of faith. But Israel, which followed after the law of righteousness, hath not attained to the law of righteousness. Wherefore? Because they sought it not by faith, but as it were by the works of the law. For they stumbled at the stumblingstone; As it is written, Behold, I lay in Sion a stumblingstone and rock of offense: and whosoever believeth on him shall not be ashamed"—Romans 9:30-33.

In the epistle to the Romans, Paul systematically proves that not only the Gentiles but the Jews were in a state of entire depravity. He then introduces the *moral law,* explaining it shows that works of the law cannot save man's soul. Sanctification, or holiness, is by faith, and all acceptable obedience is based on faith.

In the eighth and ninth chapters, he introduces the subject of divine sovereignty. Then, in the last part of the ninth chapter, he sums up the whole matter and asks, "What shall we say, then?" The Gentiles, who never thought of the law, had become pious and obtained the holiness which is by faith; but the Jews, attempting it by the law, had entirely failed. Why? Because they made the fatal mistake of attempting to become pious by obeying the law and had come short, while the Gentiles became righteous through faith in Jesus Christ. Jesus is here called "that stumblingstone" because the Jews were opposed to Him.

The difference between the religion of law and Christianity does not lie in the fact that under the law men were justified by works, without faith. The method of salvation in both covenants has been the same. Sinners were always justified by faith. The Jewish religion pointed to a Savior to come. If men were saved at all, it was by faith in Christ. And sinners now are saved in the same way.

God's Moral Government

The gospel has not canceled or set aside the obligations of the moral law. It *has* set aside the claims of the ceremonial law or law of Moses. The ceremonial law was nothing but a set of types pointing to the Savior and was set aside when the great ante-type appeared.

Many people maintain that the gospel has set aside the moral law so that believers are under no obligation to obey it. Such was the doctrine of the Nicolaitans, who were severely rebuked by Christ. (See Revelation 2.) The Antinomians, in the days of the apostles, believed that they were without any obligation to obey the moral law. They held that Christ's righteousness was imputed to believers. Since He had fulfilled the law for them, they were under no obligation to obey it themselves.

In modern times, *Perfectionists* have held that they were not under obligation to obey the law. They suppose that Christ has delivered them from the law and given them the Spirit. They believe the leadings of the Spirit are now their rule of life instead of God's law. The Bible says that sin will not have dominion over believers, but these people think the same acts that would be sin if done by an unconverted person are not sin in them.

All such notions are radically wrong. God has no right to give up the moral law. He cannot discharge us from the duty of love to God and love to man, for this is right *in itself.* Unless God alters the whole moral constitution of the universe to make that right which is wrong, He cannot give up the claims of the moral law. Besides, this doctrine represents Jesus Christ and the Holy Spirit as having taken up arms openly against the government of God.

Some people talk about gospel liberty as though they had a new rule of life allowing more liberty than the law. The gospel has provided a new method of justification, but it insists that the rule of life is the same with the law. The very first sentence of the gospel—the command to repent—is in effect a reenactment of the law. It is a command to return to obedience. The idea that the liberty of the gospel differs from the liberty of the law is absurd.

Legalists depend on their own works for justification either by profession or in fact. If they do depend on Christ for salvation, their dependence is a false dependence. They depend on Him, but their faith doesn't work by love, purify the heart, or overcome the world. They have a *kind* of faith, but not the kind that makes men real Christians and brings them under the terms of the gospel.

Legal Obedience And Love

Several different classes of people have a legal religion. Some *profess* to depend on their own works for salvation. Such were the Pharisees. I want you to distinguish between works of law and works of faith. This is the main distinction to remember—some works are produced by legal considerations and some are produced by faith.

Two principles can produce obedience to any government. One is the principle of *hope and fear,* under the influence of conscience. Conscience points out what is right or wrong, and the individual is induced by hope and fear to obey. The other principle is *confidence and love.* You see this illustrated in families where one child always obeys from hope and fear and another from affectionate confidence. In the government of God, the only thing that ever produced even the appearance of obedience is one of these two principles.

A multitude of things address our hopes and fears such as character, interest, heaven and hell, etc. These may produce external obedience or conformity to the law. But filial confidence leads men to obey God from love. This is the only obedience that is acceptable to God. God requires a certain course of conduct, and it should spring from love. There never was and never can be, in the government of God, any acceptable obedience but the obedience of faith. Some people think that faith will be done away with in heaven, as if there will be no occasion to trust God in heaven or no reason to exercise confidence in Him!

Here is the great distinction between the religion of law and Christianity: Legal obedience is influenced by hope and fear and is hypocritical, selfish, outward, and constrained. Gospel obedience is from love and is sincere, free, cheerful, and true. Legalists depend on works of law for justification, defying what they call a principle of right and setting themselves to do right—not out of respect to the law of God or out of love to God but just because it is right.

The religion of law is the religion of *purpose or desires* founded on legal considerations and not the religion of *preference* or *love to God.* The individual *intends* to put off his sins and purposes to obey God and be religious. His purpose does not grow out of love to God but out of hope and fear. A purpose founded on such considerations is very different

86

from a purpose growing out of love. Christianity is not a mere purpose but an actual preference consisting in love.

Some Legalists depend on Christ, but their dependence is not gospel dependence because the works that it produces are works of law from hope and fear. Gospel dependence may produce the very same outward works, but the motives are radically different. The Legalist drags on a painful, irksome, moral, and outwardly religious life. The gospel believer has an affectionate confidence in God that leads him to obey out of love. His obedience is prompted by his own feelings. Instead of being dragged to duty, he goes to it cheerfully because he loves it, and doing it is a delight to his soul.

The Legalist expects to be justified by faith, but he has not learned that he must be *sanctified*, or set apart, by faith. Modern Legalists do not expect to be justified by works, for they know these are inadequate. They know that the way to be saved is by Christ. But they have no practical belief that justification by faith is only true when men are first sanctified by faith. And, therefore, while they expect to be justified by faith, they perform works that are works of law.

Jesus' Yoke Of Love

True Christians and Legalists may agree on the necessity of good works and theoretically in what constitutes good works—that is, obedience springing from love to God. They may agree in aiming to perform good works of this kind. But the difference lies in the different influences that enable them to perform good works. The consideration they expect to affect their minds is different. They look to different sources for motives. The true Christian alone succeeds in actually performing good works. The Legalist, aiming to perform good works, is influenced by hope, fear, and a selfish regard to his own interest. He obeys the voice of conscience because he is afraid to do otherwise and falls entirely short of loving God with all his heart, soul, and strength.

The motives under which the Legalist acts have no tendency to bring him to the obedience of love. The true Christian, on the contrary, appreciates God and perceives and understands His character. In Christ he has such an affectionate confidence in God that he finds it easy to obey from love. The commandments are not grievous. The yoke is easy and the burden light. He finds the ways of wisdom to be ways of pleasantness, and all her paths to be peace. (See Proverbs 3:17.)

Is it so with you? Do you feel, in your duties, constrained by love? Are you drawn by such strong cords of love that it would give you more trouble to disobey than to do His will? Do your affections flow out in strong currents to God?

What is the matter with individuals who find it hard to obey and harder still to love? Ask the wife who loves her husband if she finds it hard to try to please him? Suppose she answers, in a solemn tone, "Yes, I find it hard to obey and harder still to love my husband." What would her husband think?

What would you parents say if you heard one of your children complaining, "I find it hard to obey my father and harder still to love"?

A radical defect lies in the religion of people who love such expressions and live as if they were true. If any of you find serving Jesus a painful thing, you have the religion of law. Did you ever find it painful to do what you love to do? No. It is a pleasure to do it.

Christianity is not labor, it is the feeling of the heart. What would you do in heaven if serving God is such a painful thing here? Suppose you were taken to heaven and obliged to grind out religion every week, month, and year throughout eternity. What sort of heaven would it be to you? Would it be heaven, or would it be hell? If you were required to have ten thousand times as much religion as you have here, and your whole life were to be filled up with such duties, wouldn't hell itself be a relief to you?

One class strives to be religious through hope and fear. Under the influence of conscience, they lash themselves if they don't do their duty. The other class acts from love to God and the impulses of their own feelings. They know what the Scripture means: "I will put my law in their inward parts, and write it on their hearts; and I will be their God, and they shall be my people" (Jeremiah 31:33).

You can see this experience in almost any convicted sinner after he has become truly converted. He was convicted, and the law was brought home to his mind. He struggled to fulfill the law. He was in agony, but then he was filled with joy and glory. Why? He agonized under the law. He had no rest and no satisfaction and tried to please God by keeping the law. He went about in pain, read the Bible, and tried to pray. But the Spirit of God was upon him showing him his sins, and he had no relief. The more he attempted to help himself, the deeper he sank in despair. The whole time his heart was cold and selfish.

Now let him be influenced by love to God. The same Holy Spirit is upon him, showing him the same sins that grieved and distressed him so before. But now he hits his knees, tears flow like water as he confesses his guilt, and his heart melts. Now he performs the same duties, but what a difference! The Spirit of God has broken his chains, and now he loves and is filled with joy and peace in believing.

Faith Works By Love

Here is the difference between the slavery of law and the liberty of the gospel. The liberty of the gospel does *not* consist in being freed from doing what the law requires but in a man's being in such a state of mind that doing it is itself a pleasure. What is the difference between slavery and freedom? The slave serves because he has to do so, but the free man serves from *choice*. The man who is under the bondage of law serves because conscience thunders in his ears if he does not obey, and he hopes to go to heaven if he is obedient. The man who is in the liberty of the gospel serves because he loves to. One is influenced by selfishness, and the other by selfless love.

If we believe the words and actions of most professing Christians, they have made a mistake and have the religion of law. They are not constrained by the love of Christ but moved by hopes, fears, and the commandments of God. They have gone no further than to be convicted sinners. I have witnessed the regeneration of so many false converts that I fear great multitudes in the Church are still under the law. Although they profess to depend on Christ for salvation, their faith does not work by love.

Some people are all faith, without works. These are *Antinomians*. Others are all works and no faith. These are *Legalists*. In all ages of the Church, men have inclined first to one of these extremes and then over to the other. Sometimes they pretend to be all faith, awaiting God's time. Then they get zealous about works, without regard to the motive from which they act.

The true character of these false converts is to cry out, "Legality!" as soon as they are challenged with holiness. When I first began to preach, I found this spirit in many places. The moment Christians were urged to work, the cry would rise, "This is legal preaching. Preach the gospel; salvation is by faith, not by works; you ought to comfort the saints, not distress them.'' All this was nothing but rank *Antinomianism*.

On the other hand, the same people now complain if you preach the true nature of gospel faith. Now they want to do something and insist that no preaching is good unless it stirs them up to good works. They are all for doing, doing, doing and will be dissatisfied with preaching that discriminates between true and false faith and urges obedience of the heart out of love to God. The Antinomians wait for God to produce right feelings in them. The Legalists want to get right feelings by going to work.

Going to work is the way, when the Church feels right, to bring about right feelings. But to dash right out into work without any regard to the motives of the heart is not the way to get right feelings in the first place.

Real Christians are a stumbling block to both parties—to those who wait for God's time and do nothing and to those who bustle about with no faith. The true Christian acts under love to God and his fellowmen, and he labors to pull sinners out of the fire with earnestness.

If the Church is awakened and has the spirit of prayer and zeal for the conversion of sinners, there will be some who sit still and complain that the Church is depending on its own strength. Others will be very busy and noisy but without any feeling. The third class will be so full of love and compassion to sinners that they can hardly eat or sleep, yet so humble and tender that you would imagine they felt themselves to be nothing. The Legalist, with his dry zeal, makes a great noise, deceives himself, and thinks he is acting just like a Christian. The true Christian is stirring and active in the service of Christ but moves with the holy fire that burns within his own bosom.

Some people's religion is steady and uniform while that of others is fitful and unstable. You will find some individuals always excited about Jesus. Talk to them any time, and their souls will kindle. Others are awake only now and then. Once in a while, you may find them full of zeal. When one has the anointing that abides, he has something that is durable. But if his religion is only that of the law, he will have only as much of it as he has of conviction at the present moment.

Some are anxious to get to heaven, while others are happy here. True Christians have a love for souls. They have such a desire to have Christ's Kingdom built up on earth that they are perfectly happy to live and labor for God as long as He chooses to have them. If they were sent to hell and permitted to labor there for souls, they would be happy. Others talk as if people weren't meant to enjoy life; but when they get to heaven, they expect to be happy. They have no enjoyment except in hope. The other already has the reality, the very substance of heaven begun in the soul.

What kind of Christianity do you have? True Christianity is always the same and consists in disinterested love to God and man. Does this describe you? Does your faith consist of the pursuit of happiness as the great end? The fruits of the Spirit are love, joy, and peace. There is no condemnation in true Christianity. But if any man doesn't have the Spirit of Christ, he is none of His.

Please don't make a mistake and go down to hell with a lie in your right hand because you have the religion of the law. The Jews failed here, while the Gentiles attained true holiness by the gospel. How many are deceived, acting under legal considerations, while they know nothing of true Christianity?

Chapter 7

WHO ARE WE TRYING TO FOOL?

"But be ye doers of the word, and not hearers only, deceiving your own selves"—James 1:22.

Anyone who does not practice what he admits to be true is self-deceived.

Two classes of hypocrites exist among professing Christians—those that deceive others and those that deceive themselves. One class of hypocrites has a deceptive show of religion, cover up the enmity of their hearts against God, and lead others to think they are very pious people. Thus the Pharisees obtained the reputation of being remarkably pious by their show of religion, their alms, and their long prayers.

The other class does not deceive others but *themselves*. Their religion consists of a parcel of *notions* without regard to practice, and they deceive themselves to think they are good Christians. But they are destitute of true holiness. They are hearers of the Word but not doers. They love orthodox preaching and take great pleasure in hearing abstract doctrines exhibited. With imagination and glowing feelings, they view the character and government of God; but they are not careful to practice the precepts of God's Word.

It is highly probable that a number of readers are of this character. I do not know your names, but I want you to understand that if you are of this character, you are the person I am speaking to. I mean you. You hear the Word and believe it in theory, while you deny it in practice. You *deceive yourselves.* The Scripture proves it. Here you have an express "Thus saith the Lord" that all hearers are not doers and are self-deceivers.

True Saving Faith

In the first place, you hear the Word and admit it to be true, but you do not truly *believe* it. Two things are necessary for evangelical or saving faith. The first is intellectual conviction after hearing truth. I do not mean merely the abstract truth but its bearing *on you.* The truth, in its relation to you, or its bearing on your conduct, must be received intellectually. True faith includes a corresponding change of heart. When a man's mind is convinced, and he admits the truth in relation *to himself,* then there must be an application of it to himself. Both these states of mind are indispensable to true faith.

Intellectual conviction of the truth is not saving faith. But intellectual conviction, accompanied by a change of the affections, *is* saving faith. Therefore, true saving faith always brings a change in conduct. Just as certain as the will controls the conduct, men will act as they believe. Suppose I say to a man, "Do you believe this?" "Yes, I believe it." What does he mean—a mere intellectual conviction? He may have that but not have faith.

A man may even approve or agree with *abstract truth*. Many persons suppose faith is applauding for the character and government of God and the plan of salvation. They view it, however, abstractedly. When they hear an eloquent sermon on the attributes or government of God, they are excited about the glory and excellency displayed. They do not have a particle of true faith. The rational mind is so formed that it naturally approves of truth when viewed abstractedly.

The most wicked devils in hell love it, as long as they do not see it in relation to themselves. If the gospel did not interfere with their own selfishness, they would not only see it as true but would heartily approve it. The reason why wicked men and devils hate God is because they see Him in relation to themselves. Their hearts rise up in rebellion because they see Him opposed to their selfishness.

This is the source of a grand delusion among men in regard to Christianity. They see it as truth, and they rejoice in contemplating it. They do not apply it to themselves, and so they love to hear such preaching and say they are fed by it. But they go away and do not practice it!

Imagine a man who is sick, and his feelings are

tender. In view of Christ as a kind and tender Savior, his heart melts, and he feels strong emotions towards Jesus Christ. Why? For the very same reasons that he would feel strong emotions towards the hero of a romance. But he does not *obey* Christ. He never practices one thing out of obedience to Christ but views Him abstractedly and is delighted with His glorious and lovely character. He himself remains in the gall of bitterness. Faith must be an efficient, moving faith that produces good works, or it is not the faith of the gospel and is no real faith at all.

Doers Of The Word

True Christianity *consists in obedience*. However much you may approve of Christianity, you have no faith unless you obey it. In saying that true faith consists in obedience, I do not mean *outward* obedience. But faith itself, true faith, works *by love* and produces action. There is no real obedience but the obedience of the heart. Love fulfills the law, and Christianity consists in the obedience of the heart with a corresponding change of life.

The man who hears the truth and approves it but does not practice it deceives himself. He is like the man beholding his natural face in a glass—he sees himself, goes his way, and immediately forgets what he looks like. (See James 1:23-24.)

The state of mind that you mistake for Christianity—an intellectual conviction of truth and approval of it in the abstract—is as common to the wicked as to the good. This is why it is so difficult to convince sinners that they are opposed to God and His truth. Men are created so that they do approve of virtue and admire the character and government of God. They would approve and admire every truth in the Bible, *if* they could view it abstractedly and without any application to themselves. They can sit for years under preaching that holds up the truth in such a way that it has no practical bearing on themselves. Then they will never consider that *they* are opposed to God and to His government.

I am persuaded that great multitudes of unconverted souls can be found in all congregations where the abstract doctrines are preached. No doubt many come to church because they love orthodox preaching. But after all this preaching, still they are not doers of the Word. And here is the difficulty: they have not had that searching preaching that made them see the truth in its bearing *on themselves.*

Now that they are in the Church, whenever the truth is preached in its practical relation to them, they show that their hearts are unchanged by opposing the truth.

They took it for granted that they were Christians and joined a church to hear sound doctrinal preaching. They read the Bible and approve of it. If their faith is not practical enough to influence their conduct, or if they do not view the truth in relation to their own practice, then their faith does not affect them as much as the faith of the devil. (See James 2:19.)

Great injury has been done by false representation of the wickedness of real Christians. Many impressions suggest that real Christians are the most wicked beings on the face of the earth. When they sin, they incur great guilt. For a Christian to sin is highly criminal. Enlightened Christians see great wickedness in their sins. When they compare their obligations with their lives, they are greatly humbled and express their humility in very strong language.

But it is not true that they are as bad as the devil or anywhere in the neighborhood of it. When they do sin, their sins have great aggravation and appear extremely wicked in the sight of God. But to suppose that men are true Christians while they live in the service of the devil is not only false but very dangerous.

Heretics And Pharisees

The truth is that those who do not obey God are *not* Christians. The contrary doctrine is ruinous to the churches, filling them with multitudes whose claim to piety depends on their adoption of certain notions, while they never truly intended to *obey* the requirements of the gospel in their lives.

Professing Christians who never like to hear about God or His attributes but lay all stress on religious practice to the exclusion of Christian doctrines are *Pharisees*. They practice outward piety but will not receive the great truths that relate to God, and they deny the fundamental doctrines of the gospel.

Wherever you find a man's *practice* heretical, you may be sure his *belief* is heretical too. The faith that he hides in his heart is just as heretical as his life. He may not be heretical in his *notions and theories.* He may be right there, even on the very point where he is heretical in his practice. But he does not really *believe* it. For example, if you ask a careless sinner if he expects to die, he will reply, "Oh, yes, I know I must die; all men are mortal." As soon as he thinks about it, he assents to the truth. And if you could fasten the conviction on his mind until he is really and permanently impressed with it, he would undoubtedly change his conduct and live for another world instead of this one. But he does not really believe he is going to die, and he continues grasping for wealth. A man's belief controls his practice, just as his will governs his conduct.

The Church has for too long been concerned with abstract doctrines and left the more practical out of view. Look at the creeds of the Church and see how the main emphasis lies on those doctrines that have little to do with our practice. A man may be the greatest heretic on points of practice, provided he is not openly profane or vicious, and maintain a good standing in the Church. When we attempt to purify the Church in regard to practical errors, he cannot bear it.

Why is it so difficult to get the Church to do anything for the conversion of the world? When will the Church be purified and the world converted?

Not until it is agreed that heresy in practice is the proof of heresy in belief. Not while a man may *deny the whole gospel* in his practice every day and yet maintain his standing in the Church as a "good Christian."

A minister can be deceived in regard to the state of his congregation. If he preaches a good deal on abstract doctrines that do not immediately relate to practice, his people rejoice; and he thinks they are growing in grace. In fact, it is no certain sign that there is any Christianity among them. But if he preaches practical doctrines and his people show that they love the truth in regard to themselves practicing it, then they show they love the truth.

If a minister finds that his people rebel when he comes to press the practical doctrines, he can be sure that their Christianity is in a low state.

Practice What You Believe

Many people suppose they are Christians from the *emotions* they feel in view of truth. But what they receive is truth presented to their minds in such a way that they do not see its bearing on *themselves*. If you present the truth to them, destroy their pride, and cut them off from their worldliness, they will resist it. Look at the Church. Many orthodox churches and orthodox Christians live and feed upon the abstract doctrines of religion from year to year. Then look further at their lives and see how little influence their professed belief has upon their *prac-*

tice. Do they have saving faith? It cannot be. I don't mean to say that none of these church members are virtuous but that those who do not practice what they admit in theory deceive themselves.

Are you conscious that the gospel is producing a practical effect upon you, according to your knowledge? Is it weaning you from the world? When you receive any practical truth into your minds, do you love its application to yourself? Do you take pleasure in practicing it? If you are not growing in grace, becoming more and more holy, and *yielding yourselves* up to the influence of the gospel, you are deceiving yourselves.

Woe to that man who admits the truth and yet turns away and does not practice it. He is like the man who, seeing his natural face in a mirror, turns away and forgets what he looks like.

Chapter 8

IDOLATRY AND THE FEAR OF GOD

"They feared the Lord, and served their own gods"—2 Kings 17:33.

When the ten tribes of Israel were carried away by the king of Assyria, their land was repopulated with strangers of different idolatrous nations who knew nothing of the religion of the Jews. Very soon, the wild beasts increased in the country, and the lions destroyed multitudes of the people. They thought it was because they did not know the god of that country and had therefore ignorantly transgressed and offended him.

So they applied to the king, who told them to get one of the priests of the Israelites to teach them the manner of the god of the land. They took this advice and obtained one of the priests to come to Bethal and teach them the religious ceremonies and modes of worship that had been practiced there. And he taught them to fear Jehovah as the god of that country. But still, they did not receive Him as the only God. They feared Him, that is, they feared

His anger and His judgments; and to avert these they performed the prescribed rites.

But they *served* their own gods. They kept up their idolatrous worship, and this was what they loved and preferred, although they felt obliged to pay some reverence to Jehovah as a god of that country. Multitudes of persons still profess a certain kind of fear of the Lord who nevertheless *serve* their own gods—other things to which their hearts are supremely devoted and in which they mainly put their trust.

Serving In Bondage And Selfishness

There are two kinds of fear. There is the fear of the Lord, which is the beginning of wisdom and is founded in love. There is also a slavish fear, which is a mere dread of evil and is purely selfish. This is the kind of fear that was possessed by those people spoken of in the text. They were afraid Jehovah would send His judgments upon them if they did not perform certain rites, and this was the motive they had for worshipping Him. Those who have this fear are supremely selfish and, while they profess to reverence Jehovah, have other gods whom they love and serve.

To *serve* a person is to be obedient to the will and devoted to the interests of that individual. To serve God is to make Christianity the main business of life and to devote one's self, heart, life, powers, time, influence, and *all* to build up the Kingdom of God and advance His glory. Who are they who profess to fear the Lord but serve their own gods? Anyone who has not heartily and practically renounced the *ownership* of his possessions and given them up to the Lord.

Suppose a gentleman were to employ a clerk who continued to attend to his own business. When asked to do what is necessary for his employer, who pays him wages, he replied, "I really have so much business of my own that I have no time to do these things." Such a servant was not serving his employer at all. His time was paid for by another, but he served himself. Where a man has not renounced the ownership of himself, not only in thought but *practically*, he has not taken the first step in Christianity. He is not serving the Lord but serving his own gods.

The man who does not make his business a part of his Christianity does not serve God. Sometimes men say that they are engaged all day in business and don't have time to serve God. They think they serve God a little while in the morning and then attend to their worldly business. They are not serving God. It is a shame for them to pretend to serve God. They are willing to give God the time before breakfast or before they go to work, but as soon as that is over, away they go. They fear the Lord enough to pray morning and night, but they serve their own gods.

Their religion is the laughing stock of hell. While they pray devoutly, they serve themselves instead of engaging in business for God. No doubt the idols are well satisfied with the arrangement, but God is wholly displeased.

Many of you make religion consist in certain acts of piety that do not interfere with your selfishness. You pray in the morning with your family because you can do it then very conveniently. But don't interfere with the service of your own god or stand in the way of your getting rich and enjoying the world. The gods you serve make no complaint of being slighted or neglected for the service of Jehovah.

Sunday Christians

Multitudes of people suppose that the week is man's time and the Sabbath is God's. They think they have a right to do their own work during the week and promote their own interests, if they will only serve God on Sunday.

A celebrated preacher, in illustrating the wickedness of breaking the Sabbath, used this illustration: "Suppose a man having seven dollars in his pocket should meet a beggar in great distress and give him six dollars, keeping only one for himself. And the beggar, seeing that he retained one dollar, should turn and rob him of that—would not every heart despise his baseness?" This illustration embodies the idea that it is ungrateful to break the Sabbath since God has given to men six days for *their own* and only reserved the Sabbath for Himself.

You that do this do not serve God *at all*. If you

are selfish during the week, you are selfish altogether. To suppose you had any real piety would imply that you were converted every Sunday and unconverted every Monday. But is the Sabbath a day to serve God, exclusive of other days? Is God in need of your services on Sunday to keep His work going?

God requires all your services *as much* on the six days as on the Sabbath! He has appropriated the Sabbath to peculiar duties and required its observance as a day of rest from toil, cares, and labors that concern the present world. But because God uses men to accomplish His purpose, and the gospel is to be spread and sustained by the things of this world, God requires you to work all the six days at your secular employments. It is *all* for His service as much as the worship of the Sabbath.

Sunday is no more given for the service of God than Monday. You have no more right to serve yourselves on Monday than you have on Sunday. If any of you have imagined that the six days of the week are your own time, it shows that you are supremely selfish. Do not consider that in prayer and on Sunday you are serving God if the rest of the time you are serving yourself. You have never known the radical principle of serving the Lord.

Anyone serving themselves or their own gods will make few sacrifices of personal ease and comfort. When a man enters into service, he gives up his ease and comfort for the interest of his employer. Is a man supremely devoted to the service of God when he shows that his own ease and comfort are dearer than the Kingdom of Jesus Christ? He would rather sacrifice the salvation of sinners than sit on a hard pew or be separated from his family for an hour or two!

Do you give your time and money to God's service grudgingly or by constraint? What would you think of your servant if you had to push him all the time to do anything for your interest?

Many people do everything grudgingly. If they do anything, it comes hard. If you go to one of these characters and want his time or money, it is difficult to get him interested. He does not consider the interests of Christ's Kingdom higher than his own. He may make a show of fearing the Lord, but he *serves* gods of his own.

Holiday Or Sacrifice?

Those who are aiming to elevate their own families into a different sphere by storing up wealth show that they have some other object to live for than bringing this world under the authority of Jesus Christ. They have other gods to serve. They may pretend to fear the Lord, but they *serve* their own gods.

Many people profess to be the servants of God but are eagerly gathering property and planning to retire in the country. Has God given you a right to a perpetual Sabbath as soon as you have made a lot of money? Did God tell you, when you professed to enter His service, to work hard for so many years and then have a continual holiday? Did He promise to excuse you after that from making the most of your time and talents and let you live at ease the rest of your days? If your thoughts are set upon this, you are not serving God but your own selfishness and sloth.

You can find people who greatly love things that do them no good, and others even form artificial appetites for positively loathsome things. No arguments will prevail upon them to abandon their habits for the sake of doing good. Are such persons absorbed in the service of God? Certainly not. Will they sacrifice their lives for the Kingdom of God? Why, you cannot make them even give up bad habits to save a soul from death.

Selfishness reigns in such people. It shows the astonishing strength of selfishness. You often see selfishness showing itself in little things. The true state of a man's mind stands out so strongly that it will not give place to those great interests for which he ought to be willing to lay down his life.

People who are most readily moved to action by appeals to their own selfish interests show that they are serving their own gods.

Suppose I want a man to build a church. How can I convince him? Must I show him how it will improve the value of his property, advance his business, or gratify his selfishness in some other way? If he is more excited by these motives than he is by a desire to save perishing souls and advance the Kingdom of Christ, he has never given himself to serve the Lord. He is still *serving himself.* He is more influenced by his selfish interests than by all those benevolent principles on which Christianity turns. The character of a true servant of God is opposite to this.

Many people are more excited by other subjects than the Lord. You find them talking about politics or philosophy, and if you bring up Christianity, the conversation immediately stops. They would rather talk about animal feelings, showing that the Lord is not the subject that is nearest their hearts. A man is always most easily excited about that subject that lies nearest his heart. When you can talk early and late about the news and other worldly topics but cannot *possibly* be interested in the Lord, you know that your heart is not in it. If you pretend to be a servant of God, you are a hypocrite.

When a man is more jealous for his own fame than for God's glory, it shows that he lives for himself and serves his own god. Who is his God, himself or the Lord? Imagine a minister thrown into a fever because somebody criticizes his scholarship or his dignity, while he is as cool as ice at all the indignities thrown upon the blessed God. Is that man a follower of Paul, willing to be considered a fool for the cause of Christ? If he understood Christ, he would rejoice to have his name cast out as evil for His cause.

Cushioned Pews And Folded Hands

That which gives value to a Christian institution

is the salvation of sinners and the sanctification of saints. The end for which Christ lives, and for which He has left His Church in the world, is to draw all men to Himself. This is the business to which God calls His servants. If any man is not doing this as the main object of his life, he is not serving the Lord but is serving his own gods.

People who seek for happiness in Christianity, rather than for usefulness, are serving their own gods. Their religion is entirely selfish. They want to *enjoy* religion and are always asking how they can be happy and pleasurably excited in religious exercises. They will only go to meetings that will make them happy, never asking whether that is the way to do the most good or not. They are content to do nothing but sit on their cushioned pews and have the minister feed them.

Instead of seeking how to do good, they are only seeking to be happy. Their daily prayer is not that of the converted Saul of Tarsus, ''Lord, what wilt thou have me to do'' (Acts 9:7) but, ''Lord, tell me how I can be happy.'' Is that the Spirit of God? No. He said, ''I delight to *do thy will,* O my God'' (Psalm 40:8). Is that the spirit of the apostle Paul? No. He threw off his upper garments at once and made his arms bare for the field of labor.

Those who make their own salvation their supreme object are serving their own gods. Many people in the Church show by their conduct and their language that their leading object is to secure their own salvation. Their grand determination is

112

to get their own soul planted on the firm battlements of the heavenly Jerusalem and walk the golden fields of Canaan above. If the Bible is not in error, all such characters will go to hell. Their religion is pure selfishness. For "whosoever will save his life shall loose it: and whosoever will lose his life for my sake shall find it" (Matthew 16:25).

Very little is accomplished in the world for Jesus Christ because so few do anything for Him. Jesus has few real servants in the world. How many people do you think there are in the Church that are really at work for God and striving to advance the Kingdom of Christ? The reason that Christianity advances no faster is that there are few to advance it and many to hinder it.

You see a crowd of people at a fire trying to get the goods out of a store. Some are determined to get the goods, but the rest are not doing anything. They divert their attention by talking about other things or hinder the workers by finding fault with their way of doing it. The Church is very similar. Those who are trying to do the work are greatly hindered by the backwardness, the objections, and the *resistance* of the rest.

Few Christians have the spirit of prayer. How can they have the spirit of prayer? And why should God give it to them? Suppose God gave a man engaged in his worldly scheme the spirit of prayer. Of course he would pray for things nearest his heart: his worldly schemes to serve his own gods. Will God give him the spirit of prayer for such purpose? Never!

113

Where Do You Stand?

Many professing Christians have not begun to serve the Lord *at all*. A man said to one of them, "Do you feel that your property and your business are all God's, and do you hold and manage them for God?" "Oh, no," he said, "I have not gone as far as that yet." Not got as far as that! That man had been professing Christianity for years and still did not consider all that he had as belonging to God! No doubt he was serving his own gods.

I insist that this is the very beginning of Christianity. What is conversion but turning from the service of the world to the *service of God*? And yet this man had not discovered that he was God's servant. He seemed to think it would be a big step to feel that all he had was the Lord's.

You who are performing religious duties from selfish motives are in reality trying to make God your servant. If your own interests are supreme, all your services are performed to induce God to promote your interests. Why do you pray, go to church, or give money to Christian causes? You answer, "For the sake of promoting my own salvation." Indeed! *Not to glorify God but to get to heaven!*

Don't you think the devil would do the same if he thought he could gain his end by it—and be a devil still? The highest style of selfishness is to try to get God, with all His attributes, enlisted in the service of your mighty self!

Are you serving the Lord, or are you serving your

own gods? How are you doing? Have you done anything for God? Have you been living as a servant of God? Is Satan's kingdom weakened by what you have done? Could you say now, "Come with me, and I will show you this sinner converted or that backslider reclaimed or this weak saint strengthened and aided?" Could you bring living witnesses of what you have done in the service of God?

Or would your answer be, "I have been to church every Sunday and heard a great deal of good preaching, and I have generally attended the prayer meetings. I have prayed with my family and read the Bible." And in all that, you have been merely passive. You have feared the Lord and served your own gods.

"Yes, but I have sold so many goods and made so much money, of which I *intend* to give a tenth to the missionary cause."

Be not deceived. If you loved souls and were striving to serve God, you would think of souls *here* and do the work of God *here*. What are we to think of a missionary going to another country who has never said a word to sinners at home? Does he love souls? The man that will do nothing at home is not fit to go to the mission field. And he that pretends to be saving money for missions while he will not try to save sinners here is an outrageous hypocrite.

Chapter 9

CAUGHT IN THE PUBLIC EYE

"For they loved the praise of men more than the praise of God"—John 12:43.

A plain distinction exists between *self-love*, or the simple desire for happiness, and *selfishness.* Self-love, the desire for happiness and dread of misery, is a part of our frame as God made us and intended us to be. Its indulgence, within the limits of the law of God, is not sinful. But whenever it is pursued contrary to the law of God, it becomes sinful.

When the desire for happiness or the dread of misery becomes our controlling principle, and we prefer our own gratification to some greater interest, it becomes selfishness. If to avoid pain or procure happiness we sacrifice greater interests, we violate the great law of *disinterested benevolence.* It is no longer self-love, acting within lawful bounds, but selfishness.

Professing Christians who are moved by hope or fear are moved sometimes by self-love and sometimes by selfishness. Their supreme object is not to glorify God but to secure their own salvation. The friends of God and the friends of man agree in many things, and if you look only at the things in which they agree, you cannot distinguish between them. Only a close observation of those things in which they differ will reveal that the main design of the latter class is not to glorify God but to secure their own salvation. In that way we can see their supreme object. When they do the same thing, outwardly, as the servants of God, they do them from entirely different motives. Consequently, the acts themselves are, in the sight of God, of an entirely different character.

Commitment To Self

Some professing Christians "love the praise of men more than the praise of God." I don't mean that a mere regard for reputation has led this class to profess the faith. Christianity has always been too unpopular with most people to render it a general thing to become professing Christians from a regard to reputation. But when becoming a Christian increases popularity, a complex motive operates— the hope of securing happiness in a future world and an increase in reputation here.

Many are led to profess Christianity when, on close examination, the *leading* object is the good *opinion* of their fellowmen. Their commitment turns on this. Although they profess to be sincere Christians, you can see by their conduct that they won't do anything to forfeit this good opinion of men. They will not encounter the persecution that they must to root sin out of the world.

Impenitent sinners are always influenced by one of two things in their attempts to mimic Christianity. Either they do them out of regard to natural principles—as compassion or self-love—or from self-ishness. They are done either out of regard to their own reputation or happiness or the gratification of some natural principle that has no moral character. They love the praise of men more than the praise of God.

People who make the praise of men their idol do what the apostle Paul says certain persons did in his day. For that reason they remained ignorant of the true doctrine: they "measuring themselves by them-selves, and comparing themselves among themselves are not wise" (2 Corinthians 10:12).

Instead of making Jesus Christ their standard of comparison and the Bible their rule of life, many individuals aim at no such thing. They never seri-ously dreamed of making the Bible their standard. Their great concern is to do as many things and be as pious as the other people in their churches. Their object is to maintain a *respectable profession* of Christianity. Instead of seriously seeking what the Bible requires and asking how Jesus Christ would act in such and such a case, they look at "common" Christianity and are satisfied with mimicking it. Their object is not to do what the Bible says but what is respectable.

These people do not trouble themselves about *elevating the standard* of holiness around them. They are not troubled that the general standard of holiness is low in the Church or that it is difficult to bring sinners to repentance. They think the standard at the present time is high enough. While the real friends of God and man are complaining about the standard and trying to wake up the Church, it seems to them like a meddlesome, uneasy disposition.

When Jesus Christ denounced the scribes and Pharisees, they said, "He hath a devil" (John 10:20). Today they may say, "Why, he is denouncing our doctors of divinity and our best men, and he even dares to tell us that except our righteousness exceeds theirs, we cannot enter the Kingdom of heaven. What a bad spirit he has!"

A large part of the Church has this spirit, and every effort to open the eyes of the Church and to make Christians see that they live like hypocrites only excites malice and causes reproach. They say, "What a bad spirit he shows, so unkind, nothing like the meek, kind, and loving spirit of the Son of God." They forget how Jesus Christ cursed those who had the reputation of being the most pious people in that day. It was the hypocritical spirit exhibited by professing holy men that roused His soul, moved His indignation, and called forth His burning torrents of denunciation. Jesus complained about people who set up patterns of piety, and He called them hypocrites and thundered over their heads the terrible words, "How can ye escape the damnation of hell!" (Matthew 23:33).

A Religion Of Reputation

Too many people are scrupulous in observing what the public considers acceptable, while they easily forget what public sentiment does not enforce.

Consider, for example, prohibition. How many are there who yielded to public sentiment what they never would yield to God or man? At first they waited to see what would happen. They resisted giving up alcohol. But when that became popular, and they found that they could do very well without it, they gave it up. But they were determined to yield no further than public sentiment drove them. It was not their objective to slay the monster but to maintain a good character. They loved the praise of men more than the praise of God.

Many individuals keep the Sabbath not because they love God but because it is respectable. This is obvious because they keep it while they are among their acquaintances or where they are known. But when they travel to where they are not known—where it will not be a public disgrace—you will find them skipping church altogether.

This class of people abstain from all sins that are abhorred by the public, but they do other things just as bad that are not frowned upon. They neglect things that are ordained in the Word of God. Where an individual habitually disobeys any command of

God, it is certain that the obedience he *appears* to render is not from love to God but from other motives. He does not, in fact, obey any command of God.

The apostle James has settled this question: "Whosoever shall keep the whole law, and yet offend in one point, he is guilty of all" (James 2:10). Obedience to God's commands implies an obedient state of the heart; therefore, nothing is obedience that does not imply a supreme regard to the authority of God.

If a man's heart is right, then he regards whatever God commands as more important than anything else. And if a man regards anything as superior to God's authority, that is his idol. *Whatever we supremely regard is our God*—reputation, comfort, riches, honor, or whatever we place first in our hearts.

Whatever a man's reason is for habitually neglecting anything he knows to be the command of God or sees to promote the Kingdom of Christ, he regards that as supreme. There is nothing acceptable to God in any of his services. His religion is the religion of public sentiment. It is public sentiment to which he yields obedience, in all his conduct, and not the glory of God.

How about you? Do you habitually neglect God's requirements because they aren't sustained and enforced by public sentiment? If you claim to be a Christian, I presume that you do not neglect any requirement that is strongly urged by public sentiment.

But do you habitually neglect some duties? Do you practice things accepted by men that you know are contrary to the law of God? If you do, then you regard the opinions of men more than the judgment of God.

A man who is obedient at home will often toss off a glass of brandy or step up to a bar and order liquor the second he is away. When I was in the Mediterranean, at Messina, a gentleman asked me if I would go to a bar with him. "What! A minister go to a bar?"

"Why, you are away from home, and no one would know it."

"But would not God know it?" It was plain that he thought that, although I was a minister, I could go to a bar when I was away from home. No matter if God knew it, as long as men did not know it. And how did he get that idea? By seeing ministers who do just such things!

If you allow yourselves any secret sins and think nobody knows about it, know that *God sees it* and has already written down your name—*hypocrite*. You are more afraid of disgrace in the eye of mortals than of disgrace in the eye of God. If you loved God supremely, it would be a small thing to you that everybody else knew your sins, in comparison with having them known to God. If tempted in anything, you would exclaim, "What! Shall I sin under the eye of God?"

Professing Christians may not practice any secret sins, but they neglect duties like private prayer. They go to communion and appear very pious on Sunday, but their prayer closet is unknown to God or man. Reputation is their idol. They dread to lose their reputation more than to offend God.

These people have a conscience in things that are popular and no conscience at all on things that are not scrutinized by the public. You can preach to them and clearly prove it—even make them confess that it is their duty. If, however, it is not a matter of reputation, they will go on as before. Show them a "Thus saith the Lord" and make them see that their actions are inconsistent with Christian perfection and contrary to Jesus' interests, and still they will not change. They regard the requirements of public opinion and love the praise of men more than the praise of God.

Fanatical Or Fashionable?

This class of people generally dread the thought of being considered fanatical. They are ignorant that the world is *wrong!* The public sentiment of the world is against God, and everyone who intends to serve God must set his face against the sentiment of the world. In a world of rebels, public sentiment is obviously as wrong as the controversy with God. The world is wrong, and God's ways are directly against their ways. Consequently, it is true, and always has been true, that "all that will live godly in Christ Jesus shall suffer persecution" (2 Timothy 3:12). They will be called fanatical, superstitious, irrational, etc; they always have been, and they always will be.

But these opinion-oriented people will never go further than is consistent with the expectations of worldly men. They say they must do this or that in order to influence such men. Opposite this are the true friends of God and man. Their leading aim is to turn the world upside down, bring all men to obey God, and remold opinions of men to conform to the Word of God.

Many professing Christians are intent on making friends on both sides and always take the middle course. They avoid the reputation of being over righteous on the one hand and, on the other hand, of being lax or irreligious. For centuries a person could maintain a reputable profession of religion without ever being called fanatical. And the standard is still so low that probably the great mass of the Protestant churches are trying to occupy this middle ground.

They mean to have friends on both sides. They are not considered reprobates or fanatics. They are *fashionable Christians!*

They may be called fashionable Christians for two reasons. One is that their style of religion is popular and fashionable; and the other is that they generally follow worldly fashions. Their aim is to please the world. No matter what God requires, they are determined to keep peace with the enemies of God. They have more regard to men than to God. And if they ever have to choose between displeasing their friends and neighbors and offending God, they will offend God. If public sentiment clashes with the commands of God, they will yield to public sentiment.

Although they will not exercise self-denial to gain the applause of God, they will exercise great self-denial to gain the applause of men. The men who gave up liquor because public sentiment rendered it necessary will give up wine, also, whenever a powerful public sentiment demands it—and not until then.

If a minister of this class preaches a sermon, he is more anxious to know what the people thought of it than to know what God thought of it. And if he fails, the disgrace of it with men cuts him ten times more than the thought that he has dishonored God or hindered the salvation of souls.

When some secret sin has been found, he is more distressed about it because *he* is disgraced than because God is dishonored. Or, if he falls into open sin, he cares as much about the disgrace as the sin.

These fashionable Christians are more anxious about their appearance in the eyes of the world than in the eyes of God. Females of this character are vastly more anxious how the body appears in the eyes of men than how the heart appears in the eyes of God. Such a one will take all week getting everything in order to make herself appear lovely, but will not spend half an hour in her closet to prepare her heart before God.

Everybody can see what this religion is the moment it is held up to view. Nobody is at a loss to say what that man or that woman's name is—*hypocrite*. They will go into the house of God with their heart dark as midnight, while everything in their external appearance is attractive and respectable. They must appear well in the eyes of men, no matter what God sees. The heart may be dark, disordered, and polluted, and they don't care as long as the eye of man detects no blemish.

Opposing The Light

Many people refuse to confess their sins in the manner that the law of God requires. If they are required to confess more than they think consistent with their reputation, they are more anxious how it will affect their character than whether God is satisfied.

Search your hearts, you that have made confessions, and see what most affects your minds—what God thought of it or what men thought of it. Have you refused to confess what you knew God required because it would hurt your reputation among men? Will not God *judge your hearts?*

People who profess Christ are often so ashamed to do their duty that they will not do it. When a person is too ashamed to do what God requires, it is plain that his own reputation is his idol. How many people are ashamed to acknowledge Jesus Christ, ashamed to reprove sin, and ashamed to speak out when Christ is attacked? If they supremely regarded

God, could they ever be *ashamed* of doing their duty?

Suppose a man's wife was slandered, would he be ashamed to defend her? By no means. If his children were abused, would he be ashamed to help them? Not if he loved them. It would not be *shame* that would deter him from defending his wife or children.

These people will not take decided ground when they are among the enemies of truth, where they would be subject to reproach for doing it. They are bold when among friends and make a great display of their courage. But when put to the trial, they will deny the Lord Jesus Christ before His enemies. They will put Him to open shame rather than rebuke wickedness or speak out in His cause among His enemies.

Many oppose all advancing light on practical subjects. They are disturbed by every new proposal that draws on their wallets or breaks in upon their habitual self-indulgence. You may talk and preach as much in favor of it as you please. There is only one way to reach these people, and that is by creating a new public sentiment. When you have convinced—through the Holy Spirit—a sufficient number in the community to create a public sentiment in its favor, *then* they will adopt your new proposals, but not before.

Some professing Christians are often opposed to men, measures, and things that are unpopular and subject to reproach; but when they become popular, they fall in with them. Let a minister go through the churches in any state and wake them up. While he is little known, these people are not afraid to speak against him. But if he gains influence, they will commend him and profess to be his warmest friends. Before Jesus' death, He had a certain degree of popularity. Multitudes followed Him through the streets, crying, "Hosanna, Hosanna!" But as soon as He was arrested, they all turned and began to cry, "Crucify Him, crucify Him!"

As they flow with the tide when a man is reproached, they will flow with the tide when he is honored. One exception is when they have become so committed to the opposition that they cannot change without disgrace. Then they will be silent until another opportunity comes up for letting out the burning fires within them.

Very often when a revival begins, it is opposed by certain members of the church. They do not like to have such things carried on and are afraid there is too much excitement. But the work goes on, and soon they seem to fall in and go with the multitude. Then, when the revival is over and the church grows cold again, you will find them renewing their opposition to the work. In the end, they may induce the church itself to criticize the very revival that they had so much enjoyed.

The same has been true in regard to missions, and if anything unfavorable to missions occurred, you would find plenty of these fair weather supporters turning to the opposition.

The Fear Of Man

If anything is proposed to promote Christianity, opinion-loving people are very sensitive and careful not to have anything done that is unpopular. They ask what the other churches will think. If it is likely to bring reproach on their church or their minister, in view of the ungodly or the other churches, they are distressed about it. No matter how much good it will do or how many souls it will save, they do not want to have anything done to injure the *respectability* of their church.

The true friends of God and man are always *forming and correcting public sentiment* on all points where it is wrong. With all their hearts, they search out evils in order to reform the world and drive iniquity from the earth. The other class are always following public sentiment *as it is*. They are ready to brand as imprudent or rash any man or anything that goes to stem the tide of public sentiment and turn it the other way.

People can easily make themselves believe certain things are acts of piety that are actually only acts of hypocrisy. They do the things that outwardly pertain to piety, and they give themselves credit for being holy. Their motives are all corrupt and hollow, not one of them drawn from a supreme regard to God's authority. This is manifest from the fact that they do nothing *except* where God's requirements are backed by public sentiment. Unless you aim to do *all* your duty and yield obedience *in everything*, the piety you claim is sin against God.

How many of you would break out into open sin if not for the restraints of public sentiment, the fear of disgrace, and the desire to gain the credit of virtue? True holiness is from a regard to the authority of God, despite public sentiment. Otherwise, you do it for the sake of gaining credit in the eyes of men. But if you expect any favor from God, you will assuredly be disappointed. The only reward He will bestow upon such hypocrisy is damnation.

Who of you will agree to take the Bible for your standard, Jesus Christ for your example, and do what is *right* whatever man may say or think? Everyone that is not willing to take this ground must regard himself as a stranger to the grace of God. He is by no means in a state of justification. If he is not resolved upon doing what he knows to be right, it is positive proof that he loves the praise of men more than the praise of God.

To be a Christian is to be governed by the authority of God *in all things,* to live not by hopes and fears but by supreme consecration of yourself unto God. If you intend to be a Christian, you must count the cost. I will not flatter you. I will never try to coax you to become religious by keeping back the truth. You must give yourselves wholly unto Christ. You cannot float along to heaven on the waves of public sentiment.

Who is on the Lord's side? Who is willing to say, "We will no longer do evil but are determined to do the will of God in all things—let the world think or say of us what it may''? If you are willing to do this, then kneel and pray that God would accept and seal your solemn covenant to obey Him in everything.

Chapter 10

LEGAL RELIGION: PRINCIPLES OF FEAR

"Who is on the Lord's side?"—Exodus 32:26.

The conduct of men invariably shows what their true and main design in life is. A man's character is as his supreme object is. If you can learn by his conduct what his leading object is, then you can know with certainty what his character is.

For those motivated by self-love or selfishness, hope and fear are the main springs of all they do in religion. These individuals are actuated by a supreme regard to their own good and the fear of evil. The hope of advantage to themselves is the foundation of all their conduct.

They make the Lord a secondary concern. Their conduct shows that they do not regard Christianity as the principal business of life but as subordinate to other things. They consider religion something that ought to come in and find a place among other things, rather like a Sabbath-day business to be confined to the closet. Christianity and business are considered as entirely separate concerns.

If they had right views of the matter, they would consider the Lord's business the *only* lawful business in life. Then Christianity would characterize everything they did and would obviously be an act of obedience.

Cracking The Whip Of Conscience

People motivated by selfishness perform their religious duties as a task. Such a one does not delight in communion with God. He performs prayer as a task. He does religious duties as sick people take medicine—not because they love it but because they hope to derive some benefit from it.

They possess a *legal spirit* and not a *gospel spirit.* They do what they are obliged to do for the Lord and not what they love to do. They obey God's commands but do not love them. They always inquire, in regard to duty, not how they can do good but how they can be saved. The difference between them is the same as between a convinced sinner and a true convert. The convinced sinner asks, "What *must* I do to be *saved?*" The true convert asks, "Lord, what *do You want me to do?*"

Fear, much more than hope, motivates them. They perform their duties chiefly because they *dare not* omit them. They go to communion not because they love Christ or their brethren but because they dare not stay away. They fear criticism from the Church, or they are afraid they will be damned if they neglect it. They pray not because they enjoy

133

communion with God but because they dare not neglect Him. They have the spirit of slaves and serve God like slaves, fearing to be beaten with many stripes.

These "believers" feel as if they were obliged to perform many religious duties or be lashed by conscience and lose their hopes. Therefore, they painfully and laboriously perform many works a year and that they call Christianity!

Their religion is not only produced by the fear of disgrace or the fear of hell, it is mostly of a *negative character*. They satisfy themselves with doing nothing that is very bad. Having no spiritual views, they regard the law of God chiefly as a system of prohibitions to guard men from certain sins rather than a system of benevolence fulfilled by love. If they are moral in their conduct, relatively serious and decent in their general attitude, and perform the required amount of religious exercises, they are satisfied.

Their conscience harasses them, not so much about sins of *omission* as sins of *commission*. They make a distinction between *neglecting* to do what God positively requires and *doing* what He positively forbids. The most you can say of them is that they are not bad. They seem to think little or nothing of being useful to the cause of Christ as long as they cannot be convicted of any positive transgression.

Where they have enlightened minds and tender consciences, you often find them the most rigid of all "believers." They tithe everything and are perfect Pharisees, carrying everything to the greatest extremes as far as outward strictness is concerned.

But despite all their strictness, they cannot help realizing that they are great sinners after all; and, having no just sense of gospel justification, this leaves them very unhappy. The more enlightened and tender their conscience, the more unhappy they are. Regardless of their strictness, they feel they have come short of their duty. Not having any gospel faith or annointing of the Holy Spirit that brings peace to the soul, they are unsatisfied, uneasy, and miserable.

Perhaps many of you have seen such people. Perhaps some of you *are* such, and you have never known what it is to feel justified before God through the blood of Jesus Christ. You don't know what it is to feel that Jesus Christ has accepted and owned you as His. You never felt in your minds what is spoken of in this text: "There is therefore now *no condemnation* to them which are in Christ Jesus, who walk not after the flesh, but after the Spirit" (Romans 8:1).

Does such language bring this reality home to you because you experience it in your soul? Or do you, after all, still feel condemned and guilty, with no sense of pardoned sin and no peace with God or confidence in Jesus Christ?

Comfortable Hopes

Legalists are encouraged and cheered by reading about saints who fell into great sins. They feel wonderfully instructed and edified when they hear the

135

sins of God's people set forth in a strong light. Then they are comforted and their hopes are wonderfully strengthened. Instead of being humbled and distressed, feeling that such conduct is so contrary to Christianity that they could hardly believe they were saints if it had not been found in the Bible, they feel gratified and strengthened by these things. I once knew an elder who was brought before the session of a church for the crime of adultery. He excused himself by this plea: "I did not know," he said, "why I should be expected to be better than David, the man after God's own heart."

Many professing Christians are pleased if their minister adopts a low standard and is ready to hope that almost everybody is a Christian. It is easy to see why they are pleased with such an exhibition of Christianity—it serves their main design and helps them maintain what they call a "comfortable hope," although they *do* so little for God.

Opposite them is the man whose main design is to rid the world of sin. He wants all men to be holy and wants to have the true standard of holiness held up. He wants all men to be saved but knows they cannot be saved unless they are truly holy. A godly man would just as soon think of Satan's going to heaven as getting a man there by cheapening the Bible standard of holiness.

Selfish people are fond of the doctrine of saint's perseverance and the doctrine of election. Often, all they want is what they call the doctrines of grace. If these doctrines can be preached comfortably without threatening their consciences too much, then they are fed.

Legalists love to have their minister preach sermons that feed Christians. Their main object is not to save sinners but to be saved themselves. Therefore, they always choose a minister not for his ability in preaching for the conversion of sinners but for his talents in feeding the church with mere abstractions.

In their prayers, they ask mainly for assurance of going to heaven. Their great object is to secure their hopes. They pray for evidence, instead of praying that their faith may be strengthened and their souls full of the Holy Spirit to pull sinners out of the fire.

Great stress is laid on emotions. If at any time they have intense religious feelings, they dwell on them and make this evidence last a long time. One season of excitement will prop their hopes as long as they can distinctly remember. It doesn't matter if they are not doing anything *now*, for they remember the time when they had these feelings, and that keeps their hopes alive.

If there has been a revival, and they got so involved that they could weep, pray, and exhort with feeling, they will have a *comfortable hope* for years on the strength of it. After the revival is over, they do nothing to promote Christianity, and their hearts become hard. They have a comfortable hope, patiently waiting for a revival to come and give them another move.

If you could listen at the door of their closets, you

would hear eight-tenths of all their petitions going up for themselves. It shows how they value their own salvation in comparison with the salvation of others. At a prayer meeting it will often be the same. You would not suppose, from their prayers, that they knew there was a sinner on earth traveling the road to hell. They pray for themselves just as they do in the closet, only they link the rest of the church with them and say *we*.

Living To Honor God

Selfish people are more anxious to be prepared to die than to save sinners around them. If they ask for the Spirit of God, they want it to prepare them to die. Compare this with David's prayer: "Then will I teach transgressors thy ways; and sinners shall be converted unto thee" (Psalm 51:13).

How many of you are of this character? An individual who made it his great absorbing object to do good and save sinners would not think as much about when, where, or how he will die as how he may do the most good while he lives. And as to his death, he leaves that all to God. He has long ago given his soul up to Him. Now the great question is not, "When shall I die?" but, "How shall I live to honor God?"

Many professing Christians are characterized by a fear of punishment and an unconcern for sin. True friends of God and man are more afraid of sin than of punishment. They don't ask, "If I do this, will

138

I be punished?" Instead, they ask the question that Joseph asked: "How can I do this great wickedness, and sin against God?" (Genesis 39:9). This was the spirit of a child of God—so much afraid of sin that he had no thought of punishment.

False converts often indulge in sin if they can persuade themselves that God will forgive them or when they think they can repent of it afterwards. They often reason in this way: "The pastor does this," or "The elders do this, so why shouldn't I do the same?" They fear punishment not sin. They *know* they sin, but they hope to escape the punishment. This is contrary to the spirit of the true friends of God, whose absorbing object it is to get all sin out of the world. Such people are not half as afraid of hell as they are of committing sin.

Selfish people are more fond of receiving good than doing good. These people do not have the true gospel. They have never entered into the Spirit of Jesus Christ: "It is more blessed to give than to receive" (Acts 20:35). A person actuated by true love to God and man enjoys what he does to benefit others far more than those who receive good from his hand. He is benevolent, and it is a gratification to him to show kindness. His heart is set upon it, and when he can do it, a holy joy is shed over his mind.

The other class are more eager to receive. They want to receive instruction more than to impart it. They want to receive comfort, but they are never ready to deny themselves to give the comforts of the gospel to others. How directly contrary this is to the spirit of the gospel, which finds its supreme happiness in communicating happiness to others. But these people want everybody to impart happiness to them, instead of striving to bless others. These two classes of characters are just as opposite as light and darkness.

Selfish people are chiefly afraid of hell, and when they are strongly convicted, they are afraid others will go there, too. They seek happiness for themselves; and when self is not in the way, they seek the same for others. They pray for sinners, not because they have such a sense of the evil that sinners are committing, but because they have a sense of the terrors of hell. They want sinners converted because they are in danger, not because they dishonor God. Their great object in praying is to secure the safety of those they pray for, as it is their great object in life to secure their own safety. They pity themselves, and they pity others. If there was no danger, they would have no motive to pray either for themselves or others.

The true friends of God and man feel compassion for sinners, too, but are much more concerned for the honor of God. They are more distressed to see God abused and dishonored than to see sinners go to hell. If God must either be forever dishonored or men go to hell, they will decide that sinners must sink to endless torment sooner than God suffer dishonor.

True saints manifest their feelings in their prayers.

You hear them praying for sinners as rebels against God—guilty criminals deserving eternal wrath. While they are full of compassion for sinners, they feel holy indignation against them for their conduct toward the blessed God.

False converts are apt to talk a great deal about their doubts. This makes up a great part of their history, and they are not prepared to do anything for the Lord because of these doubts. If the devil at any time suggests that the true friends of God and man are going to hell, the first answer they think of is, "What if I should? Only let me pull sinners out of the fire while I can."

Of course, a real Christian may have doubts. But they are much less apt to have them if they are fully bent on saving sinners. It will be very hard work for Satan to get an active church to be troubled with doubts.

Rejoicing In Self-Denial

Selfish people are uneasy at the increasing calls to self-denial. The good that could be done does not enter into their thoughts because they dwell on what they would have to give up.

These aggressive attacks on the kingdom of darkness distress false converts. Their objective never was to search out and banish everything dishonorable to God or injurious to man. They never determined to clear out every evil to soul or body from the earth. Therefore, they are distressed by those who are truly engaged to search out and do away with evil.

When legalists are called upon to deny themselves for the sake of doing good, instead of it being a pleasant thing, it causes them unmingled pain. Such a one does not know anything about enjoying self-denial. He cannot understand how anybody can rejoice in denying himself for the sake of doing good to others. He thinks it is a height in Christianity that he has not attained.

Yet the true friend of God and man, whose heart is determined to do good, never enjoys spending money as much as when he gives to promote Christ's Kingdom. If he is really holy, he knows it is the best thing he can do with his money. He's even sorry to have to use money for anything else when there are so many opportunities to do good with it.

If an individual has his heart set upon something, all the money he can save for that objective is pleasing to him. The more he can save from other objectives for this cause, the happier he is. If he finds it hard to give money to the Lord, his heart is not set on it. If it were, he would give his money with joy.

What would you think of a man who protested against giving money to the Church and yet was excited about missions? After calling for money, he himself never even gave five dollars. It would be obvious that his heart was not truly set on the cause of Christ. If it was, he would give his money as freely as water.

These false converts are not concerned with

promoting revivals. They always have to be dragged into the work. When a revival begins and the excitement is great, then they come in and appear to be excited. But you never see them taking the lead or striking out ahead.

As a matter of fact, these hypocrites do not convert sinners to God. They may do good, in various ways—and so may Satan do good deeds. But as a general thing, they do not pull sinners out of the fire. The reason is that this is not their great objective. How is it with you? Do you absolutely succeed in converting sinners? Is there anyone who will look to you as the instrument of his conversion? If you were truly on fire, you could not rest satisfied without doing it, and you would work in such earnest and with such agonizing prayer that you would do it.

Whom Do You Serve?

Selfish people don't show much distress when they discover sin. They don't rebuke it. They love to mingle in scenes where sin is committed, and they can hear and join in vain conversation. Their spirit is worldly, and they love worldly company. Instead of hating even the garment spotted with the flesh, they love to hang around the confines of sin, as if it satisfied them.

If any of the missions are in need, they neither know nor feel it. If missions prosper, they take no interest in it. They very likely do not read any Christian literature. Or, if they do read it, they read only the trivial news. The true friends of God and man, on the other hand, love to learn about revivals and missions. When they hear that the Lord has poured out His Spirit on a mission, a glow of holy joy surges through them.

Lovers of self don't aim at anything higher than a legal, painful, and negative religion. The love of Jesus doesn't constrain them to constant warfare against sin and a desire to do all the good in their power. What they do is done only because they think they *must,* and they maintain a formal, heartless, and worthless piety.

If an extended meeting is proposed, you will generally find these people making objections. If any other special effort is proposed, they come reluctantly and prefer the "good old way." They feel angry at being obliged to add so much every year to their religion in order to maintain their hope.

These selfish people don't pray in their closets because they *love* to pray; they think it's their duty, and they dare not neglect it. The Bible isn't sweet to their souls. They don't *enjoy* the reading, as a person enjoys exquisite delights, but read it because it's their duty to read it. They know it's not right to profess to be a Christian and not read the Bible; but they find it a dry book.

Slight excuses keep them away from prayer meetings. They never go unless they find it necessary to keep up appearances or maintain their hope. And when they do go, instead of having their souls melted and fired with love, they are cold, listless, and dull—and glad when it is over.

Their hearts are not agonized with such thoughts as this: How long will wickedness prevail? When will this wretched world be free from sin and death? When will men stop sinning against God? Instead they ask, "When will I go to heaven and be free from all my trials and cares?"

This *religion* describes the religion of the *majority* of professing Christians, and they are *radically defective*.

True Christianity is far from this. It differs as much from Christianity as much as the Pharisees differed from Christ—as much as the true gospel differs from legal religion.

To which of these classes do you belong? It is *eternally important* that you know for certain what your true character is—whether you are motivated by true love to God and man or whether you are religious out of regard to yourself. Are you the true friend of God and man or not? Settle this, and then go to work for God.

Chapter 11

CONFORMITY TO THE WORLD

"Be not conformed to this world"—Romans 12:2.

Christians should not refuse to benefit by the useful arts, improvements, and discoveries of the world. The friends of God are not only privileged but bound to avail themselves of these. We must use all the useful arts and improvements of mankind for the Lord.

Christians, however, must not conform to the world in the following things: *business, fashion,* and *politics*. In these areas, Christians should not do as the world does or adopt its principles or practices. We are by no means to act from the same motives or pursue our objectives in the same manner that the world does.

Looking Out For Number One

The first reason why you must not conform to this world in business is that the principle of the world is *supreme selfishness*. This is universally true. Worldly business is governed and regulated by supreme and unmixed selfishness, with no regard to the commands of God, the glory of God, or the welfare of men.

The businessmen of the world consult their own interest and seek their own benefit, not the benefit of those they deal with. Whoever heard of a worldly businessman doing business for the benefit of those he dealt with? It is always for his own benefit.

Christians are required to act exactly opposite to worldly business principles: "Let no man seek his own, but every man *another's* wealth" (1 Corinthians 10:24). They are required to copy the example of Jesus Christ. Did He ever make bargains for His own advantage? Can His followers adopt the principles of the world, which contain in them the seeds of hell?

Conformity to the world is *totally inconsistent* with the love of God and man. The whole system recognizes only the love of self. Go through all the ranks of businessmen, from the man who sells candy on the sidewalk to the greatest wholesale merchant in the United States, and you will find this maxim—*look out for number one.* The norm is to do, as far as the rules of honesty will allow, all that will advance your own interest regardless of the interest of others.

Ungodly men will not deny that these are the principles on which business is done in the world. The man who pursues this course is universally regarded as doing business on *business principles.*

Are these rules of conduct consistent with holiness, the love of God and man, the spirit of the gospel, or the example of Jesus Christ? Can a man conform to the world in these principles and still love God? Impossible! No two things can be more opposite.

What did the Spirit of Jesus exemplify on earth? It was self-denial, benevolence, and sacrifice of Himself for others. He exhibited the same Spirit that God does, who gratifies His benevolent heart in doing good to others. The faith of the gospel is to be like God, joyfully denying self to do good. This is the gospel maxim: "It is more blessed to give than to receive" (Acts 20:35).

Biblical Business Principles

"Look not every man on his own things, but every man also on the things of others" (Philippians 2:4). In contrast to this verse, the businessman of the world says, "Look out for number one." This maxim was made by men who knew and cared no more for the gospel than the heathen do. Why should Christians conform to a principle such as this?

To conform to the world in the pursuits of business is a flat contradiction of the confirmations that Christians make when they enter the Church. What vows do you make when you enter the Church? Is it not to renounce the world and live for God, to be led by the Holy Spirit, to possess supreme love to God, to renounce self, to give yourself to glorify God, and to do good to men? You profess not to love the world, its honors, or its riches. Around the communion table, with your hands on the broken body of your Savior, you confess these to be your principles and pledge yourself to live by them.

Then what do you do? Go away and follow rules invented by men, who love the world and whose stated objective is to gain the world? Is this your way? If so, repent! You are sworn before God to a different course, and when you pursue the business principles of the world, you show that you are perjured wretches.

Conformity to the world is such an obvious contradiction of the principles of the gospel that sinners cannot understand its true nature and object. The object of the gospel is to raise men above the love and influence of the world and place them on higher ground. When sinners see professing Christians acting on the same principles as other men, how can they understand the true principles of the gospel or know what heavenly-mindedness, self-denial, and benevolence is?

This spirit of conformity to the world has already eaten out the love of God from the Church. Show me a young convert, while his heart is warm and the love of God glows out from his lips. What does he care about the world? Call his attention to it, point him to its riches and honors, and try to engage him in their pursuit—he loathes the thought.

Then, if he goes into business on the principles of the world for one year, you will no longer find the love of God glowing in his heart. His faith will become the religion of conscience. Dry, meagre, and uninfluential, it will have no glowing love of God moving him to acts of benevolence.

Conformity to the world in business is one of the greatest stumbling blocks to converting sinners. What do wicked men think when they see professing Christians pretending to believe what the Bible teaches and yet as eager as anybody to make the best bargains and deal as hard as the most worldly? They say, "I see these Christians doing the same thing we do, looking out for number one."

These are not false accusations. Many Christians pursue the world in the same spirit, by the same maxims, and to the same degree that the ungodly do. The world says, "Look at the church! I don't think they are any better than I am. They're as *worldly* as I am."

If professing Christians act on the same principles as worldly men, they will have the same reward. They are set down in God's book of remembrance as hypocrites pretending to be the friends of God. For whoever loves the world is the enemy of God. (See James 4:4.)

If Christians would turn the tables over and do business on gospel principles, it would shake the world. It would ring louder than thunder. If the ungodly could see Christian businessmen concerned with seeking not their own wealth but every man another's wealth, and setting no value on the world any further than it can be a means of glorifying God, what do you think the effect would be?

What effect did it have in Jerusalem when the early Christians gave up their businesses and turned out *en masse* to pursue the salvation of the world? A few ignorant fishermen and a few humble women turned the world upside down. If the Church lived so now, it would cover the world with confusion and overwhelm them with convictions of sin. Infidelity would hide its head, dissension would be driven from the Church, and this charming, blessed spirit of love would go over the world like ocean waves.

When Pride Reigns

The world of *fashion* is directly at war with the spirit of the gospel. What *is* minding earthly things if it is not to follow the fashions of the world that continually fluctuate in their forms? Many men of wealth think they care nothing for fashion. They are occupied with their businesses, and they trust their tailors. But if they made an unfashionable garment, you would see that the affluent do care about fashions.

Although their thoughts are not much on the fashions, they have a higher object in view. They think it beneath the dignity of a minister to preach about fashion. They overlook the fact that with most men fashion is everything. Most people are not rich and never expect to be, but they try to make a *respectable* appearance. Nine-tenths of the population looks to the world and follows the fashions. For this they strain every nerve. And this is what they set their hearts on and what they live for.

The rich man deceives himself, therefore, if he supposes that fashion is a little thing. Most people set their mind upon it. The thing they look for in life is to have their dress, hair, furniture, car, etc., like other people's—*respectable,* as they call it.

When people join the Church, they profess to give up the spirit that gives rise to fashion. They profess to renounce the vanities of the world, repent of their pride, follow the meek and lowly Savior, and to live for God. And now what do they do? Nothing will satisfy them that is not in the height of fashion.

What lies at the bottom of all this shifting scenery? What produces all this gaudy show and display? *It is the love of applause.* When Christians follow the changes of fashion, they pronounce all this innocent. The waste of money, time, and thought, the feeding and cherishing of vanity, and the love of applause is approved by the Church when she conforms to the world.

Like the ungodly, many professing Christians show that they love the world by their conduct. They give evidence that they are motivated by one principle: the love of fashion. When "Christians" do this, they show most clearly that they love the praise of men. Like sinners, they love admiration and flattery. Isn't this inconsistent with Christian principle, to follow the very things that are set up by the pride, fashion, and lust of the ungodly?

Stewards Of Reputation

Conforming to the world in fashion shows that you do not hold yourself accountable to God for the way you spend money. You practically disown the stewardship of your wealth. By spending money to gratify your own vanity and lust, you take off the keen edge of truth that ought to cut sinners in two. You practically deny that the earth is the Lord's!

The cry comes to our ears on every wind from the lost of all nations, "Come over and help us, come over and help us." Every week brings some call for tracts and Bibles from missionaries. If you choose to spend money in following the fashions, it is obvious that *reputation is your idol.*

Take the case of a woman whose husband has died. There she is, toiling and saving, rising up early and sitting up late. She eats the bread of carefulness because the father of her children is dead. Go to that woman and tell her that it is innocent for her to follow the fashions and dress like her neighbors—will she do it? Why not? She doesn't want to do it. She hardly buys what she needs, so intent is she on raising her children.

Suppose a person loved God, the souls of men, and the Kingdom of Christ—does he need a direct order from God to prevent him from spending his money and wasting his life in following the fashion? No; instead he will probably need an order to take what he needs for his own comfort and the support of his life.

Take the case of Timothy. Did he need a prohibition to stop him from indulging in wine? On the contrary, he was so cautious that it required an express injunction from God to make him drink a little wine as medicine. (See 1 Timothy 5:23.)

Many Christians have followed the world of fashion so closely that God seems to have given them over to the devil for the destruction of the flesh. They have little or no religious feeling, no spirit of prayer, and no zeal for the glory of God or the conversion of sinners. The Holy Spirit seems to have left them.

When the elders and leaders in a church are fashionable Christians, they drag the whole church along with them into the train of fashion. Once a rich Christian lady comes to the house of God in full fashion, the whole church is tempted to follow as far as they can.

Suppose a reformed alcoholic should surround himself with wine, brandy, and hard liquor and from time to time taste a little—isn't he tempting himself? Or imagine a woman who has been brought up in the spirit of pride and show but is reformed. If she keeps her wardrobe and continues to follow the fashions, pride will drag her backward as sure as she lives. She tempts herself to sin and folly.

By following the fashions, you are setting the world into a fierce and hot pursuit of these things. The very things that the world loves and are sure to have scruples about, professing Christians fall in with and follow. You thus tempt the world to continue in the pursuit of what will destroy their souls in hell.

When you follow the fashions, you open your heart to the devil. You keep it for him—empty, swept, and garnished. Every woman or man that follows the fashions may rely upon it: they are helping Satan to tempt them to pride and sin.

If professing Christians would show their contempt for these things and not follow or regard them, it would shame and convince the world that *they* were striving for God and for eternity! How irresistible it would be. What an overwhelming testimony in favor of Christianity. What thunders it would pour into the ears of the world to wake them up to follow God!

Electing Godly Candidates

Christians also must not be conformed to the world in politics. The politics of the world are entirely dishonest. The policy of every party is to cover up the defects of their own candidate and the good qualities of the opposing candidate. Isn't this dishonest? Every party holds up its candidate as a piece of perfection and then aims to ride him into office by any means, fair or foul. No man that is committed to a party can be *entirely* honest. Can a Christian do this and keep a clear conscience?

By falling in with the world in politics, Christians are guilty of setting up rulers over them (by their own vote) who do not fear or love God and who defy the law of God. Some politicians break the Sabbath, commit adultery, fight, swear profanely, and leave the laws unexecuted. *Christians put them into office!* Where parties are divided, as they are in this country, there are enough Christians to tip the scale in *any* election.

By following the present course of politics, you are helping to undermine all government and order in the land. This great nation staggers and reels because the laws are broken and trampled under foot, and the executive power refuses to act. Either politicians don't want to put down disorder, or they compromise and let the devil rule. This is true in all parts of the country and in all parties. Can a Christian be consistent with his profession of faith and still vote for men like this? What greater stumbling block can we place before sinners?

No wonder the world has a hard time believing "Christian candidates." I myself often doubt whether many of them believe the Bible. They show, as far as evidence goes, that there is *no change of heart*.

What is Christianity? Is it going to the communion table once a month and sometimes to a prayer meeting? Is that a change of heart? The world would be foolish to believe in a change of heart on such evidence.

If Christians acted perfectly conscientious and consistent in this matter, they would say, "We will not vote for any man unless he fears God and will rule the people in righteousness." Then ungodly men wouldn't nominate candidates who set themselves against the law. Every candidate would be obliged to show that he was prepared to act from higher motives. Then he would strive to make the country prosperous, promote virtue, and put down vice, oppression, and disorder. They would have to do all they could to make the people happy and *holy*. It would shame dishonest politicians to show that the love of God and man is the motive that Christians have in view. What a blessed influence would flow over the land!

If we had a *holy* ministry, it would be far more important than an *educated* ministry. If ministers were holy, they wouldn't need so much education. I don't mean to undervalue an educated ministry. Let ministers be educated as much as they can—the more the better, as long as they are holy.

But to suppose that education can convert the world is a farce. Let the ministry have the spirit of prayer, and let the baptism of the Holy Spirit be upon them. Then they will spread the gospel. If Christians lived as they should, the Church would *shake the world*. The report would soon fill every wind, until the earth was full of excitement and inquiry. Conversions would multiply like the drops of morning dew.

Be Ye Separate!

Christians must be singular. They are called to be a peculiar people, essentially different from the rest of mankind. To argue that we are not to be singular is to maintain that we *are* to be conformed to the world. This is the direct opposite of the command in the text.

The nearer you bring the Church to the world, the more you annihilate the reasons for their changing sides and coming to Jesus Christ. Unless you separate from them and show that you are not of them in any respect, how can you make the ungodly feel that a great change is necessary? The change that is necessary is a change of heart.

Many people may argue that if Christians are too separate, then people will become disgusted and take to the world altogether. This is about as reasonable as it would be for a sober man to get drunk now and then to avoid offending alcoholics or to retain his influence over them. People must see in the lives of Christians that they have given up the love of the world and its pride. We must live holy lives in watchfulness, self-denial, and *active benevolence*.

Your heart is not right unless your conduct is right. What is outward conduct but the acting out of the heart? If your heart was right, you would not *want* to follow the world.

By non-conformity to the world, a great deal of time may be saved for doing good that is now consumed and wasted in joining in the pursuits of the world. At the same time, Christians would preserve their peace of conscience, enjoy communion with God, have the spirit of prayer, and possess far greater usefulness.

Something must be done! You say that you want to have sinners converted. But what help is it if they sink right back again into conformity to the world? I am filled with pain at the Church's conduct. What are the results of the glorious revivals we have had? I believe they were genuine revivals and outpourings of the Holy Spirit, yet many converts are a disgrace to the Lord.

One holy church crucified to the world would do more to promote Christianity than all the churches in the country, living as they now do. If I had strength to go through the churches, I would preach to bring them up to the gospel standard of *holy living*. Of what use is it to convert sinners and make them such Christians as these? Of what use is it to try to convert sinners and make them feel that there is something in *religion,* and then by your conformity to the world prove that there is nothing in it?

Where shall the Lord look for a church—like the first Church—that will be separate and serve God?

Do you believe that God commands you not to be conformed to the world? Do you believe it? And *dare you* obey it, regardless of what people say about you? Will you separate yourself from the world and never again be controlled by its principles and practices? Will you do it?

Chapter 12

THE DANGER OF DECEPTION

"He that is unjust in the least is unjust also in much"—Luke 16:10.

Jesus lays down a principle in connection with the parable of the unjust steward: One who is dishonest in small matters is not really honest in anything.

I don't mean that if a person is dishonest in small matters and takes advantage of people that he won't deal openly and honestly in greater matters. Neither do I mean that a man who commits petty theft will necessarily commit highway robbery. One who holds a grudge against a person won't necessarily commit murder. And so on.

What I do mean is that if a man is dishonest in small matters it shows that he is not governed *by principle* in anything. Real honesty of heart would lead him to act right all the time. If he appears to act honestly in larger things yet acts dishonestly in small matters, he must have other motives than honesty of heart.

Moral Inconsistency

Many people believe that a person can be honest in great matters and deserve the character of honesty, even though he is dishonest in "little things."

If a supreme regard to the authority of God was the habitual state of his mind, it would be as evident in small matters as well as large. Where the temptation is small, he would be more certain to act conscientiously than in greater matters because there is less to influence him.

What is honesty? If a man has no other motive for acting honestly than mere selfishness, the devil is as honest as he is. Satan is honest with his fellow devils, as far as it is in his interest or policy to be so. Is that honesty? If a man doesn't act honestly from higher motives than this, he is not honest at all; and if he appears to be honest in certain important matters, he has other motives than the honor of or love for God.

Does he love his neighbor as the law of God requires? If he did, he would not defraud him in small things any more than in great. Where the temptation is small, it cannot be that one who truly loves his neighbor would act dishonestly.

Take the case of Job. Job truly loved God, and he endured much distress before he would say a word that even seemed like complaining to God. When the temptation was overwhelming and he could not see any reason for his affliction, his distress became intolerable. His wife told him to curse God and die, but he would not do it. Instead, he said, "Thou speakest as one of the foolish women speaketh. What? shall we receive good at the hand of God, and shall we not receive evil?" (Job 2:10).

Do you suppose Job would have swerved from his integrity in little things or for small temptations? Never. He loved God. And if you find a man who truly loves his neighbor, you will not see him deceiving or defrauding his neighbor for anything.

The Lord has laid down the principle that if a man is dishonest in small matters, he is not strictly honest at all. Many facts appear to contradict this. We see many men who exhibit a great lack of principle in small matters while in larger things they appear to be honorable and even holy. Their conduct in regard to larger matters can be accounted to other principles than honesty of heart. If we can account for their "honesty" on principles of mere selfishness, then they are not really honest at all. Jesus' principle must be consistent, or else He has affirmed a falsehood.

The Deception Of Fear

A man may act honestly in larger matters for fear of disgrace. He may know that certain small things about him are not likely to be mentioned in public, and so he may do them. But the fear of disgrace deters him from doing more obvious things because it will disgrace him. What is this but one form of selfishness overbalancing another form? It is still self-ishness, not honesty.

A man may fear that honesty will injure his business. He deals honestly in important matters, while in little things he is ready to take advantage of anyone he can. Thus a man will take advantage of a seamstress and pay her less than he knows she deserves for making a garment. The same individual, in buying supplies, wouldn't think of cheating because it would injure his business. In dealing with an abused and humble person, he can gripe and squeeze out a few cents without fear of public disgrace, while he wouldn't be publicly spoken of as disreputable and base under any circumstances.

Fear of human law may influence a man to act honestly in obvious things, while in such small matters that the law is not likely to notice, he will defraud any time.

The love of praise influences many men to act honestly and even piously in noticeable things. Many men will cheat a poor person out of a few cents in the price of labor, and then, in some great public display, appear to act generously. Why would a man habitually take advantage of everybody and then give hundreds of dollars to charities? He may do it for the love of praise and not the love of God or man.

A man may be afraid of divine wrath if he commits great dishonest acts and still suppose that God will overlook little things and not notice dishonesty in small matters.

Often individuals who act dishonestly in small affairs will act uprightly and honorable to save their character. Many men are looked upon as honorable dealers by their business associates but are well known by intimate acquaintances to be greedy and overreaching in small matters. It is not real honesty of heart that makes him act with apparent honesty in his public transactions.

An individual may habitually entertain unclean thoughts yet never actually commit adultery. He may be restrained by fear or lack of opportunity and not by principle. If he *indulges* in unclean thoughts, he would certainly act uncleanly if it were not for other reasons than purity of principle.

He may manifest a covetous spirit yet not steal. But he has the spirit that would lead him to steal if not restrained by other reasons than honesty or principle.

A man may be angry, yet never murder anybody. But his hatred would lead him to do it, as far as principle is concerned. If it is not done, it is for other reasons than true principle.

An individual may oppress his fellowman, enslave him, deprive him of instruction, and compel him to labor without compensation for his own benefit, yet not commit murder. But if he will ruin someone's life to gratify his own pride or promote his own interest, it cannot be *principle*. Neither love to God or man keeps him from doing anything dishonest.

Anyone who defrauds the United States' treasury

of postage would rob the treasury of all its gold if he had the chance. The same motive that led him to do the one would lead him to do the other if he had an opportunity, and if it were not counteracted by some other motive equally selfish.

A man may be guilty of little misrepresentations yet not dare to tell a downright *lie*. But if he is guilty of coloring the truth to make facts appear other than they really are, he is lying. The individual who does this would manufacture many lies if it were in his interest or he were not restrained by reasons other than a sacred regard to truth.

Maintaining False Appearances

Individuals often manifest a lack of principle in regard to the payment of small debts, while they are extremely careful and punctual in paying notes at the bank and in their commercial transactions.

For instance, if a man subscribes to a newspaper and the price is a small sum, he may never pay it. The same man having a debt at the bank would certainly have been punctual. Why? Because if he does not pay, his credit will be injured; but the little debt of five dollars will not be protested. He forgets about it, and the publisher has to send for it or go without his money. Obviously this man does not pay his debts at the bank from honesty or principle but purely from a regard to his own credit and interest.

Some manifest this lack of principle by committing petty theft. If they live in an apartment house, they will steal little things, perhaps light bulbs from the halls. Instead of buying them for himself, he pilfers them one at a time. The individual who does this shows himself to be radically rotten at heart.

I once heard about a similar case. A man was sitting in a room where another gentleman had a tumbler of wine and a pitcher of water. The gentleman stepped out of the room for a moment but accidently left the door ajar. Looking back, he saw the other man drink a part of the wine in the tumbler; then, to conceal it, he filled up the tumbler with water and took his seat. The individual who did this showed that he loved wine and thought nothing of stealing. As far as principle was concerned, he would get drunk if he had the means and steal if he had a chance; at heart he was both a drunkard and a thief.

People often manifest great dishonesty when they find articles that have been lost, especially articles of small value. One will find a penknife or an umbrella and never make the least inquiry, even among those he has reason to believe were the losers. The man who would do this would keep a checkbook if he should find it. Yet this same individual, if he found five thousand dollars, would advertise it in the newspaper and make a great noise *if* he knew he'd be found out.

Many individuals conceal little mistakes that are made in their favor, for example, in giving change. If a man would say nothing and let it pass, only opportunity would prevent him from taking any advantage whatever or cheating to any extent.

The real state of a man's heart is often more obvious in small matters than in business of greater importance. Men are often deceived and think that being honest in greater things will prove their honesty of heart, despite their dishonesty in smaller things. They are sure to be on their guard in great things, while they are careless in little matters and so act out their true character.

Sin Is Sin!

The individual who indulges in any one sin does not abstain from sin *because* it is sin. If he hated sin and was opposed to it because it was sin, he would no more indulge in one sin than another. If a person goes to pick and choose among sins, avoiding some and practicing others, it is certain that he does not regard the authority of God or hate sin.

The man who will not practice self-denial in little things to promote Christianity would not endure persecution for its sake. Those who will not deny their appetite would not endure the scourge or the stake. If persecution were to arise, some might endure it for the sake of the applause it would bring or to show their spirit. There is a natural spirit of obstinancy often roused by opposition that would rather go to the stake than yield a point. But it is not true love to the cause that prompts a man to endure opposition, if he will not endure self-denial in little things for its sake.

Where you find people wearing great amounts of jewelry from vanity, consider them rotten. Men strut with their fancy designer clothes, and woman pose in cakes of makeup—it is astonishing how many ways these little things show pride and rottenness of heart.

You say these are little things. I know they are little things, and because they *are* little things, I mention them. They show a person's character clearly. If their pride was not deeply rooted, they would not show it in little things.

Keep a watch over these little things so you will know your character as it appears to God.

Cultivate strict integrity that will affect small things as well as large. Something beautiful happens when you see an individual acting in little things with careful and conscientious holiness. Until believers cultivate universal honesty, they will always be a reproach to the Lord.

How much would be gained if Christians would display purity and honesty on all occasions and to all people! Sinners often fix their eye on professing Christians' petty offenses. What an everlasting reproach to Jesus!

Of what use is it for a woman to talk to her neighbors about the Lord, when her neighbor knows that she will not hesitate to cheat in petty things? Or why should a merchant talk to his clerks, when they know that however honorable he may be in his public transactions, he is cheap and stingy in little things? It is worse than useless.

Chapter 13

DOUBTFUL ACTIONS ARE SINFUL

"He that doubteth is damned if he eat, because he eateth not of faith: for whatsoever is not of faith is sin"—Romans 14:23.

It was a custom among the idolatrous heathen to offer the bodies of beasts in sacrifice. A part of every beast that was offered belonged to the priest. The priests used to sell their portion at the market as any other meat. The scattered Christian Jews were particular about what meats they ate. They wouldn't run the least danger of violating the Mosaic law, and they raised doubts and created disputes and difficulties among the churches because of their belief. This was one of the subjects that divided the church of Corinth, until they finally wrote to the apostle Paul for directions.

A part of the first epistle to the Corinthians was doubtless written as a reply to such inquiries. Some carried their scruples so far that they thought it improper to eat any meat, for they were continually in danger of buying meat that was offered to idols.

Others thought it made no difference. They had a right to eat meat, and they would buy it in the market as they found it.

To quell the dispute, they wrote to Paul. In the eighth chapter, he discusses the subject in full. "Now as touching things offered unto idols, we know that we all have knowledge. Knowledge puffeth up, but charity edifieth. And if any man think that he knoweth any thing, he knoweth nothing yet as he ought to know. But if any man love God, the same is known of him. As concerning therefore the eating of those things that are offered in sacrifice unto idols, we know that an idol is nothing in the world, and that there is none other God but one. For though there be that are called gods, whether in heaven or in earth, (as there be gods many, and lords many,) But to us there is but one God, the Father, of whom are all things, and we in him; and one Lord Jesus Christ, by whom are all things, and we by him. Howbeit there is not in every man that knowledge: for some with conscience of the idol unto this hour eat it as a thing offered unto an idol; and their conscience being weak is defiled" (1 Corinthians 8:1-7).

The believer's conscience "is defiled"—that is, he regards it as meat offered to an idol, and he is really practicing idolatry. The eating of meat is a matter of total indifference, in itself.

"But meat commendeth us not to God: for neither, if we eat, are we the better; neither, if we eat not, are we the worse. But take heed lest by any means this liberty of yours become a stumblingblock to them that are weak. For if any man see thee which hast knowledge sit at meat in the idol's temple, shall not the conscience of him which is weak be emboldened to eat those things offered to idols; And through thy knowledge shall the weak brother perish, for whom Christ died?'' (1 Corinthians 8:8-11).

Some Christian's might know that an idol is nothing and cannot make any change in the meat itself. Yet if they should be seen eating meat that was known to have been offered to an idol, those who are weak might be encouraged to eat the sacrifices as such or as an act of worship to the idol. And the whole time they think they are only following the example of their more enlightened brethren.

''But when ye sin so against the brethren, and wound their weak conscience, ye sin against Christ. Wherefore, if meat make my brother to offend, I will eat no flesh while the world standeth, lest I make my brother to offend'' (1 Corinthians 12-13).

This is Paul's benevolent conclusion. He would rather forego eating meat altogether than be the occasion of drawing a weak brother into idolatry. For, in fact, to sin so against a weak brother is to sin against Christ.

Understanding Your Motives

In writing to the Romans, Paul takes up the same subject—the same dispute had existed there. After laying down some general principles, he gives this rule:

"Him that is weak in faith receive ye, but not to doubtful disputations. For one believeth that he may eat all things: another, who is weak, eateth herbs" (Romans 14:1-2).

Among the Romans, some chose to live entirely on vegetables rather than run the risk of buying flesh that had been offered to idols. Others ate as usual, asking no questions for conscience' sake. Those who lived on vegetables charged the others with idolatry. Those who ate flesh accused the others of superstition and weakness. This was wrong.

"Let not him that eateth despise him that eateth not; and let not him which eateth not, judge him that eateth: for God hath received him. Who art thou that judgest another man's servant? to his own master he standeth or falleth. Yea, he shall be holden up: for God is able to make him stand" (Romans 14:3-4).

A controversy also arose about observing the Jewish festival days and holy days. Some supposed that God required this, and therefore they observed them. The others neglected them because they supposed God did not require the observance.

"One man esteemeth one day above another: another esteemeth every day alike. Let every man be fully persuaded in his own mind. He that regardeth the day, regardeth it unto the Lord; and he that regardeth not the day, to the Lord he doth not regard it. He that eateth, eateth to the Lord, for he giveth God thanks; and he that eateth not, to the Lord he eateth not, and giveth God thanks. For none of us liveth to himself, and no man dieth to himself. For whether we live, we live unto the Lord; and whether we die, we die unto the Lord: whether we live therefore, or die, we are the Lord's. For to this end Christ both died, and rose, and revived, that he might be Lord both of the dead and living. But why dost thou judge thy brother? or why dost thou set at nought thy brother? for we shall all stand before the judgment seat of Christ. For as it is written, As I live, saith the Lord, every knee shall bow to me, and every tongue shall confess to God. So then every one of us shall give account of himself to God. Let us not therefore judge one another any more: but judge this rather, that no man put a stumblingblock or an occasion to fall in his brother's way'' (Romans 14:5-13).

Now mark what Paul says:

''But if thy brother be grieved with thy meat, now walkest thou not charitably: Destroy not him with thy meat, for whom Christ died'' (Romans 14:15).

The distinction of meats into clean and unclean is not binding under Christ. But to him that believes in the distinction, it is a crime to eat indiscriminately because he does what he believes to be contrary to the commands of God. ''All things indeed are pure; but it is evil to him that eateth with offence'' (Romans 14:20). *Every man should be fully persuaded in his own mind that what he is doing is right.* If a man ate unclean meat, not being clear in his mind that it was right, he offended God.

''It is good neither to eat flesh, nor to drink wine,

nor *any thing* whereby thy brother stumbeleth, or is offended, or is made weak. Hast thou faith? have it to thyself before God. Happy is he that condemneth not himself in *that thing* which he alloweth. And he that doubteth is damned if he eat, because *he eateth* not of faith: for whatsoever is not of faith is sin'' (Romans 14:21-23).

The word rendered *damned* means *condemned,* or judged guilty of breaking the law of God. If a man doubts whether it is lawful to do a thing, and while in that state of doubt he does it, he displeases God, breaks the law, and is condemned whether the thing is right or wrong. I have been careful to explain the text in its context because I want to satisfy your minds of the correctness of the principle.

If a man does what he doubts to be lawful, he sins and is condemned for it in the sight of God. Whether it is lawful itself is not the question. If he doubts its lawfulness, it is wrong in him.

One exception ought to be noted here. If a man honestly and fully doubts the lawfulness of omitting to do something as much as he does the lawfulness of doing it, he must act according to the best light he can get. But where he doubts the lawfulness of the act and has no cause to doubt the lawfulness of the omission, yet does it, he sins and is condemned before God.

Responsibility And Action

An individual is condemned if he does what he

doubts because if God makes him doubt the lawfulness of an act, he is bound to stop, examine the question, and settle it to his satisfaction.

Suppose your child is invited by his companions
to go somewhere, and he doubts whether you would
let him go. Do you not see that it is his duty to ask
you? If one of his schoolmates invites him home,
and he doubts whether you would like it, yet he
goes, is this not wrong?

Or suppose a castaway on a desolate island takes
up his abode in a cave, considering himself alone
and destitute of friends, relief, and hope. But every
morning he finds a supply of nutritious and whole-
some food prepared for him by the mouth of his
cave. What is his duty? Does not gratitude require
him to find his unseen friend and thank him for his
kindness? He cannot say, ''I doubt whether anyone
is here; therefore, I will do nothing but eat my al-
lowance and relax.'' His refusal to search for his
benefactor would convict him of wickedness, as if
he knew who it was and refused to return thanks
for favors received.

Or imagine an atheist opens his eyes on the blessed
light of heaven and breathes air that sends health
and vigor through his frame. Such a vision is enough
evidence to set him on the search for that great Being who provides all these means of life and happiness. If he does not seek after God, he shows that
he has the heart as well as the intellect of an atheist. He has, to say the least, evidence that there *may
be* a God. What then is his business? Plainly, it is

to honestly, with a childlike spirit, search the Scriptures and pay God reverence. If he still acts as if there were no God, he shows that his heart is wrong; it says, ''Let there be no God.''

It is the same with the Unitarian. He is bound to search the Scriptures humbly and satisfy himself. No intelligent and honest man can say that the Scriptures afford *no evidence* of the divinity of Christ. They do afford evidence that has convinced and fully satisfied thousands of the most acute minds, who have been before opposed to the doctrine. No man can reject the doctrine, without a doubt, because there is evidence that it *may be* true.

Let us also consider the Universalist. Where is one who can say he *knows* there is not a hell where sinners go after death into endless torment. He is bound to search the Scriptures. It is not enough for him to say he does not believe in hell. There may be one, and if he rejects it and goes on reckless of the truth whether there is or not, that itself makes him a rebel against God. He doesn't know whether there is a hell which he ought to avoid, yet he acts as if he was certain and had no doubts. He is condemned.

I once knew a physician who was a Universalist. He has entered eternity to try the reality of his speculations. Before he died, he told me that he had strong doubts of the truth of Universalism. He had mentioned his doubts to his minister, who confessed that he, too, doubted its truth; and he did not believe there was a Universalist in the world who did not doubt.

For a man to do a thing when he doubts whether it is lawful shows that he is selfish and has other objects besides doing the will of God. It shows that he wants to do it to gratify himself. He doubts whether God will approve of it, yet he does it. Is he not a rebel? If he honestly wished to serve God, he would stop, inquire, and examine until he was satisfied. But to go forward while he is in doubt shows that he is selfish and wicked. He is willing to do it whether God is pleased or not, and he wants to do it whether it is right or wrong. He does it because he wants to do it and not *because it is right*.

The man who ignores his doubts manifests a reckless spirit. This shows a lack of conscience, an indifference to right, a setting aside of the authority of God, and a disposition not to do God's will. He does not care whether God is pleased or displeased, and desperate recklessness and headlong temper is the height of wickedness.

The principle, then, which is clearly laid down in the text and context, and also in the chapter which I quoted from Corinthians, is fully sustained by examination. For a man to do a thing, when he doubts the lawfulness of it, is sin for which he is condemned before God.

Legitimate Doubts

In some cases, a person may be equally in doubt about the lawfulness of a thing and whether he is bound to do it or not.

Take the subject of wine at the communion table. Some strongly believe that wine is an essential part of the ordinance and that we ought to use the best wine we can get. Others say that we ought not to use alcoholic or intoxicating wine at all. As wine is not in their view essential to the ordinance, they think it is better to use some other drink. Both these classes are undoubtedly equally conscientious and desirous to do what they have most reason to believe is agreeable to the will of God.

Each man must decide, according to the best light he can get, what is most pleasing to God. He must pray over the matter, search the Scriptures, obtain the best understanding he can, and then act. When he does this, he is by no means to be judged or censured by others for the course he takes. "Who art thou that judgest another man's servant?" No man is authorized to make his own conscience the rule of his neighbor's conduct.

In these cases the design is to honor God, and the sole ground of doubt is which course will really honor Him. Paul says, in reference to all laws of this kind, "He that regardeth the day, regardeth it unto the Lord; and he that regardeth not the day, to the Lord he doth not regard it." The design is to do right, and the doubt is as to the means of doing it in the best manner.

Examining Selfish Desires

In some cases the *design* is wrong. The object is

to gratify self, and the individual has doubts whether he may do it lawfully.

Take, for instance, the making or vending of strong alcoholic drinks. After all the light has been thrown upon the question, is there a man living in this land who can say he sees no reason *to doubt* the lawfulness of this business. But take the most charitable supposition possible for the distiller or the vender, and suppose he is not fully convinced of its unlawfulness. He must at least *doubt* its lawfulness.

What is he to do then? Is he to shut his eyes to the light, regardless of truth as long as he can keep from seeing it? No. He may raise objections, but he *knows* that he has doubts about the lawfulness of his business. And if he doubts and persists in doing it without taking the trouble to examine and see what is right, he is just as sure to be damned as if he went on in the face of knowledge.

Men say, "Why, I don't know that the Bible forbids making or selling liquor." Well, suppose you are not fully convinced, and all your possible and conceivable objections are not removed—what then? You know you have *doubts* about its lawfulness. It is not necessary to take such ground to convict you of doing wrong. If you doubt its lawfulness, yet persist in doing it, you are on the way to hell.

The same remarks apply to all sorts of lottery and casino gambling. Men have *doubts*.

Take the case of controversial indulgences of appetite. Consider the drinking of wine, beer, and other fermented intoxicating liquors. Is it not questionable, at least, whether using these drinks is not transgressing the rule laid down by the apostle: "It is good neither to eat flesh, nor to drink wine, nor any thing whereby thy brother stumbleth, or is offended, or is made weak"? No man can make me believe he has no doubts of the lawfulness of doing it. No certain proof exists of its lawfulness, but there is strong proof of its unlawfulness. Every man who does it while he doubts is condemned.

Can any man pretend that he has no doubt about the will of God for him to use tobacco? No man can pretend that he doubts the lawfulness of his *omission* of these things. Does any man think that he is *bound* to make use of wine, strong beer, or tobacco as a luxury? No. The doubt is all on one side. What shall we say, then, of that man who doubts the lawfulness of it and still fills his face with the poisonous weed? He is condemned.

Consider parties where they eat and drink to excess. Is there no reason to doubt whether this is a practical use of time and money as God requires? Look at the starving and the poor, consider the effect of this extravagance, and see if you will ever go to another such party, or have one, without doubting its lawfulness. Where can you find a man or woman who will say they have no doubt? And if you doubt, and still do it, you are condemned.

This principle touches a whole class of controversial things where people attempt to excuse themselves by saying it is not worse than to do this or that. Thus, they get away from the condemning sentence of God's law. But, in fact, if there is a doubt, it is their duty to abstain.

Take the case of dances, novel reading, and other methods of wasting time. Is this God's way to spend your lives? Can you say you have no doubt of it?

People say we should have holidays. That is very well. But when they are abused and produce so much evil, I ask every Christian if you can help doubting their lawfulness? And if it is doubtful, it comes under the rule: "If meat makes my brother to offend." If keeping holidays leads to gluttony, drunkenness, and wickedness, does it not bring the lawfulness of them into doubt? Yes, that is the least that can be said, and they who doubt yet do it sin against God.

Intermarriages of Christians with impenitent sinners must also be considered. This answer always comes up: "But it is not certain that these marriages are unlawful." Does not the Bible and the nature of the case make it *doubtful* whether they are right? It can be demonstrated, indeed, to be unlawful. But suppose it could not be. What Christian ever married an unbeliever and did not doubt whether it was lawful? He that doubts is condemned.

No Doubt About It

This principle will stand by you when you attempt to rebuke sin and the power of society attempts to put you on the defensive to prove the sinfulness of

181

a cherished practice. Remember, *the burden of proof does not lie on you.* If you can show sufficient reason to question its lawfulness and create a valid doubt whether it is according to the will of God, you shift the burden of proof to the other side. Unless they can remove the doubt and show that there is no room for doubt, they have no right to continue. If they do, they sin against God.

The knowledge of duty is not indispensable to moral obligation, but the possession of the means of knowledge is sufficient to make a person responsible. If a man has the means of knowing whether something is right or wrong, he is bound to use the means, inquire, and get the facts.

If men who do what they doubt the lawfulness of are condemned, what will we say of the multitudes who continually do what they *know and confess to be wrong?* Woe to that man who practices what he condemns. And "happy is he that condemneth not himself in that thing which he alloweth."

Hypocrites often attempt to shelter themselves behind their doubts to get clear of their duty. The hypocrite is unwilling to be enlightened and doesn't want to know the truth. He doesn't want to obey the Lord, and he hides behind his doubts and turns his eye from the light. But God will drag him out from behind this refuge of lies by the principle laid down in the text—their very doubts condemn them.

It is obvious that very little conscience exists in the Church. Multitudes continue to strongly doubt the lawfulness of many of their actions.

And less love to God exists than conscience. It cannot be pretended that love to God is the cause of all this following of fashions, practicing indulgences, and other things of which people doubt the lawfulness. They do not persist in these things because they love God. They persist because they wish to gratify themselves, and they would rather run the risk of doing wrong than to have their doubts cleared up.

Do not say in your prayers, "O Lord, if I have sinned in this thing, forgive me the sin." If you have done what you believed was wrong, you have sinned, whether the thing itself is right or wrong. You must repent and ask forgiveness.

Are you convinced that to do what you doubt the lawfulness of is sin? If you are, I have one more question to ask you. Will you from this time relinquish everything of which you doubt the lawfulness— every amusement, indulgence, practice, and pursuit? Or will you stand condemned before the solemn judgment seat of Jesus Christ? If you will not relinquish these things, you show that you are an impenitent sinner and do not *intend* to obey God. If you do not repent, you bring God's condemnation and wrath down upon your head forever.

Chapter 14

EXPOSING YOUR INNER SELF

"Examine yourselves, whether ye be in the faith; prove your own selves"—2 Corinthians 13:5.

We must understand our own hearts and take the proper steps to prove our real characters as they appear to God. Scripture doesn't refer to a trial or proof of our strength or knowledge but our *moral character*. It implies that we should know how God regards us and what He thinks of us. Does He consider us saints or sinners? We must settle the question definitively for ourselves: Are we heirs of heaven or heirs of hell?

The individual who is uncertain about his real character can have no peace of mind. He may have apathy, but apathy is different from peace. And very few professing Christians, or people who continue to hear the gospel, can have apathy for any length of time or suppress uneasy feelings. I am not speaking of hypocrites, who have seared their consciences. But in regard to others, it is true that they *must* settle this question in order to enjoy peace of mind.

Anxiety Is No Virtue

A man who is not truly settled in his mind about his own character is hardly honest. If he professes Christ when he does not honestly believe he is a saint, he is half a hypocrite. When he prays, he always doubts whether his prayers are acceptable to God.

Some people maintain that keeping saints in the dark makes them humble. But one of the most weighty considerations in the universe to keep a believer from dishonoring God is to *know* that he is a child of God. When a person is in an anxious state of mind, he can have little faith, and his usefulness cannot be extensive until the question is settled.

Many think the question of salvation never can be settled in this world. They make a virtue of their great doubt, which they always have, even if they are Christians. For hundreds of years believers have been looked upon with suspicion unless they were filled with doubts. But I maintain that Christians can test themselves to know their own selves and understand their true character. This is evident from the command in the text, "Examine yourselves, whether ye be in the faith; prove your own selves." Does God require us to examine and prove ourselves when He knows it is impossible for us to learn our true character?

Consciousness gives the highest possible certainty about the facts that determine our characters. We can and ought to have the same kind of evidence of our state before God that we have of our existence; and that is *consciousness*. We cannot help having the evidence. Consciousness continually testifies to our state of mind. We only need to notice what consciousness testifies to, and we can settle the question as certainly as we can our own existence.

If men were shut up in dungeons with no opportunity of being influenced by circumstances, they could not be blamed for not knowing themselves. But God has placed them in circumstances to prove them and know what is in their hearts—to know whether they will keep His commandments or not. The things around us produce impressions on our minds and lead us to feel and act in some way. When we see how we feel and how we are inclined to act in particular circumstances, it produces self-knowledge.

God's law is a true standard by which to try our characters. We know exactly what His standard is; and, therefore, we have an infallible and invariable rule by which to judge ourselves. We can bring all our feelings and actions and compare them with this standard and know exactly what their true character is in the sight of God. God Himself tries them by the same standard.

When Pride Blinds

Nothing but dishonesty can possibly lead us to self-deception. The self-deceived individual is not only careless and negligent but dishonest, or he would not deceive himself. He must be greatly prejudiced by pride and blinded by self-will, or he would have to know that he is not what he professes to be. Many various circumstances call forth the exercises of his mind, and it must be willful blindness. If he never had any opportunities to act, or if circumstances did not call forth his feelings, he might be ignorant. A person who had never seen a beggar might not be able to tell what he thought about beggars. But put him with beggars every day, and he is either blind or dishonest if he doesn't know how he feels about them.

Many *wait* for evidence to come to them to decide whether they are Christians or not. They appear to be waiting for certain feelings to come to them. Perhaps they pray earnestly about it and then wait for the feelings to come that will let them know they're saved. Many times they won't do anything until they get this evidence. They sit and wait in vain expectation for the Spirit of God to come and lift them out of this stupor. They may wait until doomsday.

The human mind is so constituted that it will never feel by *trying* to feel. You can try hard to feel in a particular way. Your efforts to put forth feelings are unphilosophical and absurd. Feeling is always awakened in the mind by the mind's being intensely fixed on some *object* calculated to awaken feeling. But when the mind is fixed, not upon the object but on direct attempts to put forth feeling,

187

this will not awaken feeling. It is impossible. You may as well shut your eyes and try to see.

When the mind's attention is taken up with looking inward and attempting to examine the nature of the present emotion, that emotion at once ceases to exist; the attention is no longer fixed on the object that causes the emotion. When I hold my hand before a lamp, it casts a shadow; but if I take the lamp away, there is no shadow. There must be light to produce a shadow. If the mind is turned away from the object that awakens emotion, the emotion ceases to exist. The mind must be fixed on the object, not on the emotion, or there will be no emotion and no evidence.

You will never get evidence by spending time in mourning over the state of your heart. Some people spend their time complaining, "Oh, I don't feel; I can't feel; my heart is so hard." What are they doing? Perhaps they are trying to work themselves up into feeling. This is as philosophical as trying to fly!

While they are mourning and thinking about their hard hearts, they are the ridicule of the devil. Suppose a man shut himself outside and then went around complaining how cold he was—children would laugh at him. He would freeze if he shut himself out from the warmth. And all his complaining would not help the matter.

When we concentrate on any object calculated to awaken feeling, it is impossible not to feel. The mind is made so that it must feel. Don't stop and ask, "Do I feel?" If you put your hand near fire, do you need to stop and ask, "Do I really feel the sensation of warmth?" You *know* that you do!

Where the impression is slight, it requires an effort of attention to notice your own consciousness. The passing feeling of the mind may be so slight that it escapes your notice, but it is still real.

The Horror Of Sin

If the mind is fixed on an object calculated to excite emotions of any kind, it is impossible not to feel those emotions to some degree. If the mind is *intently fixed,* it is impossible not to feel the emotions to such a degree that you are conscious of them. These principles show you how we are to discover our characters and know the real state of our feelings toward any object.

Be sure that the things you fix your mind on are realities. A great deal of imaginary religion prevails in the world. People have high feelings—their minds are much excited and the feeling corresponds with the object contemplated. But here is the source of the delusion—*the object is imaginary*. The feeling is not false or imaginary. It is real feeling and corresponds perfectly with the imaginary object. But the object is fiction. The individual has formed a *notion* of God, of Jesus Christ, or of salvation that is opposite to the truth. His *feelings* are correct, but his object is wrong. This is undoubtedly a major source of the false hopes and conversions in the world.

You will not discover the true state of your heart merely by finding in your mind a strong feeling of abhorrence for sin. All intelligent beings disapprove of sin, *when viewed abstractly* and detached from their own selfish gratification. Even the devil feels it. The devil no more loves sin, when viewed abstractly, than Gabriel. He blames sinners and condemns their conduct; and whenever he has no selfish reason for being pleased at what they do, he abhors it.

A striking difference exists between the natural disapproval of sin, as an abstract thing, and the intense detestation and opposition that is founded on love to God. It is one thing for a young man to feel that a certain act is wrong and quite another thing to view it as an injury to his father. Here is something in addition to his former feeling. He has not only indignation against the act as wrong, but his love for his father produces a feeling of *grief.* And the individual who loves God feels not only a strong loathing for sin but a feeling of grief and indignation when he views it as committed against God.

If, then, you want to know how you feel toward sin, consider how you feel when you hang around sinners and see them break God's law. When you hear them swear profanely or see them get drunk, how do you feel? Do you feel as the psalmist did when he wrote, "I beheld the transgressors, and was *grieved*; because they kept not thy word"? And, "Rivers of water run down mine eyes, because they keep not thy law." And again, *"Horror* hath taken hold upon me because of the wicked that forsake thy law'' (Psalm 119:158, 136, 53).

Look back on your past sins and see whether you feel as an affectionate child would feel when he remembers how he has disobeyed or dishonored a beloved parent. It is one thing to feel a strong conviction that your former conduct was wicked—and quite another thing to have this feeling attended with *grief* because you sinned against God.

Most Christians look back on their former conduct toward their parents with deep emotion. In addition to a strong disapproval of their conduct, a deep emotion of *grief* often overwhelms them accompanied by gushing tears. This is true repentance toward a parent. And repentance toward God is the same thing. If genuine, it will correspond in degree to the intensity of attention with which the mind is fixed on the subject.

Examine Yourself

If you want to test your feelings toward impenitent sinners, then converse with them about the state of their souls and warn them. See what they say and discover the state of their hearts, and then you will know how you feel about sinners. Don't shut yourself up in your closet and try to imagine them. You may imagine something that will affect your sympathies and make you weep and pray.

Fix your thoughts intently on God. Don't try to imagine a God after your own foolish hearts, but take the Bible and learn who God is. Don't imagine how He looks, but fix your mind on the Bible description of how He feels, what He does, and what He says. Here you will detect the real state of your heart, which you cannot mistake.

You are *bound* to know whether you love the Lord Jesus Christ or not. Review the circumstances of His life and see whether they appear as realities to your mind—His miracles, sufferings, character, death, resurrection, ascension, and intercession at the right hand of the throne of God. Do you believe all these? What are your feelings in view of them? When you think of His willingness and ability to save, His atoning death, and His power, are these things realities to you? If so, you will have feelings and will be conscious of them.

What are your feelings toward the saints? If you want to test your heart on this point, don't let your thoughts run to the ends of the earth, but fix your mind on the saints near you. Do you love them and desire their holiness? Can you bear them in your heart to the throne of grace in faith and ask God to bestow blessings on them?

What is the state of your feelings toward revivals? Read about them, think of them, fix your mind on them, and you will have feelings that will manifest the state of your heart. The same is true of the unsaved, of drunkards, of the Bible, or any object of concern. The only way to know the state of your heart is to fix your mind on the reality of things until you feel so intensely that there is no mistaking the nature of your feelings.

If you find it difficult to produce feelings about any of these things, either your mind is taken up with the Lord's work and won't allow fixed attention to the specified object, or your thoughts wander with a fool's eyes to the ends of the earth. I have known some Christians to be very distressed because they did not feel as intensely as they think they ought to on some subjects. A person's mind may be so taken up with anxiety, labor, and prayer for sinners that it requires an effort to think enough about his own soul to feel deeply. When he hits his knees to pray about his own sins, a sinner comes to mind; and he can hardly pray for himself. Don't regard it as evidence *against you* if the reason you don't feel is because your mind is engrossed in something equally important.

If your thoughts run all over the world and you don't feel deeply enough to know your true character—if your mind won't come to the Bible and fix on *any* object of Christian feeling—lay a strong hand on yourself and fix your thoughts with a death-grasp until you do feel. You can command your thoughts: God has put the control of your mind in your own hands. You can control your own feelings by turning your attention upon the object you wish to feel about. Fasten your mind on the subject until the deep foundations of feeling break up in your mind and you understand the state of your heart and your real character in the sight of God.

The Religion Of Imagination

An individual can never know the true state of his heart unless he is active in the Church. Shut up in his prayer closet, he can never tell how he feels toward objects that are outside, and he can never feel right toward them until he goes out and acts. How can he know his real feeling toward sinners if he never brings his mind in contact with sinners? His imagination may make him feel, but his feelings are not produced by a reality.

Individuals shut out from the world of reality and living in worlds of imagination become perfect creatures of imagination. A similar thing happens in Christianity with those who don't bring their mind in contact with reality. They think they love mankind yet do them no good. They imagine they abhor sin but do nothing to destroy it. How many people deceive themselves by exciting their imagination about missions but do nothing to save souls? Women will spend a whole day at a prayer meeting for the conversion of the world, while their impenitent servant in the kitchen is not spoken to all day.

This is all a fiction of the imagination! There is no reality in such "Christianity." If they loved God and man, the pictures drawn by the imagination about the unsaved in other countries would not create any more feeling than the reality around them.

They are surrounded by sinners, and they hear profane oaths and see vices as a naked reality every day. If these produce no feeling, it is vain to pretend that they feel what God feels for sinners in foreign lands or anywhere.

People love to talk about the heathen, but they have never converted a soul at home. If they don't promote revivals at home, where they understand the language and have direct access to their neighbors, how can they be depended upon to promote the work of Jesus on the mission field? The Church must understand this and keep it in mind in selecting men to go on foreign missions. They ought to know that if the reality at home doesn't excite a person to action, the devil will only laugh at a million such missionaries.

The same delusion often manifests itself in regard to revivals. An individual may be a great friend to revivals, but they are always the revivals of former days or revivals that are yet to come. But as to any present revival, he is always aloof and doubtful. He can read about revivals and pray, "O Lord, revive thy work; O Lord, let us have such revivals when thousands shall be converted in a day."

But get him into the reality of things, and he never sees a revival he can take interest in. He is friendly to the fictitious imaginings of his own mind and can create a state of things that will excite his feelings. But no reality ever brings him out to cooperate in actually promoting a revival.

In the days of our Savior, the people said, and no

doubt really believed, that they abhorred the actions of those who persecuted the prophets. They said, "If we had been in the days of our fathers, we would not have been partakers with them in the blood of the prophets" (Matthew 23:30). No doubt they wondered that people could be so wicked. But they had never seen a prophet and were moved by their imagination.

When Jesus appeared, the greatest of prophets, on whom all the prophecies centered, they rejected Him and put Him to death with as much cold-hearted cruelty as their fathers killed the prophets. "Fill ye up," said our Savior, "the measure of your fathers. . . .That upon you may come all the righteous blood shed upon the earth" (Matthew 23:32,35).

In every age men have fallen in love with fictions of their own imaginations, over which they have stumbled into hell.

Illuminating The Past

Christianity consists in love, feeling right, doing right, and doing good. If, therefore, you want to be holy, do not think of cultivating holiness that will never cause it to grow—that is, by withdrawing from contact with mankind. If the Lord thought such circumstances would be favorable to piety, He would have directed them so. But He knew better. He has, therefore, appointed circumstances as they are so that His people may have a thousand objects of benevolence and a thousand opportunities to do good. If they deny themselves and turn their hearts upon these things, they cannot fail to grow in holiness and have increasing evidence.

We can consistently shut ourselves up in our prayer closets in only one department of self examination: that is when we want to look back and calmly examine the *motives* of our past conduct. In such cases we must limit our thoughts and keep other things from our mind. To do this effectually, it is often necessary to resort to seclusion, fasting, and prayer.

Sometimes it is impossible to vividly remember what we want to examine without association. We attempt to call up past scenes, but everything is confused and dark until we strike upon some associated idea that gradually brings the whole before us.

If I am called as a witness in court, I can sometimes only remember by going to the place. Then all the circumstances come back as though they were yesterday. Similarly, we may find that associated ideas will bring back the feelings we formerly had.

In examining yourselves, be careful to avoid expecting to find all the Christian graces in exercise in your mind at once. This is contrary to the nature of the mind. *If* you find the exercises of your mind are right, satisfy yourselves with the subject before your mind. Don't draw a wrong inference because some other right emotion isn't present. The mind can have only one train of emotions at a time.

Some Christians always have the happy kind of

feelings. Others always feel sad and distressed. They are in almost constant agony for sinners. Their thoughts are directed to different objects. One class always thinks of objects calculated to make them happy; the other thinks of the state of the Church or the state of sinners. They are weighed down with a burden as if they had a mountain on their shoulders. Both may be Christians and both classes of feelings may be right, depending upon the objects they look at.

The apostle Paul had continual heaviness and sorrow of heart on account of his brethren. No doubt he felt right. The case of his brethren, who had rejected the Savior, was the object of his thoughts. The dreadful wrath that they had brought upon themselves and the doom that hung over them was constantly before his mind. How could he be anything but sad?

Show me a joyful, happy Christian, and he is not generally a *very useful* Christian. Often, he is taken up with enjoying the sweets of religion and *does* little. Some ministers preach a great deal on these subjects and make their hearers very happy. But such ministers are seldom instrumental in converting many sinners, however much they may have refreshed, edified, and gratified their congregation.

On the other hand, you will find men who are habitually filled with deep agony of soul in view of the state of sinners, and these men will be largely instrumental in converting men. The reason is plain. Both preached the truth, both preached the gospel—in different proportions—and the feelings awakened corresponded with the views they preached. The difference is that one comforted the saints and the other converted sinners.

Do Something!

Christians who are always happy are lovely companions, but they are very seldom engaged in pulling sinners out of the fire. Others are always full of agony for sinners, looking at their state and longing to have souls converted. Instead of enjoying the foretaste of heaven on earth, they are sympathizing with the Son of God when He was on earth, groaning in spirit and spending all night in prayer. The real *revival* spirit is a spirit of agonizing desires and prayer for sinners.

People often wonder why they feel as they do. The answer is plain. *You feel so because you think so.* You direct your attention to those objects calculated to produce those feelings.

Many pious people dishonor the Lord by their doubts. They perpetually talk about their doubts and conclude that they have no faith. If, instead of dwelling on their doubts, they will fix their minds on other objects—on Jesus for instance—or go out and try to bring sinners to repentance, they will feel right and dissipate their doubts.

Never wait until you feel right before you do this. Perhaps some things that I have said have not been rightly understood. I said you could do nothing for

God unless you felt right. Don't infer that you are to sit still and do *nothing* until you are satisfied that you do feel right.

Place yourself in circumstances that will make you feel right and go to work. On one hand, to bustle about without any feeling is wrong; and on the other hand, to shut yourself up in your closet and wait for feeling to come is also wrong!

Stay active! You will never feel right otherwise. Keep your mind under the influence of objects calculated to create and keep Christian feelings alive.

Chapter 15

TRUE SAINTS

"Who is on the Lord's side?"—Exodus 32:26.

People try to serve God for many different reasons. Some serve from true love and some from other motives. They all profess to be servants of God. Yet instead of their being God's servants, they are trying to *make God their servant*. Their leading aim and object is to secure their own salvation or some other advantage for themselves through God's favor. They want to make God their friend so they can use Him to serve their own needs.

One class of professed Christians, however, are the true friends of God and man. If you observe the true design and aim of their faith, you will see that they are sincerely benevolent. That this is their character is obvious by their carefulness in avoiding sin. They hate it in themselves, and they hate it in others. They will not justify it in themselves, and they will not justify it in others. True Christians won't try to cover up or excuse their own sins, neither will they try to cover up or excuse the sins of

201

others. In short, they aim at *perfect holiness*.

This conduct makes it evident that they are the true friends of God. I don't mean to say that every true friend of God is perfect, no more than I would say that every truly affectionate and obedient child is perfect or never fails his parent. But if he is an affectionate and obedient child, his aim is always to obey. If he fails in any respect, he by no means justifies it, pleads for it, or aims to cover it up; but as soon as he comes to think of the matter, he is dissatisfied with himself and repents.

For The Love Of God

The true friends of God and man are always ready to humble, blame, or condemn themselves for what is wrong. But you *never* see them finding fault with God. You never hear them excusing themselves and throwing the blame on their Maker by telling of their inability to obey God. They always speak as if they felt that what God has required is right and reasonable with only themselves to blame for their disobedience. God does not require impossibilities of His creatures.

Christians manifest a deep abhorrence of the sins of other people. They do not cover up the sins of others or plead for them and excuse them. You never hear them *apologizing* for sin. As they are indignant at sin in themselves, they are just as much so when they see it in others. They know its horrible nature and abhor it always.

God's friends manifest this spirit in zeal for His honor and glory. They show the same ardor to promote God's honor and interest that the true patriot does to promote the honor and interest of his country. If he greatly loves his country, its government, and its interest, he sets his heart to promote it. He is never as happy as when he is doing something for his country.

A child who truly loves his father is never as happy as when he is advancing his father's honor and interest. He never feels more indignant grief than when he sees his father abused or injured. If he sees his father disobeyed or abused by those who ought to obey, love, and honor him, his heart breaks.

Multitudes of professing Christians are zealous to defend their own character and honor. But true saints feel more engaged, and their hearts beat higher, when defending or advancing God's honor. These are the true friends of God and man.

They sympathize with God in His feelings toward man and have the same love for souls that God feels. I do not mean that they feel in the same degree but that they have the same *kind* of feelings. There is such a thing as loving the souls of men but hating their conduct. You always naturally feel sympathy for a person in distress, unless you have some selfish reason for feeling malevolent. If you saw a murderer hung, you would feel compassion for him. Even the wicked have this natural sympathy for those who suffer.

The real child of God feels and manifests another

peculiar kind of sympathy toward sinners—a mingled feeling of abhorrence, compassion, and indignation against his sins and pity for his person.

Two kinds of love exist. One is the love of *benevolence*. This has no respect to the character of the person loved but merely views the individual as exposed to suffering and misery. God feels this way toward all men. The other kind, the love of *complacency,* includes esteem or approval of character. God feels this way only toward the righteous. He *never* feels this love toward sinners. He infinitely abhors them. He has compassion and abhorrence at the same time.

Christians have the same feelings but not to the same degree. They probably never feel right unless they have both these feelings at the same time. The Christian does not feel as God feels toward individuals unless both these feelings exist in his mind at the same time. You see this by one striking characteristic: the Christian will rebuke most pointedly and frequently those for whom he feels the deepest compassion. Did you ever see this? Did you ever see a parent yearning with compassion over a child and reprove him with tears but with a severity that would make the little offender shake under his rebuke?

Jesus often strongly manifested these two emotions. He wept over Jerusalem, yet He tells the reason in a manner that shows His burning indignation against their conduct: "O, Jerusalem, Jerusalem, thou that killest the prophets, and stonest them which are sent unto thee'' (Matthew 23:37). What a full view He had of their wickedness as He wept with compassion for the doom that hung over them. Similarly, a Christian's most tender appeals are accompanied with a strong rebuke for sin.

Reconciliation: A Royal Commandment

The true friend of God and man never takes the sinner's part because he never acts through mere compassion. At the same time, he is never seen to denounce the sinner without manifesting compassion for his soul and a strong desire to save him from death.

His main objective is to promote Christianity and to lead everybody to glorify God. He does this naturally if he is the true friend of God. A true friend of the government wants everybody to obey the government. A true and affectionate child wants everybody to love and respect his father. If anyone is at odds, his constant aim and effort is to bring him to reconciliation. A true friend of God makes it a *primary objective* of his life to reconcile sinners to God.

If the leading feature of your character is not the absorbing thought and effort to reconcile men to God, you have not the root of the matter in you. Whatever appearance of *religion* you may have, you lack the leading and fundamental characteristic of true piety—the character and aims of Jesus and His disciples. Look at them and see how this feature stands out, in strong and eternal relief, as the leading characteristic, the prominent design, and the objective of their lives.

What is the leading objective of your life? Is it to bring all God's enemies to submit to Him? If not, away with your pretensions. Whatever else you have, you don't have the true love of God in you.

True Christians always want to avoid everything calculated to prevent or hinder the salvation of souls. They never ask, "Is this something God forbids?" The first question that naturally suggests itself to their minds is, "How will this affect the Kingdom? Will it prevent the conversion of sinners or hinder the progress of revivals?" If so, they don't need the thunder of Sinai to be pealed in their ears to forbid it. If they see it contrary to the spirit of holiness and to their main objective, that is enough.

Take gambling, for instance. Christians don't say, "Gambling is nowhere prohibited in the Bible, and I don't feel bound to give it up." They find that it hinders the great objective for which they live, and that is enough for them.

The friends of God avoid *whatever* they see would hinder revival. Just as a merchant would avoid anything that had a tendency to impair his credit and defeat his goal of making money. Suppose a merchant was about to do something that you knew would injure his credit, and you go to him in the spirit of friendship and advise him not to do it. Would he turn around and say, "Show me the passage where God has prohibited this in the Bible"?

No. He won't ask you to show him anything else.

A person who strongly desires the conversion of sinners doesn't need an express prohibition to prevent his doing anything that would hinder it. No danger arises in his doing anything that will defeat the very purpose of his life.

Christians become distressed unless they see the work of converting sinners going on. They call it a lamentable state in the Church if sinners are not converted. No matter how rich the congregation grows or how popular their minister, their panting hearts are uneasy unless they see the work of conversion actually going on. They see that without evangelism all is vain.

The Spirit Of Prayer

God's children often trouble those who are religious from other motives and want to keep quiet and have everything go on in the "good old way." These Christians are often called "uneasy spirits in the church." If a church has a few such spirits in it, the minister will be made uneasy unless his preaching is geared to convert sinners. You sometimes hear of these men reproving the Church for living so cold and worldly. Their hearts are grieved, and their souls are in agony because sinners are pressing down to hell.

If you know people's prayer habits, it will show you how they truly feel. If a man is motivated mainly by a desire to save himself, you will hear him praying chiefly for himself—that he may have his sins pardoned and enjoy the Spirit of God.

If he is truly the friend of God and man, you will find that the burden of his prayers is for the *glory of God* in the salvation of sinners. He is never so enthusiastic and powerful in prayer as when he gets upon his favorite topic—the conversion of sinners. Go to a prayer meeting where such Christians pray. Instead of praying for themselves, you will hear them pouring out their souls for sinners.

You can tell how your prayer life is by whether you feel and pray most for yourself or for sinners. If you know nothing about the spirit of prayer for sinners, you are not the true friend of God and man. Sinners are going to hell on every side! Don't tell me men are truly holy when their prayers are droned over. This is as much a matter of form as when a priest counts over his beads. Such a man deceives himself if he talks about being the true friend of God and man.

When anything is presented to true Christians that promises success in converting sinners, they don't wait for a *command* to do it. They only want the evidence, and they will engage in it with all their soul. The question is not, "What am I commanded to do?" but "In what way can I do most for the salvation of souls and the conversion of the world to God?"

Another characteristic of such Christians is a disposition to *deny themselves* in order to do good to others. God has established throughout all the universe the principle of *giving*. Even in the natural world rivers, oceans, and clouds all give. This is true throughout the whole kingdom of nature and of grace.

This is the very spirit of Christ. He sought not to please Himself but to do good to others. Children of God are always ready to deny themselves enjoyments, comforts, and even necessities, if they can do more good to others.

They continually devise new means and new measures for doing good. This is what would be expected from their continual desire to *do good*. They are not like people who are satisfied with doing what they call their *duty*. Where an individual is aiming mainly at his own salvation, he may think that if he does his duty he is discharged from responsibility, and he is satisfied. He thinks he has escaped divine wrath and gained heaven by doing what God required him to do; *he* cannot help whether sinners are saved or lost.

But a Christian's main objective isn't to gain heaven and avoid wrath—it is to save souls and honor God. If this objective is not attained, he is in pain.

Dying To Save Souls

The friends of God are always grieved when they see a church asleep and doing nothing for the salvation of sinners. They know it is impossible to do anything considerable for the salvation of sinners while the Church is asleep. Those who have other objectives in view may think things are going on very well. They are not grieved when they see the professed people of God going after show and folly.

Christians are grieved if they think their minister compromises or does not reprove the church pointedly and faithfully for their sins. False converts are willing to be rocked to sleep and let their minister preach smooth, flowery sermons with no point or power. But God's children are not satisfied unless he preaches powerfully, pointedly, and boldly, with long-suffering and doctrine. Their souls are not fed, edified, or satisfied with anything that does not take hold and work for the ministry appointed by Jesus Christ.

They will always stand by a faithful minister who preaches the truth boldly and pointedly. Even if the truth he preaches hits *them,* they like it and say, "Let the righteous smite me . . . it shall be an excellent oil" (Psalm 141:5). When the truth is poured forth with power, their souls are fed and they grow strong in grace.

They can pray for such a minister and weep for him, that he may have the Spirit of God always with him. Others scold him and talk about his extravagance, but true Christians will stand by him and would go to the stake with him for the testimony of Jesus.

Christians are especially distressed when ministers preach sermons not adapted to convert sinners. But when a man has his heart set on the conversion of sinners and he hears a sermon not calculated to do this, he feels as if it lacked the great thing that constitutes a gospel sermon. If they hear a sermon calculated to save souls, then they are fed, and their souls rejoice.

Here you see the ground for the astonishing difference you often find in the judgment that people pass upon preaching. There is no better test of character than this. It is easy to see who is filled with the love of God and of souls by the judgment they pass upon preaching. The true friends of God and man are grieved when they hear a sermon that is not particularly designed to rouse the Church to action.

I remember a man who used to continually pray for individuals, places, and the world's conversion. Once, when he was quite exhausted from praying, he exclaimed, "Oh! my longing, aching heart! There is no satisfying my desires for the conversion of sinners, and my soul breaks with longing." Although he had been useful beyond almost any other man his age, he saw much to do. He longed so much to see sinners saved that his mortal frame could not sustain it. "I find," he said one day, "that I am dying for strength to do more to save the souls of men; how much I want strength, that I may save souls."

If you want to move true saints, you must make use of motives drawn from their great and leading objective. Hold up the situation of sinners and show how they dishonor God, and you will find that this will move their souls and set them on fire sooner than any appeal to their hopes and fears. Show them how they can convert sinners, and their longing hearts will beat and wrestle with God in prayer and travail for souls.

And now I ask you before God, do you have these characteristics of a child of God? Do you *know* they belong to you? Can you say, "O Lord, you know that I love you and that these are the features of my character!"

Chapter 16

JUSTIFICATION: THE ROYAL PARDON

"Knowing that a man is not justified by the works of the law, but by the faith of Jesus Christ, even we have believed in Jesus Christ, that we might be justified by the faith of Christ, and not by the works of the law: for by the works of the law shall no flesh be justified"—Galatians 2:16.

In its general sense, *legal justification* means "not guilty." To justify an individual in this sense is to declare that he is not guilty of any breach of the law. It affirms that he has committed no crime and pronounces him innocent.

More technically, it is a form of pleading to a charge of crime. The individual who is charged admits the fact but brings forward an excuse, on which he claims that he had a right to do as he did. Thus, if a person is charged with murder, the plea of *justification* admits that he killed the man but alleges either that it was done in self-defense or that it was by unavoidable accident. In either case, the plea of justification admits the fact but denies the guilt.

213

By the deeds of the law "there shall no flesh be justified." This is true under either form of justification.

Under the first, or *general* form of justification, the burden of proof is on the accuser. In this case, he only needs to prove that a crime has been committed once. If it is proved once, the individual is guilty. He cannot be justified, in this way, by the law. He is found guilty. To argue that he has done more good than harm or that he has kept God's law longer than he has broken it is not valid. To be justified in this way he must prove that he has fulfilled *every jot and tittle* of the law. Who can be justified by the law in this way? No one.

In the second, or *technical* form of justification, the burden of proof lies on him who makes the plea. He admits the fact alleged and must either make good his excuse or fail. Two points are to be regarded. The pleaded excuse must be *true,* and it must be a good and sufficient *excuse,* not a frivolous apology that does not meet the case. If it is not true or is insufficient, and especially if it reflects on the court or government, it will only harm him further.

The Nature Of Sin

Sinners often plead their *sinful nature* as a justification. This excuse is a good one, *if it is true*. If it is true, as they maintain, that *God* has given them a nature that is itself sinful, then it is a good excuse for sin. In the face of heaven and earth, and at the

214

day of judgment, this will be a good plea in justification. God must annihilate the reason of all rational beings in the universe before they will ever blame you for sin if God made you sin or if He gave you a nature that is itself sinful.

How can your nature be sinful? What is sin? *Sin is a transgression of the law.* Does the law say you must not have the nature that you have? This is absurd.

This doctrine overlooks the distinction between *sin* and the *occasion of sin.* The bodily appetites and tendencies of body and mind, when strongly excited, become the occasions of sin.

So it was with Adam. No one will say that Adam had a sinful nature. But he had, by his constitution, an *appetite* for food and a *desire* for knowledge. These were not sinful but were as God made them. They were necessary to fit him to live in this world as a subject of God's moral government. But being strongly excited led to indulgence, and thus became the occasions of his sinning against God. These tendencies were innocent in themselves, but he yielded to them in a sinful manner, and that was his sin.

When the sinner talks about his sinful nature as a justification, he confounds these innocent appetites and susceptibilities with sin itself. By so doing, he in fact *charges God* and accuses Him of giving him a sinful nature. In fact, his nature is essential to moral agency. God has made it as well as it could be made, perfectly adapted to the circumstances in which man lives. Man's nature is as well fitted to love and obey God as to hate and disobey Him. The day is not distant when it will be known whether this is a good excuse or not. Then you will see whether you can face your Maker in this way—when He charges you with sin, will you turn around and throw the blame back upon Him?

Do you wonder what influence Adam's sin has had in producing the sin of his posterity? It has subjected them to *aggravated temptation* but has by no means rendered their nature *in itself* sinful.

Unable To Obey?

Another excuse is *inability*. This also is a good excuse *if* it is true. If sinners are really unable to obey God, this is a good plea in justification. When you are charged with not obeying the laws of God, you have only to show that God has required what you were not able to perform, and the whole intelligent universe will resound with the verdict of "not guilty." If you don't have natural power to obey God, they must give this verdict or cease to be reasonable beings. A law of reason states that no being is obliged to do what he has no power to do.

Suppose God required you to undo something that you have done. This is a natural impossibility. Are you to blame for not doing it? God requires *repentance* of past sins—not that you should undo them.

Suppose it was your duty to warn a certain individual about his sin, but now he is dead. Are you still under obligation to warn that individual? No.

That is an impossibility. All that God can now require is that you repent. God may hold you responsible for not doing it when it was in your power, but it would be absurd to make it your duty to do what is impossible.

If God requires you to do what you have no power to do, it is tyranny. What God requires is on penalty of eternal death. He threatens an infinite penalty for not doing what you cannot do, and so He is an infinite tyrant. This plea, then, charges God with infinite tyranny and is not only insufficient for the sinner's justification but is a horrible *aggravation* of his offense.

Let's vary the case a little. Suppose God requires you to repent for failing to do what you never had natural ability to do. You must either repent, then, of not doing what you were powerless to do, or you must go to hell. You can neither repent of this, nor can He make you repent of it.

What is repentance? It is to blame yourself and justify God. But without power, you can do neither. It is a natural impossibility that a rational being should ever blame himself for not doing what he knows he couldn't do. And you cannot justify God.

Suppose God required you to repent for not flying. By what process can He make you blame yourself for not flying when you are conscious that you have no wings or power to fly? If He could cheat you into the belief that you had the power and make you believe a lie, then you might repent. But what sort of way is that for God to act with His creatures?

What do you mean by bringing up such an excuse? Do you mean that you have never sinned? It is a strange contradiction when you admit that you ought to repent but say you have no power to repent. You ought to stand your ground one way or the other. If you mean to rely on this excuse, come out with it in full, take your ground before God, and say, "Lord, I am not going to repent at all—I am not under any obligation to repent, for I don't have the power to obey the law. Therefore, I plead not guilty, for I have never sinned!"

Another excuse sinners offer for their conduct is their *wicked heart*. This excuse is true, but it is not sufficient. The first two that I mentioned would have been good if they had been true, but they were false. This is true but is no excuse.

What is a wicked heart? It is not the bodily organ we call the heart but the affection of the soul, the wicked disposition, the wicked feelings, and the actings of the mind. If these will justify you, they will justify the devil himself. Has he not as wicked a heart as you have?

Suppose you had committed murder and were put on trial and offered this plea. "It is true," you would say, "I killed the man. But then I have such a thirst for blood and such a hatred of mankind that I cannot help committing murder whenever I have an opportunity."

"Horrible!" the judge would exclaim. "Put him in jail and throw away the key!" Such is the sinner's plea of a wicked heart in justification of sin. God will condemn you out of your own mouth. (See Job 9:20.)

Shifting The Blame

People often excuse themselves by pointing to the conduct of Christians. Ask a man why he doesn't believe, and he will point to the conduct of Christians as his excuse. "These Christians," he will say, "are no better than anybody else. When I see them practice what they preach, then I will think about it." He is hiding behind the sins of Christians. He shows that he knows how Christians ought to live and cannot plead his sin through ignorance.

But does it amount to grounds for justification? I admit that Christians behave very badly and do much that is contrary to their faith. But is that a good excuse for you? *Far from it.* This is itself one of the strongest reasons why you should be saved. You know how Christians ought to live and should be an example. If you had followed them ignorantly, or didn't know any better, it would be a different case. But your plea shows that you know they are wrong and is the very reason you ought to exert a better influence than they do. Instead of following them and doing wrong because they do, you ought to rebuke them, pray for them, and try to lead them in a better way.

This excuse, then, is true but not good for justification. You only make it an excuse for charging God foolishly. Instead of clearing yourself, you only add dreadful, damning guilt.

Who can be justified by the law? Who has kept it? Who has a good excuse for breaking it? Who will dare go to God and face his Maker with such apologies?

Did Jesus Obey For Us?

Gospel justification is not the *imputed righteousness* of Jesus Christ. Under the gospel, sinners are not justified by having the obedience of Jesus Christ set down to their account as if He had obeyed the law *for them* or in their stead. People often suppose that they are accounted righteous in the eye of the law by having the obedience or righteousness of Christ imputed to them.

This idea is absurd and impossible for this reason: Jesus Christ was bound to obey the law for Himself. It was His duty to love the Lord His God with all His heart, soul, mind, and strength and to love His neighbor as Himself. If He had not done so, it would have been sin.

The only work He could perform for us was to submit to sufferings He did not deserve. This is called His "obedience unto death," and this is placed on our account. But if His *obedience of the law* is placed on our account, why are *we* called to repent and obey the law ourselves?

Does God exact triple service—first to have the law obeyed for us, then that Jesus must suffer the penalty for us, and then that we must repent and obey ourselves? No such thing is demanded! It is not required that the obedience of another should be imputed to us. All we owe is perpetual obedience to the *law of benevolence.* For this there can be no substitute. If we fail, we must endure the penalty or receive a free pardon.

Justification by faith does not mean that faith is accepted as a substitute for personal holiness or that faith is imputed to us *instead of* personal obedience to the law.

Some people think justification implies that personal holiness is set aside and God arbitrarily gets rid of the law and imputes faith as a substitute. But this is not the way. Abraham's faith was imputed to him for righteousness, worked by love, and produced holiness. Justifying faith is holiness and produces holiness of heart and life. It is imputed to the believer as holiness not instead of holiness.

Faith Works By Love

Some suppose that justification by faith is without regard to good works or holiness. They have understood this from what Paul said when he insisted so vehemently on justification by faith. But it must be remembered that Paul was combating the error of the Jews, who expected to be justified by obeying the law. In opposition to *this error,* Paul insists that justification is by faith, without works of law. He does not mean that good works are unnecessary to justification. Works of law are not good works because they spring from legal considerations, hope, and fear and not from faith that works by love.

Since a false theory had crept into the Church on the other side, James took up the matter and showed them that they had misunderstood Paul. To show this, he took the case of Abraham: "Was not Abraham our father justified by works when he had offered Isaac his son upon the altar? Seest thou how faith wrought with his works, and *by works was faith made perfect?* And the scripture was fulfilled which saith, Abraham believed God, and it was imputed unto him for righteousness: and he was called the Friend of God. You see then how that by works a man is justified, and not by faith only" (James 2:21-24).

This epistle was thought to contradict Paul, and some of the ancient churches rejected it on that account. But they overlooked the fact that Paul was speaking of one kind of works and James of another. Paul was speaking of works performed from *legal motives.* But everywhere he insists that good works springing from the righteousness of faith are indispensable to salvation. All that he denies is that works of law grounded on legal motives have anything to do with the matter of justification.

James taught the same thing when he said that men are justified not by works or by faith alone but by faith together with the works of faith. Or, as Paul expressed it, *faith works by love.* Please remember that I am speaking of *gospel justification,* which is very different from *legal justification*.

Gospel justification, or justification by faith, consists in *pardon and acceptance by God.* When we say that men are justified by faith and holiness, we do not mean that they are accepted on the ground of law. But they are treated *as if* they were righteous on account of their faith and works of faith. This is the method that God takes in justifying a sinner. Not that faith is the foundation of justification, because the foundation is in Christ. But this is the manner in which sinners are pardoned, accepted, and justified. If they repent, believe, and become holy, their past sins will be forgiven for Jesus' sake.

Justification under the gospel differs from justification under the law. Legal justification is a declaration of actual innocence and freedom from blame. Gospel justification is pardon and acceptance, *as if* he were righteous, but on grounds other than his own obedience. When the apostle says, "By works of the law shall no flesh be justified" (Galatians 2:16), he uses justification in a strictly legal sense. But when he speaks of justification by faith, he speaks not of legal justification but of a person being treated as if he were righteous.

Restored To Sonship

When an individual is pardoned, the penalty of the law is released. The first effect of a pardon is to set aside the execution of the penalty. It admits that the penalty was deserved but sets it aside. Then, as far as punishment is concerned, the individual has no more to fear from the law than if he had never transgressed. He is *entirely* released. People justified by true faith, as soon as they are pardoned, need no more be influenced by fear of punishment. The penalty is set aside as if it had never been incurred.

The next effect of pardon is to remove all the debts acquired as a consequence of transgression. A real pardon removes all these and restores the individual back to where he was before he transgressed. Under the government of God, the pardoned sinner is restored to the favor of God. He is brought back into a new relationship and stands before God and is treated by Him, as far as the law is concerned, as if he were innocent. It does not suppose or declare him to be really innocent, but the pardon restores him to the same state *as if he were*.

Another operation of pardon under God's government is that the individual is restored to sonship. In other words, it brings him into such a relationship to God that he is received and treated as a child of God.

Suppose the son of a king had committed murder and was condemned to die. A pardon would not only deliver him from death but would restore him to his place in the family. God's children have all gone astray and entered into the service of the devil. But the moment they are pardoned, they receive a spirit of adoption, are sealed heirs of God, and are restored to all the privileges of children of God.

Justification secures all needed grace to rescue themselves fully out of the snare of the devil and the innumerable sinful entanglements. If God were merely to pardon you and then leave you to get out of sin by yourselves, of what use would your pardon be to you? Imagine a child who runs away from his father's house, wanders into a forest, and falls into a deep pit. When the father finds him, he cannot merely pardon the child for running away. He must lift him from the pit and lead him out of the forest.

In the scheme of redemption, whatever help you need is guaranteed, if you believe. If God undertakes to save you, He pledges all the light, grace, and help that are necessary to break the chains of Satan and the entanglements of sin; and He leads you back to your Father's house.

Salvation Through Relationship

When individuals are first broken under a sense of sin and their hearts gush out with tenderness, they look over their past lives and feel condemned. They see that it is all wrong, break down at God's feet, and give themselves to Jesus Christ. They rejoice greatly in the idea that they are through with sin.

But soon they begin to feel the pressure of old habits and former influences. Often they become discouraged when they see what must be overcome. If God has saved you, you only have to keep near to Him, and He will carry you through. You don't have to fear your enemies. Though the heavens thunder, the earth rocks, and the elements melt, you need not tremble or fear. God is for you, and who can be against you? (See Romans 8:31.) "Who is he that condemneth? It is Christ that died, yea rather, that is risen again, who is even at the right hand of God, who also maketh intercession for us" (Romans 8:34).

Justification enlists the divine attributes in your favor as much as if you had never sinned. Imagine a holy angel, sent on an errand of love to some distant part of the universe. God's eye follows him. If He sees that angel likely to be injured in any way, all the divine attributes will at once protect and sustain him. Just as absolutely, they are all pledged for your protection, support, and salvation. Although you are not free from remaining sin and are totally unworthy of God's love, yet if you are truly justified, the only wise and eternal God is pledged for your salvation. Will you tremble and be faint-hearted with such support?

If a human government pardons a criminal, it is then pledged to protect him as a subject—as much as if he had never committed a crime. So it is when God justifies a sinner. The apostle Paul says, "Being justified by faith, we have peace with God" (Romans 5:1). God is on his side, pledged as his faithful and eternal *friend*.

Gospel justification differs from legal justification in this respect: If the law justifies an individual, it holds only as long as he remains innocent. If he transgresses again, his former justification won't help. But when the gospel justifies a sinner, it is not so: "If any man sin, we have an advocate with the

Father, Jesus Christ the righteous'' (1 John 2:1).

A new relationship is now in effect. The sinner is brought out from under the covenant of works and placed under the covenant of grace. He no longer retains God's favor by absolute and sinless obedience. If he sins, he is not thrust back again under the law but receives the benefit of the new covenant. If he is justified by faith—and so made a child of God—he receives the treatment of a child and is corrected, chastised, humbled, and *brought back again*.

Chapter 17

RECONCILIATION: A COVENANT OF GRACE

"The gifts and calling of God are without repentance"—Romans 1:29.

The meaning of this Scripture is not that God calls and saves the sinner without his repenting but that God never changes His mind once He undertakes the salvation of a soul.

Some think teaching that believers are perpetually justified is a dangerous doctrine because it will encourage men to sin. Indeed! If you tell a man that has truly repented that God will give him victory over sin, will that encourage him to commit sin?

If this doctrine inspires any man to commit sin, it only shows that he *never did repent.* He never hated sin or loved God for His own sake; he only pretended to repent. If he loved God, it was only a selfish love, because he thought God was going to do him a favor. If he truly hated sin, his heart would break in godly sorrow when he considered that despite all his unworthiness God had received him as a child.

How often the child of God has melted in adoring wonder at the goodness of God, who saved him instead of sending him to hell as he deserved! What would bring him lower in the dust than the thought that, after all God had done for him, he could wander away again when his name was written in the Lamb's book of life!

Our Loving Father's Rod

God has promised that if anyone belonging to Christ goes astray, He will use the discipline of the covenant to bring him back. In Psalm 89, God, substituting David for Christ, says, "If his children forsake my laws, and walk not in my judgments; If they break my statues, and keep not my commandments; Then will I visit their transgression with the rod, and their iniquity with stripes. Nevertheless my lovingkindness will I not utterly take from him, nor suffer my faithfulness to fail. My covenant will I not break, nor alter the things that is gone out of my lips" (Psalm 89:30-34).

Thus, Christians may always expect to be more readily visited with God's judgments if they go astray than the impenitent. The sinner may grow fat and live in riches, all according to God's established principles of government. But let a child of God forsake his God and go after any worldly object and, as certain as he is a child, God will smite him with His rod. When he has been brought back, he will say with the psalmist, "It is good for me that I have been afflicted: that I might learn thy statutes. . . . Before I was afflicted I went astray: but now have I kept thy word" (Psalm 119:71,67). Perhaps some of you have known what it was to be afflicted in this way and that it was good.

Another effect of gospel justification is to *insure holiness.* It not only insures all the means but the actual accomplishment of the work. The individal who is truly converted will surely persevere in obedience until he is fitted for heaven and actually saved.

Justification is by *faith.* Faith is the medium by which the blessing is conveyed to the believer. The proof of this in the Bible: "Knowing that a man is not justified by the works of the law, but by the faith of Jesus Christ, even we have believed in Jesus Christ, that we might be justified by the faith of Christ and not by the works of the law: for by the works of the law shall no flesh be justified" (Galatians 2:16).

The subject is too often treated in the New Testament to be necessary to go into a labored proof. It is obvious that if men are saved at all, they must be justified in this way and not by works of law, for "by the deeds of the law shall no flesh be justified."

Justifying Faith

Nowhere does the Bible say that men are justified or saved *for* faith, as the ground of their pardon.

They are justified *by* faith as the medium or instrument. Faith is confidence in God that leads us to love and obey Him. We are therefore justified by faith because we are *sanctified*—set apart—*by faith*. Faith is the instrument of our justification because it is the natural instrument of becoming holy. It brings us back to obedience and therefore is designated as the means of obtaining the blessings of that return. Faith is not *imputed* to us by an arbitrary act, but it is the foundation of all real obedience to God.

This is why faith is made the medium through which pardon comes. It first leads us to obey God from a principle of love to God. We are forgiven our sins *on account of Christ*. Our duty is to repent and obey God, and, when we do so, this is imputed to us as what it is—holiness, or obedience to God. But for the forgiveness of our past sins, we must rely on Christ.

Justifying faith does not consist in believing that your sins are forgiven. If that was necessary, you would have to believe it *before* it was done. Remember, your sins are not forgiven *until* you believe. But if saving faith is believing that they are already forgiven, it is believing a thing before it takes place, which is absurd. You cannot believe your sins are forgiven before you have evidence that they are forgiven; and you cannot have evidence that they are forgiven until it is true that they are forgiven—and they cannot be forgiven until you exercise saving faith. Therefore, saving faith must be believing something else.

Neither does saving faith consist in believing that you will be saved at all. You have no right to believe that you will be saved until you have exercised justifying or saving faith.

But justifying faith *does* consist in believing in the atonement of Christ, or believing the record that God has given of His Son. The correctness of this definition has been doubted, and I confess my own mind has undergone a change on this point.

Abraham *believed God,* and it was imputed to him for righteousness. But what did Abraham believe? He believed that he should have a son. Was this all? By no means. His faith included the great blessing that depended on that event—that the Messiah, the Savior of the world, would spring from him. This was the great subject of the Abrahamic covenant, and it depended on his having a son.

Of course, Abraham's faith included the "Desire of all nations"—this was faith in Christ. The apostle Paul has shown in detail that the sum of the covenant was "In thee shall all nations be blessed" (Galatians 3:8). In verse 16, he says, "Now to Abraham and his seed were the promises made. He saith not, And to seeds as of many; but as of one, And to thy seed, which is Christ."

The Most Excellent Sacrifice

Some people argue that in the eleventh chapter of Hebrews the saints are not all spoken of as having believed in Christ. But if you examine carefully, you will find that in all cases faith in Christ is either included in what they believed or implied by it. Take the case of Abel. "By faith Abel offered unto God a more excellent sacrifice than Cain, by which he obtained witness that he was righteous, God testifying of his gifts: and by it he being dead yet speaketh" (Hebrews 11:4).

Why was his sacrifice more excellent? Because he recognized the necessity of the atonement and that "without shedding of blood is no remission" (Hebrews 9:22). Cain was a proud infidel and offered the fruits of the ground as a mere thank-offering for the blessings of Providence. Without any admission that he was a sinner or needed an atonement, he had no ground on which he could hope for pardon.

Can an individual exercise justifying faith while denying the divinity and atonement of Jesus Christ? No! The whole sum and substance of revelation, like converging rays, all center on Jesus Christ and His divinity and atonement. All that the prophets and other writers of the Old Testament say about salvation comes to Him. The Old Testament and the New—all the types and shadows—point to Him. All the Old Testament saints were saved by faith in Him. Their faith terminated in the *coming Messiah,* as the faith of the New Testament saints did in the *Messiah already come.*

In the book of 1 Corinthians, the apostle Paul shows what place he would assign to this doctrine: "For I delivered unto you first of all that which I also received, how that Christ died for our sins according to the scriptures; And that he was buried, and that he rose again the third day according to the scriptures'' (1 Corinthians 15:3).

Mark that expression ''first of all.'' It proves that Paul preached that Christ died for sinners as the ''first'' or primary doctrine of the gospel. And you will find that from one end of the Bible to the other the attention of men was directed to this new and living way as the only way of salvation. This truth is the only truth that can make men holy. They may believe a thousand other things, but this is the great source of sanctification: ''God was in Christ, reconciling the world unto himself'' (2 Corinthians 5:19). This alone can be justifying faith.

There may be many other acts of faith that may be right and acceptable to God. But nothing is *justifying faith* except believing the record that God has given of his Son. Simply believing what God has revealed on any point is an act of faith; but justifying faith fastens on Christ, takes hold of His atonement, and embraces Him as the only ground of pardon and salvation.

Peace Like A River

As soon as you believe in Christ with the faith that works by love, you will be justified. You don't have to be under the wrath of Almighty God. You can be justified here and now if you will only believe in Christ. Your pardon is ready, made out and sealed with the seal of heaven. The gracious pardon will be delivered as soon as you, by one act of faith, receive Jesus Christ as He is offered in the gospel.

God has not revealed it in the Scriptures that you or any other individual are justified. But He has set down the characteristics of a justified person and declared that all who have these characteristics *are justified*.

All who are justified have the witness of the Spirit. They relate to the Holy Spirit. He explains the Scripture to them and leads them to see their meaning. He leads them to the Son and to the Father and reveals the Son and the Father in them. Do you have this? If you have, you are justified. If not, you are still in sin.

Do you have the fruits of the Spirit? They are love, joy, peace, etc. These are matters of human conciousness, and if you have them, you are justified.

Jesus said to His disciples, "My peace I give unto you; not as the world giveth, give I unto you" (John 14:27). And again, "Come unto me, all ye that labour and are heavy laden, and I will give you rest" (Matthew 11:28). Do you find rest in Christ? Is your peace like a river, flowing gently through your soul and filling you with calm and heavenly delight? Or do you still feel a sense of condemnation before God?

Do you feel a sense of acceptance with God, of pardoned sin, and of communion? This must be a matter of experience, if it exists. Don't imagine you can be in a justified state without evidence of it. You may have peace filling your soul yet not draw the inference that you are justified.

I remember a time when my mind was so peaceful that it seemed to me as if all nature was listening for God to speak. But I was not aware that this was the peace of God or that it was evidence of my being justified. I thought I had lost all my conviction and actually tried to bring back the sense of condemnation that I had before. I did not draw the inference that I was justified until the love of God was shed abroad in my soul by the Holy Spirit and I was compelled to cry out, "Lord, it is enough, I can bear no more." I don't believe it possible for the sense of condemnation to remain where the act of pardon is already past.

If you are justified, you are also adopted as one of God's dear children, and He has sent His Spirit into your heart. You naturally cry, "Abba, father!" (See Romans 8:15.) He seems to you just like a father, and you want to call Him Father. Do you know this? It is one thing to *call* God your Father in heaven and another thing to *feel* toward Him as a Father.

Looking Within Yourself

Do you honestly think you are justified? Would you dare to die now? Suppose the loud thunders of the last trumpet shook the universe and you saw the Son of God coming to judgment—would you be ready? Could you look up calmly and say, "This is a solemn sight, but Christ has died, and God has justified me; who will condemn me?''

Are you under the discipline of the covenant? If not, do you have any reason to believe you were ever justified? God's covenant with you, if you belong to Christ, is this: "If they backslide, I will visit their iniquity with the rod and chasten them with stripes." Do you feel the stripes? Is God awakening your mind and convicting your conscience? If not, where is the evidence that He is dealing with you as a son?

Those of you who have evidence that you are justified should maintain your relationship to God and live up to your real privileges. This is immensely important. There is no virtue in being distrustful and unbelieving. It is important to your growth in grace. One reason many Christians do not grow in grace is that they are afraid to claim the privileges of God's children that belong to them.

If you have the evidence that you are justified, press forward to holiness of heart and come to God with all the boldness that an angel would—*know* how near you are to Him. This is your duty. Why should you hold back? Why are you afraid to recognize the covenant of grace in its full extent? The provisions of your Father's house are ready and free. Are you converted, justified, and restored to His favor, yet afraid to sit down at your Father's table? Don't plead that you are unworthy. *This is nothing but self-righteousness and unbelief.*

You *are* unworthy. But if you are justified, that

is no longer a barrier. Your duty is to take hold of the promises that belong to you. Take any applicable promise in the Bible to your Father and plead it before Him, believing. Do you think He will deny it? These great and precious promises were given for this very purpose—that you may become a partaker of the divine nature. Why then should you doubt? Come along to the privileges that belong to you and take hold of the love, peace, and joy offered to you in this holy gospel!

If you are not in a state of justification, however much you have prayed and suffered, you are nothing. If you have not believed in Christ, if you have not received and trusted in Him as He is set forth in the gospel, you are yet in a state of condemnation and wrath. For weeks, months, and even years you may have been groaning with distress. But for all that, you are still in the gall of bitterness. Here you see the line drawn: the moment you pass over, you are in a state of justification.

Are you now in a state of wrath? Believe in Christ. All your waiting and groaning will not bring you any nearer. Do you want more conviction? Do you say you must wait until you pray more? What good is praying in unbelief? Will the prayers of a condemned rebel avail? Do you say you are unworthy? Christ died for people like you. He comes to you right now.

Now is the day of salvation. Hear the Word of God: "If thou shalt confess with thy mouth the Lord Jesus, and shalt believe in thine heart that God hath raised him from the dead, thou shalt be saved'' (Romans 10:9).

Believe what God says of His Son; believe those great fundamental truths that God has revealed about salvation, rest your soul on it, and you will be saved. Will you trust Jesus Christ to dispose of you? Are you confident enough in Christ to leave yourself with Him for time and eternity?

Perhaps you are trying to pray yourself out of your difficulties *before* coming to Christ. It will do no good. Cast yourself down at His feet and leave your soul in His hands. Will you do it?

Chapter 18

THE BREAD OF HEAVEN

"Do we then make void the law through faith? God forbid: yea, we establish the law"—Romans 3:31.

Paul proved that all men were in sin, refuting the doctrine generally held by the Jews that they were a holy people saved by their works. He showed that justification can never be by works but by faith.

The greatest objection to the doctrine of *justification by faith* has always been that it is inconsistent with good morals and opens the flood-gates of iniquity. It has been argued that to maintain that men are to be saved by faith will make them disregard good morals and encourage them to live in sin, depending on Christ to justify them. Others maintain that the gospel does in fact release men from obligation to obey the moral law so that a more lax morality is permitted under the gospel than was allowed under the law.

Justification by faith does not set aside the moral law, because the gospel enforces obedience to the law and lays down the same standard of holiness. Jesus Christ adopted the words of the moral law, "Thou shalt love the Lord thy God with all thy heart, and with all thy soul, and with all thy mind; and thy neighbor as thyself" (Luke 10:27).

Breaking Sinful Habits

The gospel requires repentance as the condition of salvation. What is repentance? The renunciation of sin. Man must repent of his disobedience to the law of God and return to obey it. If it did not maintain the law to its full extent, it might be said that Christ is the minister of sin!

By the gospel plan, the sanctions of the gospel are added to the sanctions of the law to enforce obedience to the law. The apostle says, "He that despised Moses' law died without mercy under two or three witnesses: Of how much sorer punishment, suppose ye, shall he be thought worthy, who hath trodden under foot the Son of God, and hath counted the blood of the covenant, wherewith he was sanctified, an unholy thing, and hath done despite unto the Spirit of grace?" (Hebrews 10:28-29). Adding the awful sanctions of the gospel to those of the law enforces obedience to the precepts of the law.

Justification by faith produces sanctification, or *holiness,* by producing the only true obedience to the law. When the mind understands this plan and excercises faith in it, it naturally produces holiness.

241

Sanctification is holiness, and holiness is nothing but *obedience to the law,* consisting in love to God and man.

True holiness can never be produced among selfish or wicked beings by the law itself, separate from the consideration of the gospel or the motives connected with justification by faith.

If the motives of the law did not restrain men from committing sin, it is absurd to suppose the same motives can *reclaim* them from sin once when they have fallen under the power of selfishness. Sin is confirmed by *habit.* The motives of the law lose a great part of their influence once a being is fallen.

They even exert an opposite influence. The motives of the law, viewed by a selfish mind, have a tendency to cause sin to abound. This is the experience of every sinner. When he sees the spirituality of the law and does not see the motives of the gospel, it raises the pride of his heart and confirms him in his rebellion.

The case of the devil is an exhibition of what the law can do to a wicked heart. He understands the law, sees its reasonableness, has experienced the blessedness of obedience, and knows that to return to obedience would restore his peace of mind. This he knows better than any sinner of our race, who never was holy. And yet it presents to his mind no motives that reclaim him. On the contrary, it drives him further from obedience.

The Terror Of Sinai

When obedience to the law is held forth to the sinner as the condition of life, immediately it starts him making self-righteous efforts. In almost every instance, the first effort of the awakened sinner is to obey the law. He thinks he must first make himself better before he embraces the gospel. He has no idea of the simplicity of the gospel plan of salvation by faith, offering eternal life as a *gift*.

Alarm the sinner with the penalty of the law, and by the very laws of his mind he tries to amend his life and self-righteously obtain eternal life, under the influence of slavish fear. The more the law presses him, the greater are his pharisaical efforts. He hopes that if he obeys he will be accepted.

What else could you expect of him? He is purely selfish, and although he ought to submit at once to God, he does not understand the gospel terms of salvation. His mind is first turned to the object of getting away from the danger of the penalty, and he tries to get to heaven some other way. I don't think there is an instance in history of a man who has submitted to God until he has seen that salvation must be by faith and that his own self-righteousness cannot save him.

If you try to produce holiness by legal motives, the very fear of failure has the effect to divert attention from the objects of love—God and Christ. The sinner is all the while dreading Mount Sinai, watching his footsteps to see how near he comes to obedience; how can he get into the spirit of heaven?

The penalty of the law has no tendency to produce love at first. It may increase love in those who already have it when they contemplate it as an exhibition of God's infinite holiness. The angels in heaven and good men on earth contemplate its excellence and see it as an expression of God's good will to His creatures. Then it appears amiable and lovely and increases their delight and confidence in God.

It is the opposite for the selfish man. He sees the penalty hanging over his head with no way of escape. He doesn't consider becoming enamored with the Being that holds the thunderbolt over his devoted head. The nature of his mind causes him to flee *from* Him, not *to* Him. The inspired writers never dreamed that the law could sanctify men. The law is more prone to slay than to make alive, to cut off men's self-righteous hopes forever and compel them to flee to Christ.

Sinners naturally and necessarily view God as an irreconcilable enemy. They are wholly selfish, and apart from the consideration of the gospel, they view God just as the devil views Him. No motive in the law can be shown to a selfish mind that will inspire love. Can the influence of the penalty do it?

This would be a strange plan of reformation, to send men to hell to reform them! Let him go on in sin and rebellion to the end of life and then be punished until he becomes holy. I wonder why the devil has not become holy! He has suffered long enough. Having been in hell these thousands of years, he is no better than he was. The reason is, no gospel and no Holy Spirit exist there to apply the truth—the penalty only confirms his rebellion.

Freedom Through Faith

Justification by faith can produce real obedience to the law. It doesn't set aside the law as a standard but sets aside the penalty of the law. The preaching of justification as a gift bestowed through the simple act of faith is the only way that obedience to the law is brought about.

It relieves the mind from the pressures that naturally tend to confirm selfishness. While the mind is looking only at the law, it feels the influence of hope and fear, which furthers selfish efforts. But justification by faith annihilates this spirit of bondage. The apostle says, ''We have not received the spirit of bondage again to fear'' (Romans 8:15). This plan of salvation produces love and gratitude to God and leads the soul to taste the sweets of holiness.

The believer in the gospel plan finds salvation full and complete, with both sanctification and eternal life already prepared. Instead of being driven to the life of a Pharisee in laborious and exhausting religion, he receives it as a free gift and is left free to exercise true love. He now can live and labor for the salvation of others, leaving his own soul unreservedly to Jesus.

The fact that God has provided and given him salvation is calculated to awaken in the believer a concern for others when he sees them dying. How far from every selfish motive are those influences. It portrays God not as an irreconcilable enemy but as a grieved and offended *Father,* desirous that His subjects should become reconciled to Him and live. This is calculated to produce love. It exhibits God as making great sacrifice to reconcile sinners to Himself from no other motive than a pure and disinterested regard to their happiness.

The law represents God as armed with wrath, determined to punish the sinner without hope or help. The gospel represents Him as offended but anxious that they should return to Him. And He has made the greatest conceivable sacrifices out of a pure disinterested love to His wandering children.

I once heard a father say that he had tried in his family to imitate the government of God. When his child did wrong, he reasoned with him and showed him his faults. When he was fully convinced, confounded, and condemned, the father asked him, ''Do you deserve to be punished?''

''Yes, sir,'' his son answered.

''I know it,'' said the father, ''and now if I were to let you go, what influence would it have over the other children? Rather than do that, I will take the punishment myself.'' So he laid the paddle on himself, and it had the most astonishing effect on the mind of the child. He had never tried anything so perfectly subduing to the mind as this. And from the laws of mind, it must be so. It affects the mind in a manner entirely different from the naked law.

Under the law, nothing but hope and fear can operate on the sinner's mind. But under the gospel, the influence of hope and fear are set aside, and a new set of considerations are presented—God's entire character, in all the attractions He can command. It gives the most heart-breaking, sin-subduing views of God and presents Him to the senses in human nature. It exhibits *disinterestedness* and love.

Death To Selfishness

Satan prevailed against our first parents by leading them to doubt God's selfless love. The gospel demonstrates the truth and corrects this lie.

The law represents God as the inexorable enemy of the sinner, securing happiness to all who perfectly obey but thundering down wrath on all who disobey. The gospel reveals new features in God's character not known before. Doubtless the gospel increases the love of all holy beings and gives greater joy to the angels in heaven, greatly increasing their love, confidence, and admiration when they see God's amazing pity and forbearance toward the guilty.

The law drove the devils to hell, and it drove Adam and Eve from Paradise. But when the believer sees the same holy God giving His beloved Son for rebels and taking unwearied pains to save sinners, it strengthens the motives in their minds to obedience and love.

The devil, who is a purely selfish being, always accuses others of being selfish. He accused Job of this: "Doth Job fear God for nought?" (Job 1:9). Satan came to our first parents and accused God of being selfish. He told them that the only reason for God's forbidding them to eat of the tree of knowledge was the fear that they might come to know as much as Himself. The gospel shows what God is. If He was selfish, He would not take such pains to save those whom He might with perfect ease crush to hell.

Nothing will make selfish people more ashamed of their selfishness than to see disinterested benevolence in others. Therefore wicked people are always trying to *appear* unselfish. Let a selfish individual who has any heart see true benevolence in others, and it is like coals on his head. The apostle Paul understood this when he said, "If thine enemy hunger, feed him; if he thirst, give him drink: for in so doing thou shalt heap coals of fire on his head" (Romans 12:20).

This is what the gospel does to sinners. It shows them that regardless of all they have done to God, He still loves them with selfless love. When he sees God stooping from heaven to save him and understands that it is indeed *true,* it melts and breaks his heart, strikes a death blow to selfishness, and wins him over to unbounded confidence and holy love.

God has so constituted the mind that it must acknowledge virtue. It must do this as long as it retains the power of moral agency. This is as true in hell as in heaven. The devil feels this. When an individual sees that God doesn't want to condemn him and offers salvation as a gift through faith, he must feel admiration for God's benevolence. His selfishness is crushed—the law has done its work, and he sees that all his selfishness has done no good. The next step is for his heart to surrender to God's love.

Suppose a man was sentenced to death for rebellion and had tried to get pardoned but failed because his reasons were hollow-hearted and selfish. He sees that the government understands his motives and that he is not really reconciled. He knows himself that they were hypocritical and selfish, moved by the hope of favor or the fear of wrath.

But now let the government offer him a free pardon on the simple condition that he receive it as a gift, making no account of his own works—what influence will it have on his mind? The moment he finds the penalty set aside and that he has no need to go to work by any self-righteous efforts, his mind is filled with admiration. The government has made great sacrifices to grant this. When his selfishness is slain, he melts like a child at his sovereign's feet, ready to obey out of love.

Motives Of The Gospel

All true obedience turns on faith, which secures

all the necessary influences to produce holiness. It gives the doctrines of eternity access to the mind and a hold on the heart. In this world the limits of time are addressed to the senses. The motives that influence the spirits of the just in heaven do not reach us through the senses. But when *faith* is exercised, the wall is broken down, and the vast realities of eternity act on the mind here with the same kind of influence that they have in eternity.

Mind is mind, everywhere. Were it not for the darkness of unbelief, men would live here just as they do in the eternal world. Sinners here would rage and blaspheme, just as they do in hell; and saints would love, obey, and praise, just as they do in heaven. Faith makes all these things realities. It frees the mind from the weight of the world. A faithful man beholds God and apprehends His law and His love.

In no other way *can* these motives take hold on the mind. What a mighty action it must have on the mind when it takes hold of the love of Christ! What a life-giving power, when the pure motives of the gospel enter the mind and stir it up with divine energy!

Every Christian knows that his mind is bouyant and active in proportion to the strength of his faith. When his faith falters, his soul is dark and listless. Faith alone places the things of time and eternity in their true perspective and sets down the things of time and sense at their real value. It breaks up the delusions of the mind, and the soul shakes itself from its errors and weights and rises up in communion with God.

To attempt to convert and sanctify the minds of sinners without the motives of the gospel is unphilosophical and unscriptural. You can press the sinner with the law and make him see his own character, the greatness and justice of God, and his ruined condition. But hide the motives of the gospel from his mind, and it is all in vain.

Some people are afraid to expose the sinner's mind to the character of God. They try to make him submit to God by casting him down in despair. This is not only against the gospel but it is absurd in itself. It is absurd to think that, in order to destroy the selfishness of a sinner, you must hide the knowledge of how much God loves him and the great sacrifices He has made to save him.

Sinners are in no danger of getting false hopes if they are allowed to know the real compassion of God. While you hide this, it is impossible to give him anything but a false hope. Withholding the fact that God has provided salvation as a gift from a convicted sinner is the best way to *confirm* his selfishness. If he gets any hope, it will be a false one. To pressure him with the law alone is to build a self-righteous foundation.

The Importance Of Understanding

The only possible way of reclaiming selfish beings is by grace. Suppose salvation was not totally a gift but that some degree of good works was taken into account in justification. Within this consideration is a stimulus to selfishness. You must bring the sinner to see that he is *entirely dependent* on free grace. A full and complete justification is bestowed on the first act of faith as a gift. No part of it is a reward for something he can do. This alone dissolves the influence of selfishness and secures holy action.

If all this is true, sinners should be given the fullest explanation, as soon as possible, of the whole plan of salvation. They should be made to see the law, their own guilt, and their helplessness to save themselves. Then the depth of the love of God should be opened. You will effectually crush his selfishness and subdue his soul in love to God. Don't be afraid to show the whole plan of salvation and give the fullest possible testimony of the infinite compassion of God. Show him that, despite his guilt, the Son of God is knocking at the door and pleading with him to be reconciled to God.

Many convicted sinners continue to embrace Mount Sinai with self-righteous efforts to save themselves by their own works. Many sinners try to get more feeling by waiting until they have prayed more and made greater efforts. They expect to reconcile themselves to God in this way.

The sinner needs to see that he is looking for salvation under the law. He must see that all this is superseded by the gospel, which offers him all he wants as a gift. He must hear Jesus saying, "I am the way, the truth, and the life: no man cometh to the Father, but by me.''Instead of trying your self-righteous prayers and efforts, here is what you are looking for. Believe and you will be saved. (See John 14:6.)

The law is useful to convict men, but it never breaks the heart. The gospel alone does that. The degree in which a convert is brokenhearted is in proportion to the degree of clearness with which he *understands* the gospel.

Converts, if you can call them so, who entertain a hope under legal preaching may intellectually approve the law and have a sort of dry zeal, but they are never brokenhearted Christians. If they have not seen God in the gospel, they are not Christians with tears trembling in their eye, shaking with emotion at the name of Jesus.

Sinners must be led to Christ and made to take hold of the plan of salvation by faith. To expect to do them good in any other way is vain.

Chapter 19

CHRISTIAN PERFECTION

"Be ye therefore perfect, even as your Father which is in heaven is perfect"—Matthew 5:48.

God has two kinds of perfections, *natural* and *moral.* His natural perfections constitute His nature or essence and are His eternity, immutability, omnipotence, etc. They are called *natural perfections* because they have no moral character. God has not given them to Himself because He did not create Himself but existed from eternity with these attributes in full possession. All these God possesses in an infinite degree.

These natural perfections are *not* the perfection required. The attributes of our nature were created in us, and we are not required to produce any new natural attributes. It would not be possible. We are not required to possess any of them in the degree that God possesses them.

Christian perfection is not freedom from temptation. James says, "Every man is tempted, when he is drawn away of his own lust, and enticed"

254

(James 1:14). The sin is not in the temptations but in yielding to them. A person may be tempted by Satan, the appetites, or by the world and yet not have sin. All sin consists in voluntarily consenting to the desires.

The perfection required is not the *infinite* moral perfection that God has: man, being a finite creature, is not capable of infinite affections. God, being infinite in Himself, must be infinitely perfect. But this is not required of us.

The Obedience Of Love

Christian perfection is perfect obedience to the law of God. The law of God requires perfect, disinterested, impartial benevolence—love to God and neighbor. It requires that we be motivated by the same feeling and act on the same principles that God acts upon. We must leave self out of the question as uniformly as He does and be as separated from selfishness as He is. We must be *in our measure* as perfect as God is.

Christianity requires that we do neither more nor less than the law of God prescribes. This is being, *morally,* just as perfect as God. Everything is here included: to feel as He feels, love what He loves, and hate what He hates—for the same reason that He loves and hates.

God loves Himself with the *love of benevolence,* or regards His own interest and happiness as the supreme good, because *it is* the supreme good. He requires us to love Him in the same way. He loves Himself with *infinite complacency* because He knows that He is infinitely worthy and excellent; and He requires the same of us. He also loves His neighbor as Himself, according to their real value. From the highest angel to the smallest worm, He regards their happiness with perfect love.

God cannot depart from this rule any more than we can without committing sin. For Him to do it would be much worse than for us to do it because he is greater than we are. God's very nature binds Him to this. He has created us moral beings in His own image, capable of conforming to the same rule as Himself. This rule requires us to have the same character as He does—to love impartially with perfect love and to seek the good of others as He does. This, and nothing less, is Christian perfection.

The command in the text, "Be ye perfect, even as your Father which is in heaven is perfect," is given under the gospel. Christ here commands the same thing that the law requires. The gospel does not require perfection as the condition of salvation, but no part of the obligation of the law is discharged. The gospel holds those who are under it to the *same holiness* as those under the law.

God cannot discharge us from the obligation to be perfect. If He were to attempt it, He would give us a license to sin. While we are moral beings, there is no power in the universe that can discharge us from the obligation to be perfect. Can God discharge us from the obligation to love Him with all our heart, soul, mind, and strength? That would be saying that God doesn't deserve such love. And if He cannot discharge us from the whole law, He cannot discharge us from any part of it, for the same reason.

How perfect are we required to be? Where do you find a rule in the Bible to determine how much less holy you are allowed to be under the gospel than you would be under the law? Should we let each man judge for himself? Do you think it is your duty to be more perfect than you are now? Can you say, "Now I am perfect enough; I have some sin left, but I have gone as far as it is my duty to go in this world"? The more holy a person is, the more strongly he feels the obligation to be perfect.

Conforming To God's Will

Christian perfection is attainable in this life. God commands us to be perfect as He is perfect. Can we say this is impossible? When God commands something, isn't there a natural possibility of doing what He commands?

I remember hearing an individual say he preached repentance to sinners because God commands it; but he would not preach that they *could* repent because God has nowhere said it was possible. What nonsense! Always understand that when God requires anything of men, they possess the faculties to do it. Otherwise, God requires of us impossibilities and sends sinners to hell for not doing what they *couldn't* do!

There can be no question of this. Perfection is to love the Lord with all our heart, soul, mind, and strength, and to love our neighbor as ourselves. It requires us to exert our own powers. The law itself goes no further than to require the *right use of the powers you possess.*

Some may object that if there is a natural ability to be perfect, there is a moral inability, which comes to the same thing. Inability is inability, call it what you will. If we have moral inability, we are as unable as if our inability was natural.

First, there is no more moral inability to be perfectly holy than there is to be holy at all. You can as easily be perfectly holy as you can be holy at all. The true distinction between natural ability and moral ability is this: *natural ability* relates to the powers and faculties of the *mind; moral ability* relates only to the *will.* Moral inability is nothing but unwillingness to do a thing.

When you ask whether you have moral ability to be perfect, if you mean, "Am I *willing* to be perfect?" I answer, "No." If you were willing to be perfect, you would be perfect, for the perfection required is only a perfect conformity of the will to God's law.

If you ask, then, "Are we able to will right?" the question implies a contradiction in supposing that there can be such a thing as a moral agent unable to choose or will. There is no such thing as *moral inability.* When we speak of *inability* to do a thing, we mean a lack of power. To say, therefore, that we are *unable* to will, is absurd.

Desperate unwillingness is the case. There is a stubborn unwillingness in sinners to become Christians and in Christians to come up to the full perfection required both by the law and gospel. Sinners may want to become Christians, and Christians may desire to be rid of all their sins, and may even agonize in prayer for it. They may think they are willing to be perfect, but they deceive themselves.

When Christians are truly willing to give up all sin and have no will of their own but merge in the will of God, then their bonds are broken. When they yield absolutely to God's will, then they are filled with all the fullness of God.

The Promise Of Holiness

The question is this: Do I have a right to expect to be perfect in this world? Is there any reason for me to believe that I can be completely subdued and love God as much as the law requires? But is perfection attainable?

I believe it is. Much has been said about Christian perfection, and individuals who have entertained it have run into many wild notions. It seems that the devil anticipated the movement of the Church and created a negative state of feeling. The moment the doctrine of sanctification is presented, people cry, ''Why, this is *Perfectionism*'' (the idea that Jesus' perfection was so imputed to us that we *cannot* sin).

But despite the errors into which Perfectionists have fallen, there is such a thing taught in the Bible as Christian perfection. Everybody needs to know this. I entirely reject the peculiarities of modern *Perfectionists.* I have read their publications, and I cannot agree with many of their views. But Christian perfection is a duty, and I am convinced that it is attainable *in this life*.

In 1 Thessalonians 4:3, we are told, "For this is the will of God, even your sanctificaton." If you examine the Bible carefully, from one end to the other, you will find it plainly taught that God wills the holiness of Christians just as He wills sinners would repent. Why should He not reasonably expect it? He *requires* it. No man can show, from the Bible, that God does not require *perfect sanctification* in this world or that it is not just as attainable as any degree of sanctification.

If you have never looked into the Bible with this view, you will be astonished to see how many more passages there are that speak of deliverance from the *commission* of sin than there are that speak of deliverance from the *punishment* of sin. The passages that speak of deliverance from punishment are nothing compared to the others.

What is *sanctification? Holiness!* When a prophecy speaks of the sanctification of the Church are we to understand that it is partial sanctification? When God *requires* holiness is it partial holiness? Surely not. He *promises* holiness! We have so long understood the Scriptures in regard to the way things are that we lose sight of the real meaning. But if we look at the language of the Bible, I defy any man to prove that the promise and prophecies of holiness mean anything short of *perfect sanctification*.

Holiness is the great blessing promised throughout the Bible. Peter says, "Whereby are given unto us exceeding great and precious promises: that by these *ye might be partakers of the divine nature, having escaped the corruption* that is in the world through lust" (2 Peter 1:4). If that is not perfect sanctification, what is? These "exceeding great and precious promises" are given for this object, and by believing, appropriating, and using them, we can become partakers of the divine nature.

The promise of the Abrahamic covenant was that his posterity would possess the land of Canaan and that through him, by the Messiah, all nations would be blessed. The seal of the covenant, circumcision, shows us what was the principal blessing intended: *it was holiness.* Peter tells us in another place that Jesus Christ was given so that He might sanctify unto Himself a peculiar people. (See 1 Peter 2:9.)

A Gospel Of Purification

All the purifications and other ceremonies of the Mosaic ritual signify the same thing; they all point to a Savior to come. Those ordinances of purifying the body were set forth, every one of them, with reference to the purifying of the mind—or *holiness.*

261

Under the gospel, the same thing is signified by baptism: the washing of the body represents the sanctification of the mind.

Ezekiel 36:25-27 promises the great blessing of the gospel: "Then will I sprinkle clean water upon you, and ye shall be clean: from all your filthiness, and from all your idols, will I cleanse you. A new heart also will I give you, and a new spirit will I put within you: and I will take away the stony heart out of your flesh, and I will give you an heart of flesh. And I will put my spirit within you, and cause you to walk in my statutes, and you shall keep my judgments, and do them."

It is the same in Jeremiah 33:8: "And I will cleanse them from all their iniquity, whereby they have sinned against me; and I will pardon all their iniquities, whereby they have sinned, and whereby they have transgressed against me." Search the Bible for yourselves, and you will be astonished to find how uniformly the blessing of sanctification is held up as the principal blessing promised to the world through the Messiah.

The great objective of the Messiah's coming was to sanctify His people! Just after the fall it was prophesied that Satan would bruise His heel but that He would bruise Satan's head. And John tells us, "For this purpose the Son of God was manifested, that he might destroy the works of the devil" (1 John 3:8).

Jesus has put Satan under His feet. His purpose is to win us back to our allegiance to God, sanctify us, and purify our minds. As it is said in Zechariah 13:1, "In that day there shall be a fountain opened to the house of David and to the inhabitants of Jerusalem for sin and for uncleanness."

In the New Testament, we are told that the Savior was called *"Jesus*: for he shall save his people *from their sins"* (Matthew 1:21). And, "He was manifested to take away our sins," and "to destroy the works of the devil" (1 John 3:5,8).

Paul speaks of the grace of God, or the gospel, as teaching us to deny ungodliness: "Looking for that blessed hope, and the glorious appearing of the great God and our Saviour Jesus Christ; Who gave himself for us, that he might redeem us from all iniquity, and purify unto himself a peculiar people, zealous of good works" (Titus 2:13-14).

In Ephesians, we learn that "Christ also loved the church, and gave himself for it; That he might sanctify and cleanse it with the washing of water by the word, That he might present it to himself a glorious church, not having spot, or wrinkle, or any such thing; but that it should be holy and without blemish" (Ephesians 5:25-27).

Christ came to sanctify the Church to such a degree that it should be absolutely "holy and without blemish." "And so all Israel shall be saved: as it is written, There shall come out of Sion the Deliverer, and shall turn away ungodliness from Jacob: For this is my covenant unto them, when I shall take away their sins" (Romans 11:26-27).

In 1 John 1:9, it is said, "If we confess our sins,

he is faithful and just to forgive us our sins, and to cleanse us from all unrighteousness.''

What is to "cleanse us from *all* unrighteous," if it is not perfect sanctification? In 1 Thessalonians 5:23, Paul prays a very remarkable prayer: "And the very God of peace sanctify you wholly; and I pray God your whole spirit and soul and body be preserved blameless unto the coming of our Lord Jesus Christ.''

What does *"sanctify you wholly"* mean? Does that mean perfect holiness? The apostle says not only that your whole soul and spirit but that your *"body* be preserved blameless.'' Could an inspired apostle make such a prayer if he didn't believe the blessing possible? He goes on to say, in the next verse, "Faithful is he that calleth you, who also *will do it"* (1 Thessalonians 5:24).

The Power Of The Holy Spirit

Perfect holiness in believers is the objective of the Holy Spirit. The whole tenor of Scripture respecting the Holy Spirit proves it. All the commands to be holy, the promises, the prophecies, the blessings, the judgments, and the duties of religion are means that the Holy Spirit employs for sanctifying the Church.

If being perfectly holy is not practical, then the devil has so completely accomplished his design in corrupting mankind that Jesus Christ is at fault and has no way to sanctify His people but to take them out of the world. Is it possible that Satan has the advantage over God? Is God's Kingdom to be only partially established, and are saints to spend half of their time serving the devil?

If holiness is not attainable in this world, it is either from a lack of motives in the gospel or a lack of power in the Spirit of God. In another life we may be like God, for we will see Him as He is. But why not here, if we have faith that is the "substance of things hoped for, the evidence of things not seen" (Hebrews 11:1)? There is a promise to those who "hunger and thirst after righteousness" that "they shall be filled." (See Matthew 5:6.) What is it to be "filled" with righteousness but to be perfectly holy? Are we to go through life hungry, thirsty, and unsatisfied?

If the power of habit can be so far encroached upon that an impenitent sinner can be converted, why can't it be absolutely broken so that a converted person may be wholly sanctified? The greatest difficulty is when selfishness has control of the mind and habits of sin are wholly unbroken. This obstacle is great, and no power but the Holy Spirit can overcome it; and in many instances, God Himself cannot, consistent with His wisdom, use the means necessary to convert the soul. But after He has broken the power of selfishness and the obstinancy of habit and actually converted the individual, God has sufficient resources to sanctify the soul altogether!

Men feel that they have fastened upon themselves appetites and physical influences that they believe

265

are impossible to overcome by moral means. Paul, in the 7th chapter of Romans, describes a man in great conflict with the body. But in the next chapter, he speaks of one who had gotten the victory over the flesh. "And if Christ be in you, the body is dead because of sin; but the Spirit is life because of righteousness. But if the Spirit of him that raised up Jesus from the dead dwell in you, he that raised up Christ from the dead shall also quicken your mortal bodies by his Spirit that dwelleth in you" (Romans 8:10-11). This quickening of the body is the influence of the Spirit of God upon the body—the sanctification of the body.

You ask, "Does the Spirit of God produce a physical change in the body?" I will illustrate it by the case of the drunkard. The drunkard has brought upon himself a diseased state, an unnatural thirst so strong that it seems impossible he can ever be reclaimed and entirely overcome this physical appetite. I have heard of cases where drunkards have been made to see the sin of drunkenness in such a strong light that they abhorred strong drink and never had the least desire for it again.

I once knew an individual who was a slave to the use of tobacco. One day he became convinced that it was a sin for him to use it. The struggle against it finally drove him to God in such an agony of prayer that he got the victory at once over the appetite and never had the least desire for it again.

I am not now giving you philosophy but *facts*. I've heard of people over whom a life of sin had a perfect mastery, but in time of revival they have been subdued and their appetites have died. The mind may be occupied and absorbed with greater things, never giving a thought to the things that would revive the vicious appetites.

Any appetite of the body may be subdued if a sufficient impression is made upon the mind to break it up. Haven't you known times when one absorbing topic has so filled your mind and controlled your soul that the appetites of the body remained, for the time, perfectly neutralized? Suppose this state of mind became constant. Wouldn't all these physical difficulties that stand in the way of perfect holiness be overcome? "For the law made nothing perfect, but the bringing in of a better hope did" (Hebrews 7:19).

Who Sets The Standard?

Paul says "Not as though I had already attained, either were *already* perfect" (Philippians 3:12). But it is not said that he continued so until his death or that he never did attain perfect sanctification. The manner in which he speaks in the remainder of the verse indicates that he expected to become perfectly holy: "But I follow after, if that I may apprehend that for which also I am apprehended of Christ Jesus" (Philippians 3:12).

John speaks of himself as if he loved God perfectly. But even if the apostles were not perfect, this does not mean others cannot be. They clearly declared holiness to be their duty and were aiming at it as if they expected to attain it *in this life*. They command us to do the same.

Why shouldn't the Church be growing better? It seems to be the prevailing idea that the Church is to look back to the early saints as the standard. I think the reverse is true. We ought to aim at a much higher standard than theirs.

I believe many saints have attained perfect holiness. Enoch and Elijah were probably free from sin before they were taken out of the world. In different ages there have been numbers of Christians who were upright and had nothing against them. Men declare that nobody would say that they were free from sin for any other motive but pride. But why can't a man say he is free from sin, if it is so, without being proud? He can say he is converted without being proud!

Won't the saints say it in heaven, to the praise of the grace of God? Then why shouldn't they say it now from the same motive? I don't profess now to have attained perfect sanctification, but if I had attained it—if I felt that God had given me the victory over the world, the flesh, and the devil and made me free from sin—would I keep it a secret and let my brethren stumble on in ignorance of what the grace of God can do? Never. I would tell them that they could expect complete deliverance if they would only lay hold of Christ. He came to save His people *from their sins.*

I have recently read John Wesley's "Plain Account

of Christian Perfection.'' I wish every member of the Church would read it. I would also recommend the memoir of James Brainerd Taylor. I have read it three times within a few months. It is plain that he believed that Christian perfection is a duty and is attainable by believers in this life.

Sometimes you hear people argue against Christian perfection on the ground that a man who was perfectly holy couldn't exist in this world. People think that if a person was perfectly sanctified and loved God perfectly, he would be in such a state of excitement that he couldn't remain in the body, eat or sleep, or attend to the duties of life. But the Lord Jesus Christ was a man, subject to all the temptations of other men. He also loved God with all His heart, soul, and strength. Yet He wasn't in such a state of excitement that He couldn't eat, sleep, or work at His trade as a carpenter.

Accepting God's Grace

Christians don't believe that God wills them to be perfectly sanctified in this world. They know He commands them to be perfect, as He is perfect. But they think He is secretly unwilling. They say, ''Why doesn't He do more to *make* us perfect?''

Sinners reason the same way. They say, ''I don't believe He wills my repentance; if He did, He would *make* me repent.'' God may prefer their continued impenitence and damnation to using influences other than those He uses to bring them to repentance.

If God were to bring all the power of His government to bear on one individual, He might save him. But at the same time, it would so derange His government that it would be a greater evil than for that individual to go to hell.

In the same way, God has furnished Christians with all the means of sanctification and requires them to be perfect. He desires that they should do exactly what He commands them to do.

Hunger and thirst after holiness *is not holiness.* The desire of a thing isn't the thing desired. If they hunger and thirst after holiness, they ought to give God no rest until He fulfills His promise that they will be made perfectly holy.

Christians think they are to remain in sin, and all they hope for is forgiveness and holiness in heaven. But the whole framework of the gospel is designed to break the power of sin and fill men with all the fullness of God. If the Church would read the Bible and lay hold of every promise, they would find them great and precious.

How many are seeking holiness by their *own* resolutions and works—their fastings, prayers, and activities—instead of taking hold of Christ by faith. It is all *work,* when it should be by *faith* in "Christ Jesus, who of God is made unto us wisdom, and righteousness, and *sanctification,* and redemption" (1 Corinthians 1:30).

When they take hold of the strength of God, they will be sanctified. Faith will bring Christ right into the soul and fill them with the same Spirit that

270

breathes through Himself. These dead works are nothing. Faith must sanctify and purify the heart. Faith is the substance of things hoped for and brings Jesus into the soul. The life that we live here should be by faith in the Son of God. It is from not knowing or not regarding this that there is so little holiness in the Church.

Instead of taking scriptural views of their dependence to see where their strength is and realizing how willing God is to give His Holy Spirit to them that ask, too many Christians sit in unbelief and sin to "wait for God's time." They call this "depending on God." The Holy Spirit is there with power to enlighten, lead, sanctify, kindle the affections, and fill the soul continually with all the fullness of God! Give up your soul to His control and hold on to the arm of God. His grace *is* sufficient!

Chapter 20

PRACTICAL CHRISTIAN LIVING

"Be ye therefore perfect, even as your Father which is in heaven is perfect"—Matthew 5:48.

The Church is not sanctified, and we ought to know why. If the defect is in God, we ought to know it. If He has not provided a sufficient revelation or if the power of the Holy Spirit is not adequate to sanctify His people, we ought to understand it so we don't perplex ourselves with vain endeavors. But if the fault is in *us,* we ought also to know it, lest we charge God foolishly by imagining He has required of us what we cannot attain.

The Religion Of Works

The first general reason for people not being sanctified is that they seek sanctification *by works* and not *by faith.* The religion of works assumes a great variety of forms, and it is interesting to see the shifting forms it takes.

One form is where men try to render their damnation unjust. It doesn't matter whether they think they are Christians or not if they are trying to live so as to make it unjust for God to send them to hell. This was the religion of the Pharisees. And there are many today whose religion is purely of this character. You will often find them ready to confess they have never been born again. But they speak of their own works in a way to make it obvious they think they are too good to be damned.

Many people are seeking by their works to recommend themselves to the mercy of God. They know they deserve to be damned and will forever deserve it. But they also know that God is merciful; and they think that if they live honest lives and do kind things for the poor, God will forgive their sins and save them.

This is the religion of most modern moralists. Living under the gospel, they know they cannot be saved by works. Yet they think that if they go to church and help support the minister, etc., it will recommend them to God's mercy. I understand this is the system of religion held by modern Unitarians. Whether they understand or admit it, it comes to this. They set aside the atonement of Christ and don't expect to be saved by His righteousness. They seem to have a sentimental religion. With their morality and their liberality, they depend on the mercy of God. On this ground they expect to receive forgiveness for their sins.

Another form of the religion of works is when people try to prepare themselves to accept Christ.

They understand that salvation is only through Jesus Christ, and they know they can't be saved by works or by the general mercy of God. But they have heard that others went through a long process of distress before they submitted to Christ and found peace in believing. They think a certain preparatory process is necessary and they must pray and run here and there to attend meetings. They lie awake many nights and suffer much distress, perhaps falling into despair. Then they feel they are ready to accept Christ.

This is the situation of many convicted sinners. When they are awakened and find they cannot be saved by their works, they then prepare to receive Christ. Perhaps some of you are like this. You dare not come to Jesus as you are. You have prayed little, attended few meetings, and felt little distress. Instead of going to Christ and throwing yourself unreservedly into His hands, you lash your mind into more conviction and distress in order to prepare yourself to accept Him.

Suppose an individual conceived this as the way to become holy. Every Christian can see this is absurd. However he may multiply such works, he is not *beginning* to approach holiness. The first act of holiness is to believe—to take hold of Christ by faith. If a Christian feels the need of holiness and tries to go through a preparatory process of self-created distress before he comes to Christ, he is just as absurd as an awakened sinner for doing it.

Working To Create Holiness

Many individuals perform works to create faith and love. We suppose them to have come to Christ, but having backslidden they set themselves to perform works to beget faith and love or to beget and perfect a right state of feeling. This is one of the most commom and subtle forms in which the religion of works shows itself today.

This is a ludicrous attempt to produce holiness *by sin*. If the feelings are not right, the act is sin. Yet people think they can create holiness by purely sinful conduct. Any act that does not spring from love is sinful. The individual acts not from the impulse of faith that works by love and purifies the heart, but he acts without faith and love, with a design to *beget* those affections by actions.

When faith and love exist and are the propelling motives to action, carrying them out in action has a tendency to increase them. This arises from the known laws of the mind, by which every power and every faculty gains strength by exercise. But these individuals have left their first love, if ever they had any. Then they set themselves, without faith or love, to bustle about doing things.

How absurd to think of waking up faith in the soul where it does not exist by performing outward acts from some other motive. It is *mocking God*. Pretending to serve God in such a way grieves the Holy Spirit and insults God.

As far as the philosophy is concerned, it is similar to the conduct of convicted sinners. But there is one difference: the sinner, in spite of all his wickedness, may eventually see his own helplessness and renounce all his own work. He may feel that his continued refusal to come to Christ is only heaping sins against God. But it is different for those who think themselves to be Christians.

Many persons who abound in religious acts are often the most hardened and removed from spiritual feeling. If performing religious duties was the way to produce right Christian feeling, we should expect that ministers and leaders would be the most spiritual. But where faith and love are not in exercise, people become hardened, cold, and full of iniquity in their outward acts. Without any spiritual life, they will become more hardened and stupid. Or if they get spiritually excited in this way, it is a superficial state of mind that has nothing holy in it.

Another reason why so many people are not holy is this: They do not receive Christ in all His functions as He is offered in the gospel. Most people are entirely mistaken here. They will never get ahead until they learn there is a radical error in the manner in which they attempt to attain holiness.

Suppose an individual is convicted of sin. He sees that God may in justice send him to hell, and that he has no way out. Now tell him of Christ's atonement. Show him how Christ died so that God could be just and yet the justifier of them that believe in Jesus. He sees it to be exactly what he needs and in faith throws himself upon Jesus for justification. He accepts Him as his justification, and that is as far as he understands the gospel. He believes, is justified, and feels the pardon of his sin.

Now, here is the very attitude in which most convicted sinners stop. They see Christ as Savior, the propitiation of their sins, to make atonement and procure forgiveness—and there they stop. After that, it is often exceedingly difficult to get their attention to what Jesus offers. Say what you will in regard to Christ as the believer's wisdom, righteousness, sanctification, and all His functions as a Savior from sin—they don't feel they need Him in these relations.

Giving Up Your Throne

The converted person feels at peace with God. Joy and gratitude fill his heart, and he rejoices in having found a Savior that will stand between him and his Judge. He may have really submitted, and for a time he follows God's commandments. But eventually he finds the workings of sin in his members—unsubdued pride, his old temper breaking forth, and a multitude of enemies assaulting his soul—and he is not prepared to meet them.

Until now, he has regarded Jesus as a Savior to save him from hell. The great mass of professing Christians lose sight, almost altogether, of many of the most important functions that Christ offers to believers. When the convert finds himself brought under the power of temptation and drawn into sin, he needs to invite Christ into these areas of his life. He needs to know more of Jesus' provision for him to resist temptation.

This is not fully understood by many Christians. They never really view Christ under His name "Jesus," who saves His people *from their sins*. They need to receive Him as a King, to take the throne in their hearts and rule over them with absolute and perfect control, bringing every faculty and every thought into subjection. The reason why the convert falls under the power of temptation is that he has not *submitted* his own will to Christ in *everything*.

Christians complain that they cannot understand the Bible, and they are always in doubt about many things. What they need is to receive Christ as wisdom and to accept Him in His function as the source of light and knowledge.

Who of you now attach a full and definite idea to the text that says we are "in Christ Jesus, who of God is made unto wisdom, and righteous, and sanctification, and redemption" (1 Corinthians 1:30)? What do you understand by it? It doesn't say He is *a* justifier, *a* teacher, *a* sanctifier, and *a* redeemer, but that He *is* wisdom, and righteousness, and sanctification, and redemption. What does that mean? Until Christians find out by experience and know what the Scripture means, how can the Church be sanctified?

The Church is now like a branch plucked from

a vine. Unless she abides in Christ, she cannot bear fruit. If a branch had power to voluntarily separate itself from the vine and then should try to produce fruit, what would you think? The Church is the same. Until Christians go to the eternal source of sanctification, wisdom, and redemption, they will never become holy. If they would become, by faith, absolutely united with Jesus, in all His offices and functions, then they would know what holiness is. He is the light and the life of the world. To be sanctified by Him, they must embrace Him and receive grace and knowledge, which alone can purify the soul and give the complete victory over sin and Satan.

If an individual isn't deeply convicted of his own depravity and his need to overcome the power of sin, he will never receive Jesus Christ into his soul as King. When men try to help themselves out of sin and feel strong enough to cope with their spiritual enemies, they never receive Christ fully or rely solely on Him to save them from sin.

But when they have tried to keep themselves by their own watchfulness and prayers, binding themselves by resolution and oaths to obey God, they find nothing but depravity. Then they feel their helplessness and begin to ask what to do.

God's Promise Book

The Bible teaches all this plainly enough. If people would believe the Bible, they would know from the beginning their need of a Savior. But they don't receive or believe the Word until they try to work out their own righteousness. They soon find out they are nothing without Christ. Therefore, they don't receive Him in this function until they have spent years in vain, self-righteous attempts to sanctify themselves. Having begun in the spirit, they try to perfect themselves in the flesh.

Others, when they see their own condition, don't receive Christ as a Savior from sin because they are unwilling to abandon all sin. They know that if they give themselves up entirely to Christ, *all* sin must be abandoned; and they have some idol they are unwilling to give up.

Many people suppose they are under a fatal necessity to sin, and they drag along this load of sin until their death. They don't directly charge God and say in words that He has made no provision for such a case as this. But they appear to suppose that Christ's atonement will cover all sins. They think that if they continue in sin all their days, He will forgive them and it will be just as well as if they had been truly holy. They don't see that the gospel *has* made provisions to rid us forever of all sin. They look at it as a system of pardon, leaving the sinner to drag his load of sin to the gate of heaven.

Oh, how little use Christians make of those great and precious promises. We have only to draw upon Him, and we will have whatever we need for our sanctification. ''What things soever ye desire, when ye pray, *believe* that ye receive them, and ye shall have them'' (Mark 11:24).

Christians do not really believe much that is in the Bible. Imagine you met God, and you knew it was God Himself. Suppose He held out a book in His hand and told you to take it. This book contained great and precious promises of all you needed to resist temptation, overcome sin, become perfectly holy, and fit yourself for heaven. Then He told you whenever you need anything, you only have to take the appropriate promise and present it to Him, and He will do it.

Now, if you were to receive such a book directly from the hand of God, and you knew that God had written it for you, would you believe it? Would you read it a great deal more than you now read the Bible? How eager you would be to know all that was in it. How ready to apply the promises in time of need! You would want to know it by heart! You would keep your mind familiar with its contents and be ready to apply the promises you read.

The Bible is that book! It is written by God and filled with such promises. Any Christian, by laying hold of the right promise and pleading it, can always find all he needs for his spiritual benefit.

Jesus is a complete Savior. All the promises of God are in Him to the glory of God the Father. God has promised them in the second Person of the Trinity and made them all certain through Him. Christians need to understand these promises and believe them.

Suppose they lack wisdom. Let them go to God and plead the promise. Suppose they cannot understand the Scriptures, or the path of duty is not plain. The promise is plain enough—take it. Whatever they lack of wisdom, righteousness, sanctification, and redemption, only let them go to God in faith and take hold of the promise.

Shattering Your Pride

Many people don't receive Jesus in all His functions because they are too proud to relinquish all self-dependence or reliance on their own wisdom and will.

How great a thing for the proud heart of man to give up its own wisdom, knowledge, will, and everything, to God! I have found this the greatest of all difficulties. Doubtless all find it so. All that God says must be true, whether we in our ignorance and blindness can see the reasonableness of it or not. If we go beyond this, we go beyond the proper province of reason.

But how unwilling the proud heart of man is to lay aside all its own vain wisdom and become like a little child under the teaching of God. The apostle says, "If any man think that he knoweth any thing, he knoweth nothing yet as he ought to know" (1 Corinthians 8:2). There is a vast meaning in this. A person that doesn't receive Christ alone as his wisdom knows nothing.

If he is not taught by Jesus Christ, he has not

learned the first lesson of Christianity. "Neither knoweth any man the Father, save the Son, and he to whomsoever the Son will reveal him" (Matthew 11:27). The individual who has learned this lesson feels that he has not one iota of knowledge of any value besides what is taught by Jesus Christ. For it is written, "And they shall be all taught of God" (John 6:45).

Christians need to be searched thoroughly, shown their defects, brought under conviction, and then pointed to where their great strength lies. With their everlasting parade of dead works, they need to be shown how poor they are. "Thou sayest, I am rich, and increased with goods, and have need of nothing; and knowest not that thou art wretched, and miserable, and poor, and blind, and naked" (Revelation 3:17).

Until Christians are shown their poverty and the infinite emptiness and abominable wickedness of their dead works, the Church will go further and further from God. It will have only the form of godliness, denying this power thereof. (See 2 Timothy 3:5).

When you see the Christian character defective in any way, you can always know that the individual needs to receive Christ more fully to supply this defect. This defect in the believer will never be remedied until he sees Christ in that part of his character. By faith he must take hold of Christ to remedy that imperfection.

Suppose a person is selfish. He will never remedy that defect until he receives Christ as his pattern.

Then the selfishness will be driven out of his heart by saturating his soul with the infinite love of the Savior. In regard to any other defect, he will never conquer it until he sees that Christ is sufficient.

Raising The Standard Of Holiness

Until the standard of holiness is greatly raised among ministers, the piety of the Church will not be elevated. Christians who understand these things should, therefore, constantly pray for ministers. The leaders of the Church must take hold of Christ for the sanctification of their own hearts, and then they will know what to say to the Church on the subject of holiness.

Many people seek holiness by works who don't know they are seeking in this way. They profess they are seeking sanctification only by faith and tell you they know it is vain to seek it in their own strength. But their results show they are seeking by works and not by faith.

If a man is seeking by works, he obviously is relying on performing certain preparatory steps and processes *before* he exercises saving faith. He is not ready *now* to accept Christ but thinks he must bring himself into a different state of mind as a preparation. It is at this he is aiming. He is trying *without faith* to get into a proper state of mind. It is all the religion of works.

How common is such a state of mind among Christians who profess to be seeking holiness. You say you must mortify sin, but the way you go about it is by a self-righteous preparation, seeking to recommend yourselves to Christ as worthy to receive the blessing. But you must come right to Christ as an unworthy and ruined beggar to receive at once, by faith, the blessing you need. Like a person in a pit of clay, every struggle of your own sinks you deeper in the clay. All your attempts, instead of bringing you nearer to Christ, are only drawing you further from God.

The sinner, by his preparatory seeking, gains no advantage. He lies, dead in trespasses and sins, removed from spiritual life like a dead corpse, until he comes to the conviction that there is nothing he can do for himself but to go now, *as he is*, and submit to Christ. As long as he thinks there is something he must do first, he never feels that now is God's time of salvation. As long as the Christian is seeking sanctification through works, he never feels that now is God's time to give him the victory over sin.

Multitudes deceive themselves because they have seen certain "faith without works" churches roused up, dragging along in death. Where such a church has been found, fed on dry doctrine until the members were as stupid as the seats they sat on, the first thing has been to rouse them up to *do something*. Perhaps that would bring such a church under conviction and lead them to repentance—not because there is any good in their *doings,* but because it shows them their deficiencies and awakens their consciences.

The same thing occurs when a careless sinner begins to pray. Everybody knows there is no piety in such prayers, but it calls his attention to the Lord and gives the Holy Spirit an opportunity to bring the truth to his conscience. But if you take a man who has been in the habit of praying from his childhood, whose formal prayers have made cold as a stone, praying will never bring him under conviction until he sees the true character of his ungodly prayers.

Where a church has sunk in stupidity, the most effective way to rouse the people has been to warn sinners of their danger. This gets the attention of the church and often brings many of the people to repentance.

If you take what is called a "working church," where they have been in the habit of enjoying revivals and holding meetings, you will find there is no difficulty in motivating the church to act. But as a general rule, unless there is great wisdom and faithfulness in dealing with the church, every succeeding revival will make their religion more and more superficial. Their minds will become more hardened instead of being convicted.

Tell such a church they are self-righteous and there is no Holy Spirit in their bustling, and they will be affronted. "Don't you know that the way to wake up is to go to work in religion?" they say. The very fact that activity has become a habit with them shows they require a different course. They need first to be thoroughly probed, searched, made

sensible of their deficiencies, and brought humble
and believing to the foot of the cross.

Growing In Holiness

When I was an evangelist, I worked in a church
that had enjoyed many revivals. It was the easiest
thing in the world to get the church to bring sinners to the meetings. The impenitent would come
and hear, but there was no deep feeling and no faith
in the church. The minister saw this was ruining the
church. Each successive revival made the converts
more and more superficial. We began to preach holiness, and the church members writhed under it. The
preaching ran directly against their former notions
about the way to promote Christianity, and some
of them were quite angry. But, after a major conflict, many of them broke and became as humble and
teachable as little children.

Multitudes in the churches insist that the way to
promote holiness is to work, and they think that by
friction they can produce the warm love of God in
their hearts. This is all wrong. Bustle and noise will
never produce holiness—least of all when people
are accustomed to this course.

Do you perform many religious duties yet fall
short of holiness? Then throw yourself on the Lord
Jesus Christ for sanctification and work to serve
Him. You are working for salvation instead of working from a principle of life within, impelling you to
the work of the Lord.

Do you have half the perseverance of a sinner? A sinner, driven by the fear of going to hell, exerts himself in works until his strength is exhausted and his self-righteousness is worked up. Feeling that he is helpless and undone, the sinner throws himself into the arms of Christ. But since you don't have as much perseverance, you don't have as much fear. If you think you are a Christian and that however short of holiness you come, you are still safe from hell and can go to heaven, you are wrong.

Christ is your only hope for sanctification. This is why convicted Christians generally fall short of that submission to Christ for holiness that the convicted sinner exercises for forgiveness.

If the Church grows in holiness, it will grow in works. But it does not always follow that growth in works promotes growth in holiness. Works of religion may greatly increase while the *power* of Christians is rapidly declining. Often a church that begins to lose its power may be willing to do even more works than ever, but it will not arrest the decline unless the people become broken before God.

Oh, that I could convince the Church they need no other help than Christ and can come to Him for all their needs—wisdom, righteousness, sanctification, and redemption. How soon they would be supplied from the depths of His infinite fullness!

Chapter 21

THE CHALLENGE OF LOVE

"Thou shalt in any wise rebuke thy neighbor, and not suffer sin upon him"—Leviticus 19:17.

Men are bound to reprove their neighbors for sin, or they become partakers or accessories to their sin. If we really love God, we will feel bound to reprove those who hate and abuse Him and break His commands.

If I love the government of the country, won't I reprove and rebuke a man who abuses or reviles it? If a child loves his parents, won't he reprove a man that abuses his parents?

If a man loves the universe and is motivated by love, he knows that sin is inconsistent with the highest good of the universe. If not counteracted, sin injures and ruins, and its direct tendency is to overthrow the order and destroy the happiness of the universe. Therefore, if a Christian sees this happening, his benevolence will lead him to reprove and oppose sin.

Love Thy Neighbor

Love for the particular people with whom you are connected should lead you to reprove sin. Sin is a reproach to any people, and the man who commits it produces a society harmful to everything good. His example has a tendency to corrupt society, destroy its peace, and introduce disorder and ruin. The duty of everyone who loves the community is to resist and reprove sin.

Love for your neighbor demands it. *Neighbor,* here, means anybody who sins within the reach of your influence—not only in your presence but in your neighborhood, your nation, or the world. If he sins, he injures himself; and if you love him, you will reprove his sins.

Love for the sinner prompts us to warn him of the consequences of his actions. Suppose we saw our neighbor's house on fire. True love would induce us to warn him so he wouldn't perish in the flames. If we saw him stay in the burning house, we would plead with him not to destroy himself. Much more should we warn him of the consequences of sin and strive to turn him to God before he destroys himself.

If you see your neighbor sin and neglect to reprove him, it is just as cruel as if you saw his house on fire and passed by without warning him. If he was in the house and the house burned, he would lose his life. If he sins, and remains in sin, he will go to hell. Isn't it cruel to let him go unwarned to hell?

Some people seem to consider it *not cruel* to let a neighbor continue in sin until the wrath of God comes on him. Their feelings are so "tender" that they cannot wound him by telling him of his sin and danger. No doubt, the tender mercies of the wicked are cruel. Instead of warning their neighbor of the consequences of sin, they actually encourage him in it.

For anyone to see rebellion and not lift his hand to oppose it is itself rebellion. It would be counted rebellion by the laws of the land. The man who knows of a treasonable plot and doesn't expose it or try to defeat it is an accessory, condemned by law. If a man sees a rebellion breaking out against God and doesn't oppose it or make efforts to suppress it, *he is himself a rebel.* God holds us accountable for the death of those whom we allow to continue in sin without reproof, and it is right that He should. If we see them sin, make no opposition, and give no reproof, we consent to it and encourage them in it. If you see a man about to kill his neighbor and do nothing to prevent it, you consent and are an accessory—in the eye of God and in the eye of the law, you are guilty of the same sin.

Likewise, if you see a man committing iniquity and do nothing to resist it, you are guilty with him. His blood will be upon his own head, but at whose hand will God require it? What does God say respecting a watchman? "Son of man, I have set thee a watchman unto the house of Israel; therefore thou shalt hear the word at my mouth, and warn them from me. When I say unto the wicked, O wicked man, thou shalt surely die; if thou dost not speak to warn the wicked from his way, that wicked man shall die in his iniquity; but his blood will I require at thine hand'' (Ezekiel 33:7-8).

This is true of all men. If you allow a neighbor who is within reach of your influence to sin unwarned, he will die in his iniquity, but his blood will be required at your hand.

If you keep silent, your silence encourages him in sin. He infers from your silence that you approve of his sin or, at least, that you don't care about it—especially if he knows you profess Christianity. Silence is consent. Sinners *do* regard your silence as approval for what they do.

Arrows Of Light

How many multitudes have been reformed by timely reproof? Most of those who are saved are saved by somebody's rebuking them for sin and urging them to repentance. You may be instrumental in saving any man, if you speak to him, reprove him, and pray for him. A single reproof has often been to the transgressor like the barbed arrow in his soul that festered until its sweet poison drank up his spirits and he submitted to God. I have known instances where even a look of reproof has done the work.

Cases have often occurred where the transgressor has not been reclaimed, but others have been deterred from following his example by the rebukes directed to him. If believers were faithful, men would fear their reproofs, and that fear would deter them from such conduct. Multitudes who now go on unblushing and unawed would pause, think, and be reclaimed and saved! Will you, with such an argument for faithfulness before you, let sinners go on unrebuked until they stumble into hell?

The language in the text is exceedingly strong. "Thou shalt *in any wise* rebuke him"—that is, without any excuse—"and not suffer sin upon him"— not be accessory to his ruin. The word is a Hebrew superlative, which leaves no doubt or excuse for not doing it. No stronger command of God exists in the Bible than this. God has given it the greatest strength of language that He can.

A man does not live conscientiously toward God or man unless he is in the habit of reproving transgressors within his influence. This is one reason why there is so little conscience in the Church. This verse from Leviticus is one of the strongest commands in the Bible, yet most Christians don't pay any attention to it. Can they have a clear conscience? They may as well pretend to have a clear conscience and get drunk every day.

No man keeps the law of God or keeps his conscience clear who sees sin and does not reprove it. He who knows of sin and does not reprove it breaks two commandments: first, he becomes an accessory to the transgression of his neighbor; second, he disobeys by refusing to reprove his neighbor.

Would you be prepared to meet your children at the judgment if you had not reproved, chastised, or watched over them? "Certainly not," you say. But why? "Because God has made it my duty to do this, and He holds me responsible for it." Then take the case of any other man that sins under your eye or within reach of your influence. If he goes down to hell, and you have never reproved him, aren't you responsible? How many souls are now groaning in hell that you have seen commit sin and have never reproved? Now they are pouring curses on your head because you never warned them. How can you meet them on the day of judgment?

How many profess to love God but never even pretend to obey His command? Are such people prepared to meet God? When He says, "Thou shalt in any wise rebuke thy neighbor," He means there is *no excuse*.

This command is addressed to all men who have neighbors. It was directed to the people of Israel, and through them it is addressed to all who are under the government of God—to high and low, rich and poor, young and old, male and female, and every individual bound to obey His commands.

Precious Pearls And Swine

He who made the law has a right to make exceptions. Some exceptions to this rule are laid down in the Bible.

God says, "Reprove not a scorner, lest he hate thee" (Proverbs 9:8). If a person is known to be a scorner—a despiser of religion and a hater of God—and has no regard to the Lord's law, why should you reprove him? It will only provoke a quarrel without any good resulting to anybody. Therefore, God makes such a character an exception to the rule.

Jesus Christ says, "Neither cast your pearls before swine, lest they trample them under their feet, and turn again and rend you" (Matthew 7:6). Whatever else this passage means, it means that sometimes men are in such a state of mind that to talk to them about the Lord would be at once irrational and dangerous, like casting pearls before swine. They have such a contempt for Christianity and such a stupid, sensual, and swinish heart that they will trample all your reproofs under their feet and turn on you in anger. Leave such men alone. Not meddling with them will be greater wisdom than to attack them. But great love and discernment must be used not to suppose those of your neighbors to be swine who do not deserve it and might be helped by reproof.

Jesus said of the scribes and Pharisees, *"Let them alone:* they be blind leaders of the blind" (Matthew 15:14). They were full of pride and conceit, satisfied with their own wisdom and goodness, and could not be reached by any reproof. If you begin to reprove them, they will put you down. These men are so full of arguments, cavils, and bullyings that you gain nothing.

When you reprove your neighbor for sin, make

him feel that it is not a personal controversy with you or a matter of selfishness on your part. Don't claim any right of superiority over him, but reprove him in the name of the Lord, for the honor of God. If you in any way give the impression that it is a personal controversy, done for any private motive with you, he will invariably rise against you and resist. But if you impress that it is done in the name of God and bring him before God as an offender, he will find it difficult to get away from you without at least confessing that he is wrong.

Above all things, don't make him think it is a little thing that you hint to him. Instead, make him realize he has sinned *against God* and that it ought to be looked on as a terrible offense. However, you should use more or less severity according to the nature of the case and the circumstances under which the sin was committed.

Using Wisdom In Reproof

Your relationship to the person who is guilty of sin should be properly regarded. If a child is going to reprove a parent, he should do it in a manner suited to the relationship. If a man is going to reprove a magistrate or an elder, the apostle says it must be in that way—"treat him as a father" (1 Timothy 5:1).

Relationship should enter deeply into the manner of administering reproof. Parents, children, husbands, wives, brothers, and sisters should all be regarded. The ages of the parties and their relative circumstances in life must be considered. For servants to reprove their masters in the same manner as their equals is improper.

This direction should never be overlooked or forgotten, for if it is, the good effect of reproof will be lost. But remember that *relative circumstances* of the parties take away the obligation of this duty. You are to reprove sin and are bound to do it in the name of the Lord. Do it not as if you were complaining or finding fault for a personal injury committed against yourself but as a sin against God. Thus, when a child reproves a parent, he is not to do it as if he was discussing an injury done to himself but because the parent has sinned against God.

If the individual is ignorant, reproof should be in the form of instruction rather than of severe rebuke. How do you treat your little child? You instruct him and strive to enlighten his mind respecting his duty. You proceed, of course, very differently than you would with a hardened offender.

You would reprove a first offender in a different manner than you would use toward a habitual transgressor. If a person is accustomed to sin and knows it is wrong, you use more severity. The first time a mere mention of it may be enough to prevent a repetition.

If he has not only often committed the sin but been often reproved, there is necessity for using sharpness. The hardening influence shows that no common rebuke will take hold. He needs to have the terrors of the Lord poured upon him like a storm of hail.

Never show any displeasure at the transgressor that he can possibly turn into personal displeasure at himself. Only show your strong displeasure at what he is *doing*. Otherwise, he will think you are not in earnest. Suppose you reprove a man for murder in a manner not expressing any abhorrence of his crime. You would not expect to produce any change. The manner should be suited to the nature of the crime; just don't let him think you have any personal feeling. This is the fault in the manner of reproving crime, both in the pulpit and out of it: for fear of giving offense, men don't express their hatred of the sin. Therefore, transgressors are seldom reclaimed.

You should always have so much of the Holy Spirit with you that when you reprove a man for sin he feels it comes from God. I have known cases where reproof from a Christian cut the transgressor to the heart and stung like the arrow of the Almighty, and he couldn't get rid of it until he repented.

Sometimes reproof is best done by sending a letter, especially if the person is at a distance. And there are times where it can be done even in your own neighborhood.

I knew an individual who chose this way of reprimanding a sea captain for drunkenness. The captain drank hard, especially in bad weather, when his services were very important. He was not only a drunk, but when he drank, he was ill-natured and endangered the lives of all on board. The Christian was concerned and made it a subject of prayer.

This was a difficult case—he did not know how to approach the captain. A sea captain is a perfect despot and has the most absolute power on earth. He sat down, wrote a letter, and handed it to the captain. He plainly and affectionately, but faithfully and pointedly, set forth the sin the captain was committing against God and man. He accompanied it with much prayer to God. The captain read it, and it completely changed his ways. He apologized to the individual and never drank another drop of anything stronger than coffee or tea the whole trip.

It may be very essential to reprove sin in many cases where there is no chance that the individual will be benefited. For example, you must act in cases where your silence would be taken for approval of his sin or where the very fact of his being reproved may prevent others from falling into the same sin. Where the offender comes properly under the description of a scorner or a swine, there God has made an exception, and you are not bound to reprove. But in other cases, the duty is yours and the consequences are God's.

People ask, "Should I reprove strangers?" Why not? Isn't the stranger your neighbor? You are not to reprove a stranger in the same way that you would a familiar acquaintance, but because he is a stranger is no reason why he should not be reproved. If a man swears profanely in your presence, his being a stranger does not excuse you from the responsibility of administering reproof or trying to bring him to repentance and save his soul.

Pulling Sinners From The Fire

Don't talk about people's sins, go and rebuke them. Christians often talk about people's sins behind their backs, and this is great wickedness. If you want to talk about a person's sins, go and talk to *him* about them, and try to get him to repent and forsake them. Don't talk to others behind his back and leave him bound for hell.

Few Christians are sufficiently conscientious to practice this duty. Thousands never think of doing it. They live in habitual disobedience to this plain but strongly-expressed command of God. Then they wonder why they don't have the spirit of prayer and why there aren't more revivals! How can they enjoy Christianity? What would the universe think of God if He granted the joys of religion to such unfaithful believers?

People have more regard for their own reputation than to the requirements of God. Rather than run the risk of being called judgmental or of creating enemies by rebuking sin, they let men remain unrebuked. It shows they have greater fear of men than of God. For fear of offending men, they run the risk of offending God. They absolutely disobey God in one of His plainest and strongest commandments rather than incur the displeasure of men by rebuking their sins.

No man has a right to say, when we reprove him

for his sin, that it's none of our business. Often transgressors tell faithful reprovers they had better mind their own business and not meddle with what doesn't concern them. God forbid that we should be silent. He has commanded us to rebuke our neighbor *in any wise* regardless of the consequences. And we will rebuke them, though all hell should rise up against us.

If a man professes to love God, he ought to have consistency enough to reprove those that oppose God. If Christians were consistent in this duty, many would be converted by it. A right public sentiment would be formed, and sin would be rebuked and forced to retire before the majesty of Christ. If Christians were not such cowards, absolutely disobedient to the plain command of God, one thing would certainly come of it—either they would be murdered in the streets as martyrs because men could not bear the intolerable presence of truth, or men would be converted.

What should we say, then, to such professing Christians? Are you afraid to reprove sinners? When God commands, are you prepared to obey? How will you answer to God?

Will you practice this duty? Will you reprove sin faithfully and not bear it for your neighbors? Will you make your whole life a testimony against sin? Or will you hold your peace and be weighed down with the guilt of all transgressors around you and within your sphere of influence? God says, *"Thou shalt in any wise rebuke thy neighbor, and not suffer sin upon him."* Think about it.

Chapter 22

HOLINESS AND THE HOLY SPIRIT

"Nevertheless I tell you the truth: It is expedient for you that I go away: for if I go not away, the Comforter will not come unto you; but if I depart, I will send him unto you. And when he is come, he will reprove the world of sin, and of righteousness, and of judgment: Of sin, because they believe not on me; Of righteousness, because I go to my Father, and ye see me no more; Of judgment, because the prince of this world is judged. I have yet many things to say unto you, but ye cannot bear them now. Howbeit, when he, the Spirit of truth, is come, he will guide you into all truth: for he shall not speak of himself; but whatsoever he shall hear, that shall he speak: and he will shew you things to come"—John 16:7-13.

Divine influence is necessary to enlighten and purify the minds of men. But very little knowledge of the gospel is available among men, and it exerts comparatively little influence. The gospel has hardly begun to produce holiness on the earth.

Do we need divine influence to attain the ends of the gospel? And if we do need it, then in what degree do we need it, and why? If our minds are unsettled on this question, we will be unsettled on all the subjects that *practically* concern our holiness.

The Importance Of Understanding

The mind of man can understand those abstractions that make up the skeleton of the gospel—the being and character of God, the divine authority and inspiration of the Scriptures, and other fundamental doctrines that make up its framework. It can understand and see the evidence that supports them as true, just as it can theories in science.

A man by his reason can understand the law of God. It requires him to exercise perfect love toward God and all other beings. He can understand this obligation because he is a moral being. He knows by experience what love is, for he has exercised love toward different objects. And he can, therefore, form or comprehend the idea of love to see the *reasonableness* of the requirement. He can understand the foundation and the force of moral obligation and see, in some measure, the extent of his obligation to love God.

Also, he can see he is a sinner and cannot be saved by his own works. He has broken the law, and it can never justify him. He knows if he is ever saved, he must be justified through mere mercy. Human understanding is capable of knowing the whole circle of theology as a system of propositions to be received and believed, on evidence, like any other science.

But *unaided reason* cannot attain any knowledge that will produce a sanctifying change. Our knowledge of the things of Christianity is defective without the aid of the Holy Spirit, for human understanding of the gospel lacks certain things to make it available to salvation.

We must distinguish between knowledge that *might be* available to one who wants to love and obey God, and what will be available to a sinner completely uninterested in holiness. One who is disposed to do right would be influenced by a far less clear and vivid view of motives than one disposed to do wrong. Whether the knowledge attainable by our present faculties would influence us to do right, if there were no sin in the world, is uncertain. The knowledge that Adam had when in a state of innocence didn't help influence him to do right. But we are now speaking of things as they are in this world, and we must show why sinners can't understand divine things that would influence them to love and serve God.

Knowledge must influence the mind. The will must be controlled. To do this, the mind must understand things and excite emotion, corresponding to the object in view. Mere intellect will never move the soul to act. A pure scientific abstraction of the intellect that does not excite any emotion is unable to move the will.

To influence sinners to love and obey God, you must have enough light to powerfully excite the mind and produce strong emotions. The reasons for obedience must appear strong and vivid and must subdue their rebellious heart and bring them voluntarily to obey God. This is helpful knowledge. This men can never have without the Spirit of God.

Limitations Of Perception

Our minds are shut up in the body and derive ideas from external objects through the senses. By ourselves we can never obtain sufficient knowledge of spiritual or eternal things to rightly influence our wills. Our bodily powers were not created for this. All the ideas we can have of the spiritual world are by analogy—figures, parables, types, etc.—comparing them with the things around us. All ideas conveyed to our minds in this way are extremely imperfect, and we do not get the *true* idea.

Words are merely signs of ideas. They are not the ideas but the representatives of ideas. It is often difficult, and sometimes impossible, to convey ideas by words. Take a little child and attempt to talk with him. Often it is difficult to get your ideas into his mind. He must have some experience of the things you are trying to teach before you can convey ideas to him by words.

Imagine you were born blind and had never seen colors. Then suppose I tried to describe a grand and beautiful painting to you. No language I could use would enable you to form a picture of it in your mind. Any subject we must describe using figurative language will come across as defective and inadequate. You have heard descriptions of people or places that you thought you had accurately pictured; but when you saw them, you found that your conception was incorrect.

Suppose an individual were to visit this world from another planet, where everything is backwards. If he learned our language and tried to describe the world he had left, we would understand it according to our ideas and experiences. If the analogy between the two worlds is imperfect, our knowledge of things there, from his description, would be imperfect in proportion. So, when we find in the Bible descriptions of heaven, hell, or anything in the invisible world, we can get no true ideas at all of the reality from mere words.

Breaking Down Obstacles

The wickedness of our hearts perverts our judgment and shuts our minds to much that we might understand. When a man's mind is so perverted on any subject that he will deny the evidence concerning it, he cannot come to a knowledge of the truth. This is our case in regard to Christianity. Perverseness of heart shuts out the light so that the intellect does not and cannot grasp the ideas it might otherwise gain.

Prejudice is a great obstacle to the reception of

correct knowledge concerning Christianity. Take the case of the disciples. They had strong Jewish prejudices respecting the plan of salvation—so strong that all the instructions of Christ Himself could not make them understand the truth. After teaching them for three years, He still couldn't get their minds in possession of the first principle of the gospel.

Until His death, Jesus couldn't make them see that He must die and be risen from the dead. Therefore, He says in His last conversation, "If I go not away, the Comforter will not come unto you; but if I depart, I will send him unto you." This was the very design of His going away from them—that the Spirit of Truth might come and *put them in possession of* the things that He meant by the words He had used in teaching them.

The general truth is this: without divine illumination, men can understand from the Bible enough to convict and condemn them but not enough to sanctify and save them.

Some may ask, "What, then, is the use of revelation?" The Bible is as plain as it can be. Jesus gave instructions to His disciples as plainly as He could, as a parent would to a little child. But without divine illumination, the unaided reason of man never did and never will attain any helpful knowledge of the gospel.

The difficulty lies in the subject. The Bible contains the gospel as plain as it can be. It contains the signs of the ideas, as far as language can represent the things of Christianity. No language but figurative language can be used for this purpose. And this will forever be inadequate to put our minds in real possession of the things themselves. The difficulty is in our ignorance, sin, and the nature of the subject. This is why we need divine illumination—to get Holy Spirit knowledge of the gospel.

The Spirit of God alone can give us this illumination. The Bible says, "No man can say that Jesus is the Lord, but by the Holy Ghost" (1 Corinthians 12:3). The abstract proposition of the Deity of Christ can be proved as a matter of science. But nothing short of the Holy Spirit can put the mind in possession of the idea that Christ is God. Only He can sanctify the heart.

"No man can come to me, except the Father which hath sent me draw him: and I will raise him up at the last day. It is written in the prophets, And they shall be all taught of God. Every man therefore that hath heard, and hath learned of the Father, cometh unto me" (John 6:44-45). Here it is evident that the drawing spoken of is teaching by the Holy Spirit. They must be taught by God and learn of the Father before they have the knowledge of the things of Christianity required to come to Christ.

The Spirit Of Truth

Jesus said, "It is expedient for you that I go away: for if I go not away, the Comforter will not come unto you." The word, *Paracletos,* here translated

Comforter, properly means a "Helper" or "Teacher."

"When he is come, he will reprove the world of sin, and of righteousness, and of judgment: Of sin, because they believe not on me; Of righteousness, because I go to my Father, and ye see me no more; Of judgment, because the prince of this world is judged. I have yet many things to say unto you, but ye cannot bear them now. Howbeit when he, the Spirit of truth, is come, he will guide you into all truth: for he shall not speak of himself; but whatsoever he shall hear, that shall he speak: and he will shew you things to come" (John 16:7-13).

And in the fourteenth chapter, the Savior said, "I will pray the Father, and he shall give you another Comforter, that he may abide with you for ever; Even the Spirit of truth; whom the world cannot receive, because it seeth him not, neither knoweth him; but ye know him; for he dwelleth with you, and shall be in you" (John 14:16-17).

Again, in the twenty-sixth verse, Jesus said, "But the Comforter, which is the Holy Ghost, whom the Father will send in my name, he shall teach you all things, and bring all things to your remembrance, whatsoever I have said unto you" (John 14:26). Here you see that the office of the Spirit of God is to instruct mankind in regard to the things of Jesus.

None but the Spirit of God can meet this need. No teaching by words, whether by Jesus Christ, by His apostles, or by any teacher coming through the senses can ever put the mind in possession of spiritual things. We need someone to teach us who doesn't have to depend on words or the medium of the senses. We need some way in which the *ideas themselves* can be brought to our minds, not merely the signs of the ideas. This the Spirit of God can do.

How the Spirit of God does this we will never know in this world. But the fact is undeniable—He can reach the mind without the use of words and can put our minds in possession of the ideas themselves. Types, figures, and words are only imperfect representatives. The human teacher can only appeal to our senses and finds it impossible to possess us of ideas we have never experienced.

·But the Spirit of God, having direct access to the mind, can, through the outward sign, impart actual ideas to us. The Spirit of God instantly reveals to us that passage of Scripture which, in all our study and effort, we never could have understood!

Take the case again of a painting on the wall. Suppose that a congregation was blind, and I was trying to describe this painting. Now suppose that while I was trying to make them understand the various distinctions and combinations of colors, all at once their eyes were opened! They could then see for themselves the thing I was vainly trying to bring to their minds by words. The Holy Spirit opens the spiritual eye and brings the things we try to describe by analogy and signs before the mind and puts it in complete possession of the thing *as it is*.

No one but the Spirit of God knows the things of God well enough to give us the idea of those things correctly. "What man knoweth the things of a man, save the spirit of man that is in him?" (1 Corinthians 2:11). I can speak to your consciousness—being a man and knowing the things of a man. But I cannot speak these things to the consciousness of a beast, and a beast can't speak of these things.

Similarly, the Bible says, "The things of God knoweth no man, but the Spirit of God" (1 Corinthians 2:11). The Spirit of God, knowing from consciousness the things of God, possesses a different kind of knowledge of these things than other beings can possess. He, therefore, can give us the instruction we need, which no other being can give.

The Divine Instructor

The needed influences of the Spirit of God may be possessed by all men, freely, under the gospel. God is more willing to give His Holy Spirit to them who ask Him than parents are to give their children bread.

"Ask, and it shall be given you; seek, and ye shall find; knock, and it shall be opened unto you" (Matthew 7:7).

"And all things, whatsoever ye shall ask in prayer, believing, ye shall receive" (Matthew 21:22).

"Therefore I say unto you, What things soever ye desire, when ye pray, believe that ye receive them, and ye shall have them" (Mark 11:24).

"If any of you lack wisdom, let him ask of God, that giveth to all men liberally and upbraideth not;

and it shall be given him" (James 1:5).

If God has made these unlimited promises to *all men,* then anyone who asks Him may have as much divine illumination as they ask for.

But men don't have as much divine illumination as they need. They don't ask for it in the manner or to the degree that they need it. They ask amiss or from selfish motives.

The apostle James says, "Ye ask, and receive not, because ye ask amiss, that ye may consume it on your lusts" (James 4:3). When an individual has some reason other than a desire to glorify God, he shouldn't expect to receive divine illumination. If his object in asking for the Holy Spirit is happiness, wisdom in the Scriptures, importance as a Christian, remarkable experience, or any other selfish motive, that is a good reason why he doesn't receive what he asks for.

Suppose a person neglects his Bible but asks God to give him knowledge. That is tempting God. God gives knowledge *through the Bible,* preaching, and the other appointed means of instruction. If a person will not use these means—when they are in his power—no matter how much he prayed, he shouldn't expect divine instruction. "Faith cometh by hearing, and hearing by the word of God" (Romans 10:17).

A person may learn the gospel and receive supernatural illumination if he is deprived of the normal means. If he was on a desolate island, he might receive direct illumination from the Spirit of God. And he might receive it in any other circumstances where he absolutely *could not* have access to any means of instruction. Some very remarkable cases of this kind have occurred.

When I was an evangelist, I participated in a revival in a neighborhood where there were many Germans. Many of them could not read. When the gospel was preached among them, the Spirit of God was poured out, and a powerful revival followed. If a meeting was appointed at any place, the whole neighborhood would come together, fill the house, and listen intently to the preacher, who tried to fill their minds with gospel truth.

One poor German woman could not read. In one of these meetings, she told this story, which was supported by her neighbors. With many tears and a heart full of joy, she said, "When I loved God, I longed to read the Bible, and I prayed, 'O Jesus! You can teach me to read Your holy Bible,' and *the Lord taught me to read!* There was a Bible in the house, and when I had prayed, I thought I could read the Bible. I got the book and opened it, and the words were just what I had heard people read. The Lord has taught me to read my Bible, blessed be His name for it."

Although I don't know anyone involved except a teacher who heard the German lady read, she was a woman of good character among her neighbors. Some of the most respectable of them afterwards told me they didn't doubt the truth of what she said. I have *no doubt* it was true.

Grieving The Holy Spirit

Many people don't receive illumination from the Spirit of God because they grieve Him. They grieve, or offend, the Holy Spirit so that He cannot consistently grant them His illuminating grace.

They rely on the instructions they receive from ministers, commentaries, books, or their own powers of research. All these things, without the Spirit of God, will only kill but can never make alive. It can only damn but never save. It seems the whole Church is in error on this point—depending on means for divine knowledge. *No means* are available without the Spirit of God. If the Church felt this—if they really felt that all the means in creation are useless without the teaching of the Holy Spirit—how they would pray, cleanse their hands, and humble their hearts until the Comforter would descend to teach them the things they need to know.

Men are responsible for what they could have of divine illumination. This is a universal truth and is acknowledged by all men. A man is just as responsible for what light he might have as for that which he actually has. Common reason admits that no man who breaks the law is to be excused for ignorance of the law, because all are responsible to know what the law is.

If your children *could* know your will and misbehave, you consider them all the more blameworthy. So it is in Christianity: men have both the outward means of instruction and the inward teach-

314

ings of the Holy Spirit absolutely within their reach. If they sin in ignorance, they are not only without excuse on that score, but their ignorance is itself a crime and is an aggravation of their guilt. All men are *plainly without excuse* for not possessing all the knowledge available for their *perfect and immediate sanctification*. (See Romans 1:20-21.)

Without the Holy Spirit, instruction may convince the Church of duty, but it will never produce holiness. It may harden the heart but will never change it. Without divine influence, it is but a savor of death unto death.

When The Blind Lead The Blind

We use all the appropriate means of instruction in our power as the *medium* through which the Spirit of God conveys divine illumination to the mind.

No reason exists why we should not use the means in our power to acquire knowledge as faithfully as if we *could* understand the whole subject without divine influence. If we don't use the means within our power, we have no reason to expect divine aid. When we help ourselves, God helps us. When we use our natural faculties to understand these things, we may expect God to enlighten us. To turn our eyes away from the light and then pray to see is to tempt God.

Blind leaders of the blind attempt to teach the things of Christianity without being themselves taught by God. No theological degree will ever make a successful teacher unless he enjoys the illuminating powers of the Holy Spirit. He is blind if he thinks he understands the Bible without this, and if he undertakes to teach, he deceives himself and all who depend on him—both will fall into the ditch together.

If an individual teaches the gospel with the Holy Spirit sent from heaven, he will be understood. He may understand the gospel himself yet not make his hearers understand it, because the Holy Spirit is not on them as well as himself. But if the Spirit of God is on them, precisely in proportion as he himself understands the real meaning of the gospel, he will make his hearers understand it.

In preaching the gospel, ministers should never use texts unless its meaning has been taught by the Spirit of God. It is presumption. And there is no excuse for it, for they can always have the teachings of the Spirit. God is more ready to bestow divine illumination than an earthly parent is to give bread to his child. If they ask, they will always receive all the light they need. This is applicable both to preachers and teachers. If any of them attempt to teach the Scriptures without being themselves taught, they are no more fit to teach than the most ignorant person in the streets is fit to teach astronomy.

I fear that most ministers and teachers have understood very little of their need of this divine teaching or the necessity of praying over their sermons and Bible lessons. If this was done as it should be, their instructions would be far more effective than we now see them.

Do you Bible and Sunday school teachers believe this? Are you in the habit of seeking the true idea of every lesson on your knees? Or do you go to some commentary and then come and peddle out your dry stuff to your classes without the Holy Spirit? If you do this, let me tell you, you had better be doing *something else*.

What would you say about a minister who never prayed over his texts? You might as well have Balaam's donkey for a minister; the dumb beast might speak with a man's voice and rebuke the madness of such a man. He could give just as much available instruction to reach the deep fountains of the heart as such a preacher. And this is just as important for a Sunday school teacher as for a minister. If you do not pray over your lesson until you feel that God has taught you the idea contained in it, *beware!* Never be satisfied with anything from a book until you are satisfied that God has put you in possession of the very idea *He* would have you receive.

The Author Of Holiness

When I studied theology, I spent many hours on my knees—perhaps I might say weeks—with the Bible before me, laboring and praying to understand the mind of the Spirit. I don't say this boastingly but as a matter of fact to show that the sentiment here

317

advanced is no novel opinion with me. And I always get my texts and sermons on my knees. Yet I am conscious that I have gained little knowledge compared with what I might have had if I had taken hold of the source of light as I ought to have done.

How little knowledge most Christians have respecting the Word of God! Ask them, for instance, to read the epistles or other parts, and they probably won't be able to give an opinion as to the real meaning of one-tenth of the Bible. No wonder the Church is not holy! They need *more truth*. Our Savior said, "Sanctify them *through thy truth*" (John 17:17). This means of holiness must be more richly enjoyed before the Church knows what entire *sanctification* means. They don't understand the Bible.

They have not gone to the Author to have it explained. Although they have the blessed privilege every day—just as often as they choose—of carrying the book to the Author for His explanation, yet how little they know of the Bible they are sure has been taught by the Holy Spirit! Read the text again, or read similar passages, and then try and tell me that Christians are not responsible for understanding the Bible.

We must all study the Bible under divine teaching. I recommend several books for you to read, such as Wesley's *Thoughts on Christian Perfection* and the memoirs of Brainerd, Taylor, and Payson. I have found that, in a certain state of mind, such books are useful to read.

But I only study *one book*. I read the others occasionally but have little time or inclination to read many books because I have so much to learn in my Bible. I find it like a deep mine—the more I work it, the richer it grows. We must read, pause, and pray over it verse by verse. We must dwell on it, digest it, and get it into our minds until we feel that the Spirit of God has filled us with the *spirit of holiness*.

Will you lay your hearts open to God and give Him no rest until He has filled you with divine knowledge? Will you *search* the Scriptures? I have often been asked by young converts and young men preparing for the ministry what they should read. I give the same answer every time: *Study the Bible!*

Chapter 23

UNFAILING CRYSTAL LOVE

"Love worketh no ill to his neighbour: therefore love is the fulfilling of the law"—Romans 13:10.

The two principal forms of Christian love are *benevolence* and *complacency*. *Benevolence* is an affection of the mind or an act of the will that desires to promote the happiness of its object. *Complacency* is esteem or approval of the character of its object. Benevolence should be exercised toward all beings, irrespective of their moral character. Complacency is due only to the good and holy.

Love may exist either as an affection or as an emotion. When love is an *affection,* it is voluntary and consists in the act of the will. When it is an *emotion,* it is involuntary. What we call feelings, or emotions, are involuntary. They are not directly dependent on the will or controlled by a direct act of will. The *virtue* of love is mostly in the form of an affection. The *happiness* of love is mostly in the form of an emotion. If the affection of love is very strong, it produces a high degree of happiness; but the emotion of holy love is happiness itself.

Choosing To Love

The *emotion* of love is involuntary. I don't mean that the will has nothing to do with it, but that it isn't the result of a mere or direct act of the will. No man can exercise the emotion of love by merely willing it. And emotions may often exist in spite of the will. Individuals often feel improper emotions rising in their minds and try to banish them by direct efforts of will. Finding that impossible, they conclude they have no control of these emotions.

But emotions can always be controlled by the will in an indirect way. The mind can bring up any kind of emotion it chooses by directing the attention to the proper object. They will be certain to rise in proportion to the attention fixed upon it, provided the will is right in regard to the object. So, the mind can be rid of improper or disagreeable emotions by turning the attention entirely away from the object and not allowing the thoughts to dwell on it.

Ordinarily, the *emotions* of love toward God are experienced when we exercise love toward him in the form of *affection*. But this is not always the case. We may exercise good will toward any object yet at times feel no sensible emotions of love. It is not certain that even Jesus exercised emotional love toward God at all times. A person can exercise affection and be guided and governed by it in all his actions without any felt emotion.

A husband and father may labor for the benefit of his family, having his very life controlled by affection for them. He may feel no sensible emotions of love for them at the time. His work may take up his mind so much that he has scarcely a thought of them. He may feel no emotion toward them, yet he is guided and governed by affection for them. Again, an affection is an *act of the will* or a volition.

Love to our neighbor naturally implies the existence of love to God, and love to God naturally implies love to our neighbor: "Owe no man any thing, but to love one another: for he that loveth another hath fulfilled the law. For this, Thou shalt not commit adultery, Thou shalt not kill, Thou shalt not steal, Thou shalt not bear false witness, Thou shalt not covet; and if there be any other commandment, it is briefly comprehended in this saying, namely, Thou shalt love thy neighbour as thyself" (Romans 13:8-9).

Love to our neighbor implies the existence of love to God; otherwise it could not be said that "he that loveth another hath fulfilled the law." James recognizes the same principle, when he says, "If ye fulfill the royal law according to the scripture, Thou shalt love thy neighbour as thyself, ye do well" (James 2:8). Here love to our neighbor is spoken of as obedience to the whole law. Benevolence, or good will to our neighbor, naturally implies love to God. So the love of complacency toward holy beings naturally implies love to God, who is a being of infinite holiness.

All that is required of man by God consists in love, in various modifications and results. (See Micah 6:8.) *Love is the sum total of all.* The Scriptures fully teach that love is the sum total of all the requirements, both of the law and gospel. Our Savior declares that the great command to love the Lord with all your heart, soul, mind and strength, and your neighbor as yourself, is the sum total of all the law and the prophets. (See Matthew 22:37-40.) It implies and includes all that the Scriptures, the law, and the gospel require.

God's Perfect Love

God is love, and to love is to be like God; and to be perfect in love is to be perfect as God is perfect. All God's moral attributes consist in love, acting under certain circumstances and for certain ends. God's justice in punishing the wicked, His anger at sin, etc., are only exercises of His love to the general happiness of His Kingdom.

All that is good in man is some modification of love. Hatred of sin is only love of virtue acting itself out in opposing whatever is opposed to virtue. True faith implies and includes love, and faith that has no love in it or does not work by love has no part in Christianity. Christian faith is an affectionate confidence in God.

One kind of faith in God has no love in it. The devil has that kind of faith. The convicted sinner has it. But there is no virtue in it. Faith might even rise to the faith of miracles, yet if there is no love in it, it amounts to nothing. The apostle Paul, in the thirteenth chapter of 1 Corinthians, said, "Though I have the gift of prophecy, and understand all mysteries, and all knowledge; and though I have all faith, so that I could remove mountains, and have not charity, I am nothing" (1 Corinthians 13:2).

Repentance that does not include love is not repentance *toward* God. True repentance implies obedience to the law of love and, consequently, opposition to sin.

The highest degree of emotion is not essential to perfect love. The Lord Jesus Christ very seldom had the highest degree of *emotion*, yet He always had perfect love. He generally manifested little emotion or excitement. Excitement always equals the strength of the emotions. The Savior generally remained remarkably calm. Sometimes His indignation was strong or His grief was overwhelming, and sometimes He rejoiced in spirit. But He was usually calm and manifested no high degree of emotion. The emotion of love in a high degree is plainly not essential to perfect love.

The growth of the mind in knowledge naturally implies growth in love. The Lord grew in stature and in favor with God and man. As He grew in knowledge, He grew in love toward God and in favor with God. His love was perfect when He was a child, but it was greater when He became a man. As a human being, Jesus probably continued to increase in love to God as long as He lived. It may be so with all the saints in glory—their perfect love will increase throughout eternity.

In perfect love, love cannot always be exercised toward all individuals alike. You cannot think of everyone you know at once. The degree of love toward an individual depends on the fact that he is present in the thoughts.

The spirit of prayer is not always essential to pure and perfect love. The saints in heaven have pure and perfect love for all beings, yet we do not know if they have the spirit of prayer for anyone. You may love any individual strongly yet not have the spirit of prayer for him. The Spirit of God may not lead you to pray for his salvation. Jesus Christ said expressly that He did not pray for all mankind: "I pray not for the world" (John 17:9).

This has been a great mistake in regard to prayer. Some suppose Christians haven't done their duty if they haven't prayed in faith for every sinner on earth. Then Jesus Christ never did His duty, for He never did this. God has never told us He will save all mankind and never gave us any reason to believe He will do it. How then can we pray in faith for the salvation of all? What does that faith have to rest on?

The Evidence Of Perfect Love

Excitement exhausts our powers. Although one may feel more like lying down and sleeping than he does like praying, his love may still be perfect. The Lord often felt this weariness and exhaustion.

If perfect love is to reign, there must be nothing in the mind inconsistent with love—no hatred, malice, wrath, envy, or any other negative emotions that are inconsistent with it. All our actions, words, and thoughts must be continually under the entire and perfect control of love.

In perfect love, the love to God is completely supreme, so entirely above all other objects that nothing else is loved in comparison. God is loved for the excellence of His character.

Love to our neighbor should be equal. His interest and happiness should be regarded by us as of equal value with our own, and he and his interests are to be treated accordingly by us.

Perfect love to God and man will certainly create delight in self-denial for the sake of promoting the interests of God's Kingdom and the salvation of sinners. Affectionate parents delight in self-denial for the sake of promoting the happiness of their children. A loving father labors from year to year, rising early and eating the bread of carefulness to promote the welfare of his family. He counts all his self-denial and toil not as a grief or a burden but as a delight because of love for his family.

Loving parents rejoice more in gifts to their children than they would in enjoying the same things themselves. What parent does not enjoy giving a piece of fruit to his little child more than eating it himself?

The Lord Jesus enjoyed more solid satisfaction in working out salvation for mankind than any of His saints can ever enjoy in receiving favors at His hands. He testifies that it is more blessed to give than to receive. (See Acts 20:35.) This was the joy set before Him for which He endured the cross and despised the shame. His love for mankind was great, and it constrained Him to undertake this work and sustained Him triumphantly through it.

The apostle Paul did not count it grief to be hunted from place to place, imprisoned, scourged, stoned, and counted the offscouring of all things for the sake of spreading the gospel and saving souls. It was his joy. The love of Christ so constrained Him that it was his highest delight to lay himself on that altar as a sacrifice.

Other individuals have had the same mind as the apostle. They would be willing to live to the end of time if they could do good, promote the Kingdom of God, and save the souls of men.

Perfect love leads a person to obey God not because he fears the wrath of God or hopes to be rewarded but because he loves God and loves to do His will. Two extremes exist on this subject. One class makes virtue to consist in doing right simply *because it is right,* without any reference to the will of God or any influence from His love. Another class makes virtue to consist in acting from love to the *employment,* without reference to God's authority as Ruler and Law-giver. Both of these are in error.

To do a thing simply because one thinks it right is not virtue. Neither is it virtue to do a thing because one loves to do it, with no regard to God's will. A woman might do something because she knew it would please her husband. But if she did the same thing because she loved to do it, with no regard to her husband, it wouldn't be virtue as it respects her husband. If a person loves God, as soon as he knows God's will, he will do it *because it is God's will.* Perfect love leads to universal obedience to God's will in all things because it *is* His will.

Dying To The World

The individual who exercises perfect love will be dead to the world. He will be cut loose from the influence of worldly considerations. Perfect love will so annihilate selfishness that he will have no will but the will of God and no interest but God's glory.

A loving wife will cut loose from her friends as if she were dead to them and not pay the least regard to what they say. She will leave all the riches, honors, and delights they can offer to join the husband whom she loves and live with him in poverty, disgrace, or exile. Her affection is so great that she will joyfully go from a palace to a cave and be perfectly happy. And all that her friends can say against the man of her affection only makes her cling more closely to him.

This one *all-absorbing* affection has actually killed all the influences that used to act on her. To attempt to influence her by such things is vain. Only one avenue can approach her mind, and only one class of motives move her—and that is through the object of her affection.

The perfect love of God operates in the same way. A mind filled with perfect love is impossible to divert from God. Take away his worldly possessions, his friends, his good name, or his children; send him to prison, beat him with stripes, bind him to the stake, fill his flesh full of pine knots, and set him on fire; and then leave him his God, and he is happy. His strong affection can make him insensible to everything else. It is as if he were dead to the world.

Cases have been known of martyrs who, while their bodies were frying at the stake, were so perfectly happy in God that they lost the sense of pain. Put such a one in hell, in the lake of fire and brimstone, and, as long as the love of God fills his soul, he is happy.

We have all witnessed or heard of cases of affection where a person lives only for a loved object. Sometimes parents live for an only child, and when that child dies, they wish themselves dead. Sometimes a husband and wife have such an absorbing affection for each other that they live for nothing else. If the husband dies, the wife pines away and dies also. The soul-absorbing object for which she lived is gone, and why should she live any longer?

When an individual is filled with the perfect love of God, he wishes to live only to love and serve God. He is dead to the world and his own reputation. He has no desire to live for any other reason—here, in heaven, or anywhere else in the universe—than to glorify God. He is willing to live anywhere and suffer throughout eternity if it will glorify God.

I often heard a friend say, "I would never think of living a single moment for any purpose other than to glorify God, any more than I should think of leaping right into hell." This was said soberly and deliberately, and his whole life corresponded with the declaration. He was intelligent, sober-minded, and honest, and I have no doubt that he expressed what had been his fullest conviction for years.

What was this but perfect love? What more does any angel in heaven do than this? His love may be greater in degree because his strength is greater. But the highest angel could not love more perfectly than to sincerely say, "I would rather leap into hell than live one moment for anything besides glorifying God." What more could Jesus Himself say?

The Fruit Of Love

Perfect joy and peace are the natural results of perfect love. Turn your attention to what Paul says in the thirteenth chapter of first Corinthians. The word translated *charity* means *love:* "Though I speak with the tongues of men and of angels, and have not charity, I am becoming as sounding brass, or a tinkling cymbal. And though I have the gift of prophecy, and understand all mysteries, and all knowledge; and though I have all faith, so that I could remove mountains, and have not charity, I am nothing" (1 Corinthians 13:1-2). He might have enough faith to move mountains from their everlasting foundations and yet have no love.

"And though I bestow all my goods to feed the poor, and though I give my body to be burned, and have not charity, it profiteth me nothing" (1 Corinthians 13:3). You see how far a man can go without love.

"Charity suffereth long." Long-suffering is meekness under opposition or injury. One of the effects of love is to bear great provocations and not retaliate or revile. Love "is kind," or affectionate in all relationships, never harsh, rude, or needlessly giving pain to any. Love "envieth not," never dislikes others because they are more thought of, noticed, honored, useful, or wise. Love "is not puffed up" with pride but is always humble and modest. (See 1 Corinthians 13:4).

"Love doth not behave itself unseemly" but is naturally pleasant and courteous toward all. However unacquainted the individual may be with the ways of society, if he is motivated by perfect love, it is natural for him to be kind, gentle, and courteous. Love "seeketh not her own" or has no selfishness, and "is not easily provoked." This is always the effect of love. A loving mother bears with her children because she loves them. (See verse 5.) If you see an individual that easily flies into a passion when anything goes wrong, he is by no means perfect in love. To be easily provoked is always a sign of pride. If a person is full of love, it is impossible to make him exercise sinful anger while love continues. He exercises such indignation as God exercises at what is base and wrong, but he will not be provoked by it.

Love "thinketh no evil" (verse 5). Show me a man who is always suspicious of the motives of others, forever criticizing the words and actions of his fellowmen, and I will show you one who has the devil in him, not the Holy Spirit. If an individual is honest and simple-hearted, he will be the last to think evil of others. He won't always be seeing heresy or mischief in others. On the contrary, such people are often easy to take advantage of. Not from any lack of good sense but from the effect of love. They don't *suspect* evil.

Love "rejoiceth not in iniquity, but rejoiceth in the truth" (verse 6). A man who exults at his neighbor's fall or cries out, "I told you so" is far from being perfect in love.

"Love beareth all things," all injustices and injuries, without revenge. Love "believeth all things" instead of doubting what is in favor of others, always ready to believe good wherever there is the least evidence of it. Love "hopeth all things," even where there is reason to suspect evil. As long as there is room for hope, love puts the best construction upon the things it will bear (verse 7).

"Love worketh no ill to his neighbour" (Romans 13:10). No ill! Perfect love never overreaches, defrauds, oppresses, or does any wrong to a neighbor. How can a man who hates or injures his neighbor pretend to love God?

James says, "If any man among you seem to be religious, and bridleth not his tongue, but deceiveth his own heart, this man's religion is vain" (James 1:26). The man that professes Christianity yet allows himself to speak against his neighbor with an unbridled tongue deceives himself if he thinks he loves his neighbors as himself.

True Christian Zeal

People often intellectually understand about the Lord and can share it with others, while it is plain they are not motivated by the spirit of love. They do not have the law of kindness on their lips.

Individuals who have great religious knowledge and zeal, without love, are unlovely and dangerous. They are always censorious, proud, heady, and highminded. They may make a strong impression but don't produce true Christianity. They zealously affect you but not well.

If the light in a man's mind is accompanied with love, his zeal will not be sectarian in its character. Show me a man full of jealousy toward those that don't belong to his denomination, and there is a man far from perfect love.

True love is never denunciatory or harsh. If it has occasion to speak of the faults of others, it does it in kindness and sorrow. Perfect love cannot speak in a rough or abusive manner, either to or of others. It will not lay great stress on the ceremonies of religion or be picky about particular measures or forms. Many contend fiercely either for or against certain things, but if they were full of love they wouldn't do it.

Zeal governed by perfect love will not spend itself in contending for or against any forms in *religion*. Love leads to laying stress on the fundamentals of Christianity. It cleaves to warm-hearted Christians, regardless of their denomination, and delights to associate with them.

True Christian zeal is never full of controversy. Find a man who loves to attend ecclesiastical meetings and enters into all the janglings of the day, and that man is not full of love. To a mind filled with holy love, it is exceedingly painful to see ministers dividing into parties and striving for the mastery. Find an individual who loves controversy in the newspaper, and he is not of love. If he was, he would rather be abused, reviled, and slandered than to defend himself or to reply. As much as possible, he would live peacefully with all men.

Much of what passes for works of Christianity is constrained by outward causes and influences instead of love. Unless love is the mainspring, no matter what the outward action may be—praying, praising, giving, or anything else—there is no truth in it. Much excitement that passes for Christianity has no love.

Religious excitements not grounded in the spirit of love aren't true revivals. People may be excited and bustle about with a great show of zeal and boisterous noise but still have no tenderness of spirit.

I once knew a young man who acknowledged that he *aimed* at making people angry. He thought that it brought them under conviction and led to their conversion. And so it might if he should go in and utter horrid blasphemies until they were frightened into a consideration of their own character. But who would defend such conduct on the ground that occasionally someone got saved?

If the character of the revival is wrath, malice, and uncharitableness, it is not Christianity. I do not mean that when some or many are "filled with wrath" it is certain evidence that there is no revival. But when the excitement has this *prevailing character,* it is not a true revival. Some among them may have the spirit of love. But certainly those filled with a bitter, malicious zeal are not Christians.

When Love Reigns

If love is not the ruling feature in a person's character, he is not truly converted. However well he appears in other respects, and no matter how clear his views or how deep his feelings, if he doesn't have the spirit of love to God and man, he is deceived.

The time will come when there will be nothing to hurt or destroy, and the spirit of love will universally prevail. What a change in society! What a change in all the methods of doing business and in all the relationships of mankind. Each man will love his neighbor as himself and seek the good of others as his own! Could one of the saints that live now revisit the earth in that day, he would not know the world—everything will be so altered. "Is it possible," he would exclaim, "that this is the same earth that used to be full of jangling, oppression, and fraud?"

The Lord Jesus Christ is working to bring all men under the influence of love. Is this not a worthy objective? He came to destroy the works of the devil, and this is the way to do it. Suppose the world was full of such men as Jesús Christ was in His human nature. Compare it with what it is now. Would not such a change be worthy of the Son of God? What a glorious end, to fill the earth with love!

Heaven is love—perfect love. It is easy to see what makes heaven on earth in those who are full of love. How sweet their temper, what delightful companions, how blessed to live near them and to associate with them. They are full of candor, kind, gentle, careful to avoid offense, and divinely amiable in all things!

Is this to be attained by men? Can we love God here in this world with all our heart, soul, strength, and mind? Is it our privilege and our duty to have the Spirit of Christ? Beloved, let our hearts be set on perfect love, and let us give God no rest until we feel our hearts full of love and all our thoughts and lives are full of love to God and man.

When will the Church come up to this standard? Let the Church be full of love, and she will be fair as the moon, clear as the sun, and terrible to all wickedness.

Chapter 24

RESTING IN OBEDIENCE

"For we which have believed do enter into rest"—Hebrews 4:3.

The apostle who wrote this was very active in the Church. Those of whom he spoke, including himself—*"we* who have believed do enter into rest"*—would know at once they had not entered into the rest of *inactivity.*

Neither are we to understand that the *perfect* rest of heaven is the rest here spoken of. He speaks of it as a present state: "we *do* enter." The perfect rest of heaven includes absolute freedom from all the pains, trials, sufferings, and temptations of this life. The rest of the believer here may be of the *same nature*, substantially, with the rest in heaven. But that rest begun on earth is not made perfect. It differs because it does not deliver from all trials, pains, sickness, and death. The apostles and early Christians did not escape these trials but still suffered their full share of them.

The word *rest* is often used in the Bible. The children of Israel rested when they were freed from their enemies and strife of war. Those who enter into this rest cease from their warfare with God, their struggle against the truth, and their war with their own conscience. The reproaches of conscience that kept them in agitation and the slavish fears of the wrath of God are done away with. They rest.

Ceasing From Selfish Works

Much *religion* in the world is made up of people's *own works*. They are working for their own lives—that is, they are working for themselves as absolutely as the man laboring for his bread. If the object of your faith is your own salvation, it doesn't matter whether it is from temporal or eternal ruin, it is for *yourself*. You have not ceased from your own works but are still multiplying them.

The *rest* spoken of in the text is entire cessation from this kind of works. The apostle affirms this: "He that is entered into his rest, hath ceased from his own works" (Hebrews 4:10). And in the text, he says, "We that believe do enter," or have entered, "into rest."

This rest is ceasing from *our own* works, not ceasing from all kind of works, for that is true neither of the saints on earth nor the saints in heaven. We have no reason to believe that any saint, angel, or God Himself is ever inactive. But we cease to perform works merely to save our own souls. By ceasing to work for ourselves we can work for God. If he question of our salvation is thrown entirely on esus Christ and our works are performed out of love o God, they are not our own works.

In entering into this rest, we cease from all works performed *from* ourselves as well as works performed *for* ourselves. Works are *from* ourselves when they result from the simple, natural principles of human nature, such as conscience, hope, fear, etc., without the influences of the Holy Spirit. Such works are universally and wholly sinful. They are the efforts of selfishness, under the direction of mere natural principles. Our conscience convicts us, and hope and fear come to our aid. Under this influence, the carnal, selfish mind acts.

People who practice their own righteousness painfully grind out religion, constrained by hope and fear, lashed to the work by conscience. They haven't the least impulse from that divine principle of the love of God shed abroad in the heart by the Holy Spirit. All such works are just as much from themselves as any work of any devil is. No matter what kind of works are performed, if the love of God is not the mainspring, life, and heart, then they are dead and provide no rest. These works set aside the gospel.

The individual who is actuated by these principles sets aside the gospel, in whole or in part. If he is motivated *only* by these considerations, he sets aside the gospel entirely. As far as he is influenced by them, he refuses to receive Christ as his Savior in that relation. Christ is offered as a complete

Savior—our wisdom, righteousness, sanctification, and redemption. If anyone dispenses with the Savior in any of these functions, he is setting aside the gospel in proportion.

To enter into rest implies that we cease from doing anything for ourselves. We are not even to eat or drink for ourselves: "Whether therefore ye eat, or drink, or whatsoever ye do, do all to the glory of God" (1 Corinthians 10:31). God requires it, and he that has entered into rest has ceased to have any interest of his own. He has wholly merged his own interest in that of Christ. He has given himself so perfectly to Christ that he has no work of his own to do. He might as well sit still until he is in hell as attempt to save himself by his own exertions. When a man fully understands this, he ceases from making any efforts in this way. The convicted sinner will strain to help himself until he learns that he is nothing. Then he ceases from all this and throws himself, helpless and lost, into the hands of Christ.

Until he feels that in himself he is without strength, help, or hope for salvation, he will never think of the simplicity of the gospel. No man applies to Christ for righteousness and strength until he has used up his own and feels that he is helpless and undone. Then he can understand the simplicity of the gospel plan, which consists in *receiving* salvation by faith, as a free gift. When he has done all that he could and finds that he is no nearer salvation and that sin is multiplied upon sin, he is crushed down with utter helplessness and gives all into the hand of Christ.

Yielding Yourself To Jesus

Everyone who has entered into rest knows that whatever he does in his own strength is an abomination to God. Unless Christ lives in him to will and to do His good pleasure, nothing is ever done acceptably to God. He who has not learned this has not ceased from his own works and has not accepted the Savior. The depth of depravity to which sin has reduced us is not understood until we know we are not able to work for ourselves.

Jesus invites us to throw all our burdens and cares on Him. "Come unto me, all ye that labour and are heavy laden, and I will give you rest" (Matthew 11:28). "Casting all your care upon him; for he careth for you" (1 Peter 5:7).

These words mean just as they say. Whether your burden is temporal or spiritual, whether your care is for the soul or body, throw it all upon the Lord.

Imagine a little child walking with his father. The father is carrying something that is heavy, and the child takes hold with his little hand to help. But how can he carry such a load? Many Christians cause a great deal of trouble by trying to help the Lord in His work. They weary and worry themselves as if everything hung on their shoulders.

Jesus Christ is as much pledged to the believer for *all* that concerns him as He is for his justification.

The Lord is as absolutely bound for his temporal as for his eternal interests. Everything that concerns the Christian can be cast on the Lord. I do not mean that the Christian has no responsibility in the matter. A man who has cast his family upon Jesus must still be concerned for his family. But he has cast himself upon God for direction, light, strength, and success. He has yielded himself up absolutely to God to guide and sustain him, and Christ will see that everything is done right.

Entering into Jesus' rest implies the yielding up of our powers so perfectly to His control that from that point all our works will be His works. I hope you will not understand anything from this language more mystical than the Bible intends. What a man does by another, he does himself. If I hire a man to commit murder, the deed is as absolutely my own as if I had done it with my own hand. The crime is not in the hand which struck the blow any more than it is in the knife that stabs the victim. The crime is in my mind. Even if I use another's hand, my mind influenced him, and it is still my act.

Apply this principle to the doctrine that the individual who has entered into rest has yielded himself up to Christ's control, and all his works are the works of Jesus. The apostle Paul says, "I laboured more abundantly than they all: yet not I, but the grace of God which was with me" (1 Corinthians 15:10). He frequently insists that it was not himself that did the works but Christ in him.

Do not misunderstand it now. Do not think that

342

the believer acts upon compulsion or that Christ acts in him without his own will. But Christ, by His Spirit dwelling in him, influences and leads his mind so that he acts voluntarily to please God.

When one ceases from his own works, he so perfectly gives up his own interest and will and places himself under the dominion and guidance of the Holy Spirit that whatever he does is done by the impulse of the Spirit of Christ. Paul describes it exactly: "Work out your own salvation with fear and trembling. For it is God which worketh in you both to will and to do of his good pleasure" (Philippians 2:12-13).

God influences the will, not by force but by love, to do what will please Him. If it was done by force, we would no longer be free agents. But it is love that sweetly influences the will and brings it entirely under the control of the Lord Jesus Christ.

Our free will isn't suspended but is employed by the Lord Jesus Christ. Our hands, feet, and powers of body and mind are all employed to work for Him. He does not suspend the laws of our constitution but directs us, and the love of Christ constrains us to will and do of His good pleasure.

All works that are really good in man are, in an important sense, Christ's works. Over and over the Bible affirms that our good works are not from ourselves or in any way by our own action without God. God directs us and influences our will to do His. They are in one sense our works, because we do them voluntarily. Yet, in another sense, they are

343

His works because He is the moving cause of all.

Insomuch as we yield our will to Christ, to that degree we cease from sin. If we are directed by the Lord, He will not direct us to sin. Just as far as we give ourselves up to God we cease from sin. If we are controlled by Him, so that He works in us, it is to will and to do of *His good pleasure.*

The True Rest Of Faith

Believers enter into rest in this life. This appears from the text and context. The author of Hebrews, in connection with the text, was reasoning with the Jews. He warns them to beware unless they fail to enter into the true rest, typified by their fathers' entering into the land of Canaan. The Jews supposed *that* was the true rest. But the author argues that there was a higher rest of which the rest of temporal Canaan was only a type. The Jews might have entered this rest except for their unbelief.

If Joshua had given them the real rest, he would not have spoken of another day. Yet another day is spoken of. Even in David's day it is spoken of in the Psalms as yet to come: "To day, after so long a time; as it is said, To day if ye will hear his voice, harden not your hearts. For if Jesus (that is Joshua) had given them rest, then would he not afterwards have spoken of another day. There remaineth therefore a rest to the people of God" (Hebrews 4:7-9).

He therefore argues that the rest in Canaan was not the real rest promised but was typical of the true rest. What then was the true rest? It was the rest of faith in Christ, a cessation from our own works. And believers enter into that state *by faith*.

Many people suppose that the rest spoken of is the heavenly rest beyond this life. But it is certainly a rest that begins *here*. "We which believe *do* enter into rest." It begins here but extends into eternity. There it will be more perfect in degree, embracing freedom from the sorrows and trials to which all believers are subject in this life. But it is the same rest of faith, the Sabbath-keeping of the soul when it ceases from its own works and casts itself upon the Savior.

Faith is essential to taking possession of this rest. The author of Hebrews warns them not to indulge in unbelief, because by faith they may take immediate possession of the rest. If this rest by faith ever begins at all, it must be in this world. Jesus said, "Come unto me, all ye that labour and are heavy laden, and I will give you rest. Take my yoke upon you, and learn of me; for I am meek and lowly in heart: and ye shall find rest unto your souls" (Matthew 11:28-29). We are told that if we will only come to Christ, we will find rest. If we will take His yoke of love and trust Him to bear all our burdens, we will find rest.

The psalmist speaks of the same rest: "Return unto thy rest, O my soul" (Psalm 116:7). What Christian does not know what it is to have peace in Christ and find rest from all the cares, perplexities, and sorrows of life?

Faith in Christ brings the soul into rest. Faith instantly breaks up slavish fear and brings the soul into the liberty of the gospel! It sets us free from selfishness and other influences we formerly acted under. By faith we confide in Christ to lead us, sanctify us, and justify us. The soul sees no need for its own selfish efforts. In itself, the soul is so far gone in sin that it is as hopeless as if it had been in hell a thousand years. Take the best Christian on earth—if the Lord leaves his soul, where is he? Will he pray or do anything good or acceptable to God without Christ? Never. The greatest saint on earth would immediately go right back into sin if abandoned by Jesus Christ. But faith throws all upon Christ, and that is rest.

Principles Of Faith

Faith makes us cease from all works *for* ourselves. By faith we see that we have no more need of doing works for ourselves than the child whose father is worth millions needs to work for his daily bread. He may work out of love to his father or love to his job, but not from any necessity to labor for his daily bread. The soul that truly understands the gospel sees no need of mingling his own righteousness with the righteousness of Christ, his wisdom with the wisdom of Christ, or his own sufferings with the sufferings of Christ. If there was any need of this, there would be much temptation to selfishness and working from legal motives. But there is none.

By faith the soul ceases from all works performed *from* itself. Faith brings a new principle into action, entirely above all considerations addressed to the natural principles of hope, fear, and conscience. Faith brings the mind under the influence of love. It takes the soul from under the influences of conscience and brings it under the influence of the same holy, heavenly principle that influenced Jesus Himself.

Faith brings the mind into rest and brings it to cease from all efforts merely for its own salvation, putting the whole being into the hands of Christ.

Faith is confidence, yielding up all our power and interests to Christ to be led, sanctified, and saved by Him. It annihilates selfishness and thus leaves no motives for our own works.

Faith is an absolute resting of the soul in Jesus for all that it needs or can need. It is trusting Him for everything. If a little child didn't trust his father, he would be miserable. He is absolutely dependent on his father for house, food, clothing, and everything under the sun. Yet that little child feels no uneasiness because he confides in his father. He rests in him and is sure he will provide. He is as cheerful and happy as if he had all things in himself because he has confidence.

The soul of the believer rests in Christ just as the infant does in the arms of its mother. The penitent sinner, like a condemned wretch, clings to Christ without the least help or hope. Only when he comes to Christ alone will He do all that is needed.

If faith does consist in thus trusting absolutely in Christ, then it is true that this rest is taken possession of when we believe. It must be in *this life,* if faith is to be exercised in this life.

Unbelief is the cause of all the sin in the world. Unbelief, itself a sin, is the fountain out of which all other sin flows. It is distrust in God or a lack of confidence. This lack of confidence constituted Adam's real crime, not the mere eating of the fruit. The distrust that led to the outward act constituted the real crime, for which he was cast out of Paradise.

The moment an individual lacks faith and is left to the simple influence of natural principles and appetites, he is like a beast. The things that address his mind through the senses alone influence him. The motives that influence the mind when it acts right are discerned by faith. Where there is no faith, there are no motives before the mind except those confined to this world. The soul is then left to give itself up to the flesh.

This is the natural and inevitable result of unbelief. The eye is shut to eternal things, and nothing before the mind is calculated to beget anything but selfishness. Left to grovel in the dust, it can never rise above its own interest and appetites; for how can the mind act without motives? But the motives of eternity are seen only by faith. Mere mental and bodily appetites can never raise the mind above the things of this world, and the result is sin—the minding of the flesh forever. The very moment Adam distrusted God, he was given up to follow his appetites. And it is so with all other minds.

Suppose a child loses all confidence in his father. He can now give no heartfelt obedience. If he pretends to obey, it is only from selfishness and not from the heart. The mainspring and essence of all loving obedience is gone. It will be so in heaven; it is so in hell. Without faith it is impossible to please God. We cannot obey God and be accepted by Him without faith. Unbelief is the foundation of all the sin in earth and hell, and the soul that is void of faith is left to work out its own damnation.

Resting In Jesus

Perfect faith would produce perfect love and perfect holiness, if we would yield ourselves up and trust all that we have and are to Christ. If an individual is not sanctified, his faith is weak.

When Jesus was on earth, if His disciples fell into sin, He always reproached them for a lack of faith: "O ye of little faith." (See Matthew 6:30; 8:26; Luke 12:28; Mark 4:40; etc.) A man that believes in Christ has no more right to expect to sin than he has a right to expect to be damned. You may startle at this, but it is true.

You are to receive Christ as your holiness just as absolutely as for your justification. You should expect to be damned unless you receive Christ as your justification. But if you receive Him, you have no reason and no right to expect to be damned. If you depend upon Him for sanctification, He will no

349

more let you sin than He will let you go to hell. And it is as unreasonable, unscriptural, and wicked to expect one as the other. Nothing but unbelief, *in any instance,* is the cause of your sin.

Take the case of Peter. When the disciples saw Jesus walking upon the water, Peter requested permission to come to Him on the water. Christ told him to come. Jesus' invitation was a promise that, if Peter attempted it, he would be sustained. Except for this promise, his attempt would have been tempting God. But with this promise, he had no reason and no right to doubt. He made the attempt; and while he believed, Jesus' energy bore him up. But as soon as he began to doubt, he began to sink.

As soon as the soul begins to doubt the willingness and the power of Christ to sustain it in a state of perfect love, it begins to sink. Take Jesus at His Word, make Him responsible, and rely on Him. Heaven and earth will sooner pass away than He will ignore a soul falling into sin.

A state of inaction is inconsistent with Christian rest. How could it be rest for one whose heart was burning and bursting with love to God and to souls to sit and *do nothing?* But it is perfect rest for the soul to burn in prayer and effort for their salvation. Such a soul cannot rest while God is dishonored, souls destroyed, and nothing is done for their rescue. But when all his powers are used for the Lord Jesus Christ, this is true rest. Such is the rest enjoyed by angels, who never cease, day or night, and who are all ministering spirits to the heirs of salvation.

"Let us therefore fear, lest, a promise being left us of entering into rest, any of you should seem to come short of it" (Hebrews 4:1).

Do any of you know what it is to come to Christ and rest in Him? Have you found rest from all your own efforts to save yourselves from the thunders of Sinai and the stings of conscience? Can you rest sweetly in Jesus and find everything essential to holiness and eternal salvation in Him? Have you found actual salvation in Him?

If you have, then you have entered into rest. If you have not found this, it is because you are still laboring to perform your own works.

Chapter 25

THE BRIDE OF CHRIST

"Wherefore, my brethren, ye also are become dead to the law by the body of Christ; that ye should be married to another, even to him who is raised from the dead, that we should bring forth fruit unto God"—Romans 7:4.

Marriage is set forth in the Bible as describing the relationship between Christ and the Church. Jesus is often spoken of as the husband of the Church: "Thy Maker is thine husband; the Lord of hosts is his name" (Isaiah 54:5). "Turn, O backsliding children, saith the Lord; for I am married unto you" (Jeremiah 3:14).

The Church is spoken of as the bride, the Lamb's wife: "The Spirit and the Bride say, Come" (Revelation 22:17). That is, Christ and the Church say, "Come." The apostle Paul says, "For I am jealous over you with godly jealousy: for I have espoused you to one husband, that I may present you as a chaste virgin to Christ" (2 Corinthians 11:2).

Faithful Husbands And Devoted Wives

In most marriages, the wife gives up her own name and assumes that of her husband. And the Church assumes the name of Christ and is baptized into His name. A married woman has no separate interest. So the Church has no right to have a separate interest from the Lord Jesus Christ. If a wife has property, it joins with her husband's.

The reputation of the wife is united to that of her husband; his reputation is hers, and her reputation is his. What affects her character affects his; and what affects his character affects hers. Their reputation is one, and their interests are one. Whatever concerns the Church is just as much the interest of Christ as if it were personally His own matter. As the husband of the Church, He is as responsible to do everything necessary to promote the interest of the Church as a husband is responsible to promote the welfare of his wife.

A faithful husband gives up his time, his labor, and his talents to promote the interest and happiness of his wife. Jesus Christ gives Himself up to promote the welfare of His Church. He is as jealous of the reputation of His Church as any husband ever was of the reputation of his wife. Never was a human being as committed and devoted to the interest of his wife as Jesus Christ feels when His Church has her reputation or her feelings injured. He declares that it would be better for a man to hang a millstone around his neck and be cast into the sea than to offend one of His little ones. (See Matthew 18:6.)

Jesus feels all the sufferings of the Church, and the Church feels all the sufferings of Jesus. When a believer has any understanding of the sufferings of Christ, nothing in the universe so affects and dissolves his mind with sorrow. No wife ever felt such distress and brokenhearted grief than when she has caused the death of her husband. The Christian feels this remorse when he views his sins as the occasion of the death of Jesus Christ. How would you feel if your husband or wife volunteered to suffer and die for you to save your life? Just to be reminded of it would melt you in brokenhearted grief!

Have you ever understood that *your sins* caused the death of Christ, and that He died for you just as absolutely as if you had been the only sinner in God's world? He suffered pain, contempt, and death *for you*. He loved His Church and gave Himself for it. He purchased it with His own blood.

In Christian marriages, the wife pledges to yield to the will of her husband. She has no separate interest and should have no conflicting will. The Bible makes it a Christian duty for the wife to conform in all things to the will of her husband. The will of the husband becomes to the faithful wife the mainspring of her activity. Her entire life is only carrying out the will of her husband.

The relationship of the Church to Jesus is precisely the same. The Church is governed by His will. When believers exercise faith, the Lord's will becomes the moving cause of all their conduct. The wife recognizes her husband as her head, and the Bible declares that he is so. The Head governs the Church.

Lord Of The Church

Every believer places himself as absolutely under the protection of Christ as a married woman is under the protection of her husband. The woman naturally looks to her husband to preserve her from injury, insult, and want. She hangs her happiness on him and expects him to protect her, and he is bound to do it.

Jesus is pledged to protect His Church from every foe. Often the powers of hell have tried to put down the Church, but He has never abandoned it. No weapon formed against the Church has ever been allowed to prosper, and none ever will. Never will the Lord forget His relationship to the Church and leave His bride unprotected. Let all earth and all hell conspire against the Church, and she will be safe.

Every individual believer is as safe as if he were the only believer on earth and has Jesus truly pledged for his preservation. The devil can no more destroy a single believer than he can put down God Almighty. He may murder them, but that is no injury. Overcoming a believer by taking his life gives Satan no triumph. Neither the grave nor hell has any more power to injure one of the Lord's little ones than they have to injure Jesus Himself.

Jesus says, "Because I live, ye shall live also" (John 14:19). And "He that believeth in me, though he were dead, yet shall he live: And whosoever liveth and believeth in me shall never die'' (John 11:25-26). No power in the universe can destroy a single believer. Jesus Christ is Lord over all things, and the Church is safe.

Jesus Christ is Lord over His Church, and if He does not restrain His Church from sin, He is brought into great trouble and reproach by the misconduct of His people. By human laws, the husband is not liable for capital crimes committed by the wife, and the law recognizes her separate existence.

But Jesus has assumed responsibility for all the Church's conduct. He took the place of His people when they were convicted and sentenced to eternal damnation. And now it is His business to take care of the Church and keep her from sin. Jesus Christ is responsible and must answer for every sin of every member.

And He does answer for them. He has made an atonement to cover all this, and He lives to make intercession for His people. He holds himself responsible before God for all the conduct of the Church. Every believer is so perfectly united to Him that whatever any of them may be guilty of Jesus takes upon Himself. This is abundantly taught in the Bible.

What an amazing relationship! The Lord has assumed the responsibility for all the civil and capital crimes of rebellion against God. There is a sense, therefore, in which the Church is lost in Christ and has no separate existence known in law. God has so given up the Church to Christ, by the covenant of grace, that the Church is not known in law. I do not mean that crimes committed by believers against the moral law are not sin, but the law cannot get hold of them for condemnation. There is now no condemnation to them that are *in* Christ Jesus. (See Romans 8:1.)

The penalty of the law is forever remitted. The crimes of the believer are not taken into account. Whatever is done falls upon Christ. He has assumed the responsibility of bringing Christians out from under the power of sin, as well as from under the law. He stands pledged to give His children all the assistance they need to gain a *complete victory*.

Bringing Forth Fruit

A principal design of the institution of marriage is the propagation of the species. The same is true in regard to the Church. Through the instrumentality of the Church, children are born to Christ, and He is to see His seed multiplied as the drops of morning dew. Through both the travail of the Redeemer's soul and through the travail of the Church, believers are born to Jesus Christ. As soon as Zion travailed, she brought forth children.

Another object of the marriage institution is the protection and support of those who are naturally helpless and dependent. If the law of power prevailed in society, females would be universally enslaved. The institution of marriage secures protection and support to those who are more frail. Jesus upholds His Church and affords her all the protection against the powers of hell that she needs.

The mutual happiness of the parties is another reason for marriage. Perhaps you will think it strange if I tell you that the happiness of Christ is increased by the love of the Church. But what does the Bible say? "Who for the joy set before him endured the cross, despising the shame" (Hebrews 12:2). What was the joy set before Him if the love of the Church was not a part of it? It would be strange to hear of a husband contributing to the happiness of his wife without enjoying it himself. Jesus Christ enjoys the happiness of His Church as much as He loves her—which is infinitely greater than any husband loves his wife.

Sharing each other's sorrow is a great relief. Jesus Christ and His Church share each other's sorrows. The apostle Paul says he was always bearing about in his body the dying of the Lord Jesus: "For as the sufferings of Christ abound in us, so our consolation also aboundeth by Christ" (2 Corinthians 1:5). And he declared that one end of all his toils and self-denials was that he might "know . . . the fellowship of his sufferings" (Philippians 3:10). Paul rejoiced in all his sufferings. The Church keenly feels every reproach cast upon Christ, and He feels every injury inflicted on the Church.

White Robes And Adultery

The principal reason for this union between Jesus and His church is that He may sanctify her: "Wives, submit yourselves unto your own husbands, as unto the Lord. For the husband is the head of the wife, even as Christ is the head of the church: and he is the saviour of the body. Therefore as the church is subject unto Christ, so let the wives be to their own husbands in every thing. Husbands, love your wives, even as Christ also loved the church, and gave himself for it; That he might sanctify and cleanse it with the washing of water by the word, That he might present it to himself a glorious church, not having spot, or wrinkle, or any such thing; but that it should be holy and without blemish" (Ephesians 5:22-27).

This is the great design of Christ in marrying the Church—that He might sanctify and cleanse it, and that it should be perfectly holy and without blemish. In Revelations, John informs us that he saw those who had washed their robes and made them white in the blood of the Lamb. How beautifully the Lamb's wife is described in the twenty-first chapter, coming down from God out of heaven prepared as a bride adorned for her husband.

Vast multitudes of those who profess to be a part of the Bride of Christ are hypocrites. They pretend to merge their self-interest with Christ's but obviously keep a separate interest. Any attempt to make them understand that they have no separate interest will plainly show that they have no such design.

Everybody knows what an abominable thing it is for a wife not to be satisfied with the love of her husband but continually seeking other lovers. Yet the Church is not satisfied with the love of Christ and always seeks after other lovers. What are we to think of members of the Church who are not satisfied with the love of Christ but must have the riches and honors of the world to make them happy?

Still more horrible would be a wife who chose her lovers from the enemies of her husband and made them her chosen friends. Yet how many professing Christians give their affections to Christ's enemies? Some will even marry those whom they know are *haters of God!* Is that the way a bride should act?

Everyone knows that it is a disgraceful thing for a wife to play the harlot. Yet God often speaks of His Church as going astray and committing *spiritual whoredom!* And it is true! He doesn't make this charge unjustly. But He makes it with tender grief and pleads with her to return.

What would you think of a married woman who *expected*, at the very time of her marriage, to get tired of her husband, leave him, and play the harlot?

Many "Christians," when they made a profession, had no more expectation of living without sin than they expected to have wings and fly. They have come into God's house, pledged themselves to live entirely for Him, and married Him in this public manner. They promised to forsake all sin, to live alone for Christ, to be satisfied with His love, and to have no other lovers—yet the whole time they are doing it, in their minds they expect to commit sin and dishonor Christ.

What are we to think of a woman who, at the very time of her marriage, expected to continue in adultery as long as she lives, in spite of all the commands and protests of her husband? Then what are we to think of "Christians" who deliberately expect to commit spiritual adultery and continue in it as long as they live?

But the most abominable part of such a wife's wickedness is when she turns around and blames her conduct upon her faithful husband! The Church does this. Although Christ has done all that He could do, short of absolute force, to keep His Church from sinning, the Church charges her sin upon Him. They act as if He hasn't made adequate provisions for preserving His people against temptation.

They are horrified at the very name of *Christian perfection,* as if it were dishonoring Christ to believe that He is able to keep His people from committing sin and falling into the snare of the devil. And so for hundreds of years the greater part of the Church has not taught that Jesus Christ really *has* provided a way for His people to live free from sin. People wonder that anybody teaches that the Bride of the Lord Jesus Christ is expected to do as she is commanded to do. Has He married a Bride and made no provision to protect her against the arts and seductions of the devil?

Jesus' Loving Patience

The reputation of husband and wife is one. Whatever dishonors one, dishonors the other. The Church, instead of avoiding every appearance of evil, continually opens opportunities for the enemies of God to blaspheme the Lord.

What other husband, in such circumstances, could suffer to remain and bear what Jesus bears? Yet he still offers to be reconciled and strives to regain the affection of His Bride. Sometimes a husband loses his affection toward his wife and treats her like a brute, and she loses her love for him. But where can anything be found in the character and conduct of Jesus to justify the treatment He receives? He has laid Himself out to capture the affections of the Church.

What more could He have done? Can any fault or any deficiency be found in Him? After everything the Church has done against Him, what is he doing now? Suppose a husband should for years follow his wandering, guilty wife from city to city beseeching her with tears to return home, and she persists after her lovers while he continues to cry after her and beg her to come back. Is there any such forbearance and humility known among men?

Your sins dishonor, grieve, and injure Christ—and then you make Him responsible for them. You sustain such a relationship to Him, and you ought to know the effect of your sin.

How does a wife feel when she has disgraced her husband? Blushes cover her face and tears fill her eyes! When her offended husband comes into her presence, she falls down with a full heart, confesses her guilt, and pours tears onto his shoulder. She is grieved and humbled; and, although she loves him, his very presence is a grief until she breaks down and feels he has forgiven her.

How can a Christian fail to recognize this? When he is betrayed into sin and has injured Jesus, how can he sleep? How can you not know that your sins take hold of Jesus Christ and wound Him!

If an individual expects to live in sin, of course he will live in sin. Many professing Christians never really meant to live without sin. Paul insists that believers should consider themselves *dead to sin*. (See Romans 6:11.) They should from now on no more expect to sin than a dead man should expect to walk. They should throw themselves upon Christ, receive Him in all His functions, and expect to be preserved, sanctified, and saved by Him. If they would do this, they would be kept from sin just as certainly as they believe in Christ for it!

To believe that Jesus will keep them insures that He will. The reason many Christians do not receive preserving grace at all times is that they do not expect it or trust Jesus to preserve them in perfect love. The man tries to preserve himself. Instead of throwing himself upon Christ, he throws himself upon his own resources. Then in his weakness he expects to sin—of course he sins! If he knew his own emptiness and would throw himself upon Christ, he would rest confidently for holiness and justification.

No one who trusted God for anything He has promised has ever failed to receive, according to his faith, the very thing for which he trusted. If you trust God for what He has *not* promised, that is tempting God.

If Peter had not been called to come out on the water, it would have been tempting God for him to get out of the ship. He would have lost his life for his presumption and folly. But as soon as Christ told him to come, it was merely an act of sound and rational faith for him to do it. It was a pledge on the part of Christ that Peter would be sustained— and he was sustained, as long as he had faith.

If the Bible has promised that those who *receive* Christ as their sanctification will be sanctified, then you who believe in Him for this have just as much reason to expect it as Peter had to expect to walk on water. We do not expect miracles to sustain the believer. But it is promised that he will be sustained, and God would move the universe and turn the course of nature upside down before one of His promises should fail those who trust Him.

Has God promised holiness to them that trust Him for it? If He has not, then to go to Him in faith for preservation from temptation and sin is tempting God. It is *fanaticism*. If God has left us to get along on our own watchfulness, firmness, and strength, then we must submit and do the best we can. But if He has made any promises, He will redeem them *to the uttermost*, although all earth and hell oppose Him.

This is true in regard to the mistakes and errors that Christians fall into. If there is no promise that they will be guided and led into truth and peace, then for a Christian to look to God for knowledge, wisdom, guidance, and direction is tempting God. But if there are promises on this subject, depend on it—they will be fulfilled in the believer who trusts in them and exercises confidence in the Word of God.

I believe that the great difficulty of the Church on the subject of Christian perfection lies here— she has not fully understood how the Lord Jesus Christ is *wholly pledged* in all these relationships. The Church has as much reason and is as bound to trust in Him for holiness as for justification.

What do the Scriptures say? "Who of God is made unto us wisdom, and righteousness, and sanctification, and redemption" (1 Corinthians 1:30).

Plainly, Jesus is promised and pledged for *wisdom* and for *sanctification* to all that receive Him. Has He promised that if any man lack wisdom, he may ask God, and if he asks in faith, God will give it to him? What then? Is there then no such thing as being preserved by Christ from falling into this and that delusion and error? God has made this broad promise, and Jesus is as much pledged for our wisdom and our sanctification, *if we only trust in Him,* as He is for our justification.

Surrendering To The King

The Church must renounce any expectation from herself and die as absolutely to her own wisdom and strength as she does to her own righteousness. Jesus Christ is pledged for one as much as for the other. The only reason why the Church does not realize the same results is that Christ is trusted for justification, but for wisdom and sanctification He is not trusted!

The truth is that most believers, having begun in the Spirit, are now trying to be made perfect by the flesh. We have thrown ourselves on Christ for justification but have been attempting to make ourselves holy. If it is true, as Paul affirms, that Christ is to the Church both wisdom and sanctification, what excuse do Christians have for not being sanctified?

If individuals do not expect to live without sin against Christ, it must be for one of three reasons:

We love our fellow men better than we do Christ and are less willing to do them an injury.

We are restrained by a regard to our own reputation—and this proves that we love reputation more than Christ.

We think we can preserve ourselves from these crimes.

Suppose I were to ask any of you if you expect to commit murder or adultery? Horrible! you say. But why not? Are you so virtuous that you can resist any temptation that the devil can offer? If you say yes, you do not know yourself. If you have real power to abstain from openly disgraceful sins, in your own strength, you have power to abstain from *all sins*. But if your only reliance is on Jesus Christ to keep you from committing murder and adultery, why do you think that He is not equally able to keep you from *all sin?*

What a horrible reproach the Church is to Jesus Christ! She is in such a state that it is no wonder those who are brought in, with few exceptions, are a disgrace to Christianity. How can it be otherwise? How can the Church, living in such a manner, bring forth offspring that will honor Christ? The Church does not, and individual believers generally do not, receive Christ in all His offices as He is offered in the Bible. If they did, it would be impossible for them to live like such loathsome harlots.

If believers would only throw themselves wholly on Christ and make Him responsible by placing themselves *entirely* at His control, then they would know His power to save and would live without sin.

Jesus loves His Church. *He loves you* and will do anything for you. Place yourself in His hands and let Him make you transparent, loving, and holy. He will not fail you.